WRITINGS OF FARM WOMEN
1840–1940
An Anthology

edited by
Carol Fairbanks
Bergine Haakenson

GARLAND PUBLISHING, INC. • NEW YORK & LONDON
1990

Library of Congress Cataloging-in-Publication Data

Fairbanks, Carol, 1935–
  Writings of farm women, 1840–1940 : an anthology / Carol
Fairbanks, Bergine Haakenson.
     p.   cm. — (Garland reference library of the humanities ; vol.
1327)
  Includes index.
  ISBN 0–8240–5170–X (alk. paper)
  1. Rural women—United States. 2. Farm life—United States.
I. Haakenson, Bergine, 1939–   . II. Title. III. Series.
HQ1410.F17   1990
305.42—dc20
                                                    90-41452
                                                    CIP

Printed on acid-free, 250-year-life paper
Manufactured in the United States of America

For
Clara
Linda and Lindsey
and Anita.

C.F.

In memory of
my mother, Ellen,
and my grandmothers,
Anna, Bertha and Bergina.

B.H.

CONTENTS

Illustrations

Preface

The stories of the homesteaders, ranchers, and farm women included in this anthology describe both the ordinary and the extraordinary. The writers discuss farming techniques, flower gardens, needlework, animals, religious beliefs, politics, friendships with Indians as well as prejudices against Indians, childbirth, spouse abuse, schools, and parties. They also describe such situations as near-starvation during a blizzard, the destruction of crops when grasshoppers descend, the mental breakdown of a neighborhood woman, and the dispossession of a farm family during a drought.

Painful experiences, however, are sometimes passed over quickly. Readers must search between the lines to detect disappointments and grief. In both the memoirs and letters, women are apt to soften the edges of a difficult situation, choosing instead to focus on the fact that—in spite of everything—they survived. And in the process of surviving they learned what one woman called "lessons for life." They discovered untapped resources, physical and emotional, within themselves. Elinore Pruitt Stewart found her comfort in nature: instead of being defeated by the deaths of cows and horses, she "planted flowers everywhere." Others emerged from traumatic experiences with renewed faith in God. Jennie Osborn proclaimed that "stick-to-it-iveness" was the determining factor. "Well," Jennie says, "We stuck." These women do not boast about their ability to endure; at the same time, there is no display of false modesty. Dignity is the dominant tone struck by women who have worked hard and developed self-confidence.

These women are not without their flaws. Both class prejudice and, to a greater degree, racial prejudice are revealed in some of their works. As editors we have chosen to eliminate some disagreeable passages not because we want to present the writers in a better light than they present themselves, but because their unsophisticated generalizations add very little to our understanding of their lives and relationships. Several women placed high value on their friendships with Indians and expressed sincere gratitude for assistance and protection provided by Indian neighbors. Those who used the terms *squaw* and *half breed* did not usually do so disapprovingly; these were the words commonly used without thought by settlers at the time. Alice Dahlin Lund described many social visits between the white women and Indian women. Their inability to speak each other's language was not an overwhelming problem. They liked being together to rejoice in the birth of a healthy new baby or to grieve over an infant's death.

Friendships among women form a recurring motif in these narratives. Hilda Rose depended on two types of female relationships. She described the happiness that comes when isolated women took off a day or two to gather in town and work on special projects which would bring relief to an old "granny" or an overworked farm woman giving birth to yet another baby. She also described the life-line formed by letters from women whom she had never met but who corresponded with her over a period of several years. In fact, her first letter, dated 21 June 1919, begins thus: "We are friends now, so we won't stand on ceremony. At last! At last! I am going to have friends who will be glad to see me when I go back to the world for a visit or to stay. Time will tell, but I presume that it will be when I am old and gray."

Another persistent theme emphasizes the commitment of writers to rural life. Hilda Rose suffered enormous worries and frustrations on her little Montana ranch, yet she says it is "better to die fasting with a flower in my hand" than to live in poverty in a city. Elinore Pruitt Stewart argues that homesteading is "the solution of all poverty's problems," although she recognizes that temperament has much to do with success in any undertaking, and persons afraid of wolves and work and loneliness had better let ranching alone." She goes on to say that

> any woman who can stand her own company,
> can see the beauty of the sunset, loves growing
> things, and is willing to put in as much time
> at careful labor as she does over the washtub,
> will certainly succeed; will have independence,
> plenty to eat all the time, and a home of her
> own in the end.

In *The First Four Years*, Laura Ingalls Wilder is quite blunt in her assessment of the hardships endured by farm women, especially during a period of drought such as the one she and Manly faced when they were first married. Nevertheless, she rose to the challenge: "It would be a fight to win out in this business of farming, but strangely she felt her spirit rising to the struggle."

In our first selection, Buffalobird-woman describes farming methods of the Hidatsa women in the 1840s. Charlotte Ouisconsin Van Cleve focuses on her family's ordeals during their first winter in Long Prairie, Minnesota, when the new town was isolated by an extensive blizzard. Two writers, Melissa Moore and Jennie Osborn, re-create the lives of young married women on the Kansas frontier in the 1860s and 1870s, while Mrs. "Doaty" Orpen recounts the excitement and responsibilities as a girl homesteader in Kansas from 1862-1865. Alice Dahlin Lund recreates the daily life and adventures of a girl in a Swedish community in western Wisconsin in the 1870s. The transition from frontier to established communities is described in Mary Bailey's memories of Alberta and in Ada Mae Brinton's Iowa history.

Dakota farms frequently have been the hardest hit by natural catastrophes, and such recurring ordeals have led many Dakota women to write about rural life. Mary Larrabee recalls the 1870s when her husband was "sentenced" to ten years on the prairie after having deserted from the U.S. Army. Laura Ingalls Wilder faced repeated hardships in the late 1880s. Edith Eudora Kohl's memoirs record the debilitating drought of 1907 and her desire to flee the sun-dried 160 acres which she and her sister were trying to "prove up." In 1914 Anne Langhorne

Waltz, a minister's wife, spent the summer on a homestead with her nine-month-old baby when the heat soared to 110 degrees every day, and she barely escaped disaster when her water supply ran out. In the same year, Era Bell Thompson's family struggled through their first year on a North Dakota farm. Thompson's story is of special interest because it shows how white neighbors, at a time of crisis, came to the aid of her parents, who were black.

Elinore Pruitt Stewart and Hilda Rose describe life on small ranches in their letters to friends; Stewart writes about Wyoming, 1909-1913, and Rose's letters begin in 1919 in Montana and end a few years later in northern Alberta. Anne Greenwood Pike and her "city boy" husband farmed—and failed—in Idaho.

Depression and drought are the dominant images of the 1930s. Meridel LeSueur describes the landscape as she rides a bus through the Dakotas: the prairies "looked like an evacuated countryside with the people running out after the enemy had passed." Grace Fairchild, however, was one of the Dakota farmers who emerged from the Depression with her farm intact, partly because she worked with country farm agents and planted crops which were suitable to the soil and climate.

Our epilogue highlights the farm experiences of a Wisconsin woman, Lynn Spielman Dummer. She deals with age-old farm problems with the assistance of unique 1980s resources, including a strong women's network.

The spirited women whose stories appear in this anthology are indeed survivors. Their situations are familiar to readers who have experienced farm life and listened to family tales of "the old times"; at the same time, many stories take curious twists and provide fresh details. Although the patterns of these farm women's lives can no longer be repeated, we can carry their solid values and determined optimism with us into the twenty-first century.

C. F.

Acknowledgments

We are indebted to Polly Emerich for her perseverance, reliability and good will as she transformed the rough drafts into camera-ready copy. Her flexibility and her commitment to the project made our task easier at every stage.

We appreciate the talents of our illustrator: Lee Fairbanks reproduced the illustrations in the first selection by Buffalobird-woman.

We are indebted to the following for permission to reprint works included in this anthology.

Buffalo Bird Woman as told to Gilbert L. Wilson, "Beginning a Garden" and "Since White Men Came," from *Buffalo Bird Woman's Garden: Agriculture of the Hidatsa Indians.* Copyright 1917 by the University of Minnesota as *Agriculture of the Hidatsa Indians: An Indian Interpretation*; reprint edition 1987 by Minnesota Historical Society Press.

Elizabeth Hampsten, ed. *To All Inquiring Friends: Letters, Diaries and Essays in North Dakota.* Grand Forks, ND: Department of English, U of North Dakota, 1979. 55-60. Mary Young, Jamestown, North Dakota, who contributes the Larrabee letters to Hampsten's anthology.

Laura Ingalls Wilder. *The First Four Years*, pp. 98-134. Illustrated by Garth Williams. Text copyright (c) 1970 by Roger L. MacBride. Pictures Copyright (c) 1970 by

Garth Williams. All selections reprinted by permission of Harper & Row, Publishers, Inc.

Mr. Hugh A. Dempsey, Historical Society of Alberta, for permission to reprint Mary C. Bailey's "Reminscences of a Pioneer," *Alberta Historical Review* 15 (1967): 17-25.

Ms. Christie Dailey for the article originally published as "Eighty-Six Years in Iowa: The Memoir of Ada Mae Brown Brinton," *Annals of Iowa* 45 (Winter 1981). Reprinted with permission of the State Historical Society of Iowa.

Edith Eudora Kohl's "The Thirsty Land," from *Land of the Burnt Thigh*. Copyright 1938 by Funk & Wagnalls; reprint edition 1986 by the Minnesota Historical Society Press.

Nancy Tystal Koupal, Director of Publications, South Dakota State Historical Society, for permission to reprint Anne Langhorne Waltz's "West River Pioneer," *South Dakota History*, Copyright (c) 1987 by the South Dakota State Historical Society. All Rights Reserved. Reprinted with permission.

Era Bell Thompson, "Testing Ground," from *American Daughter*. Copyright 1946 by the University of Chicago Press; reprint edition 1986 by the Minnesota Historical Society Press. Reprinted with the permission of the University of Chicago Press.

Elaine Maruhn, reprint from *North Star Country*, by Meridel LeSeuer, by permission of University of Nebraska Press. Copyright 1945 by Meridel LeSeuer.

University of Wisconsin-River Falls Press, to reprint from Walker D. Wyman's *Frontier Woman: The Life of a Woman Homesteader* on the Dakota Frontier (1972) pages 103-14.

Writings of Farm Women
1840–1940

"Planting a Garden"
Buffalobird-woman

The land is the common denominator in the stories collected for this anthology. It is appropriate, therefore, to begin with the narration of Buffalobird-woman, who describes the Hidatsa way of planting a garden. Buffalobird-woman (Maxi'-diwac) was the daughter of Small Ankle, one of the leaders of the Hidatsa Indians. She was born about 1839 at Knife River on the Fort Berthold Indian Reservation in North Dakota. Her son, Edward Goodbird, served an an interpreter for Gilbert L. Wilson, who recorded Buffalobird-woman's account of gardening. Wilson says in his introduction to Agriculture of the Hidatsa Indians that he "claims no credit beyond arranging the material and putting the interpreter's Indian-English translations into proper idiom." While Buffalobird-woman's narration focuses on agricultural techniques, it also provides glimpses of family and community relations, tribal values, and women's roles. The first excerpt below describes the process of breaking up land for new gardens. The second excerpt contrasts traditional Indian methods of farming in the 1840s with new methods introduced by the government in the 1870s.

Source:
Gilbert Livingstone Wilson. Agriculture of the Hidatsa Indians: An Indian Interpretation. *University of Minnesota Studies in the Social Sciences No. 9. Minneapolis: U of Minnesota P, 1917. 9-15, 119-20.*

Turtle

My great-grandmother, as white men count their kin, was named Ata'kic, or Soft-white Corn. She adopted a daughter, Mata'tic, or Turtle. Some years after, a daughter was born to Ata'kic, whom she named Otter.

Turtle and Otter both married. Turtle had a daughter named Ica'wikec, or Corn Sucker; and Otter had three daughters, Want-to-be-a-woman, Red Blossom, and Strikes-many-women, all younger than Corn Sucker.

The smallpox year at Five Villages left Otter's family with no male members to support them. Turtle and her daughter were then living in Otter's lodge; and Otter's daughters, as Indian custom bade, called Corn Sucker their elder sister.

It was a custom of the Hidatsas, that if the eldest sister of a household married, her younger sisters were also given to her husband, as they came of marriageable age. Left without male kin by the smallpox, my grandmother's family was hard put to it to get meat; and Turtle gladly gave her daughter to my father, Small Ankle, whom she knew to be a good hunter. Otter's daughters, reckoned as Corn Sucker's sisters, were given to Small Ankle as they grew up; the eldest, Want-to-be-a-woman, was my mother.

When I was four years old, my tribe and the Mandans came to Like-a-fishhook bend. They came in the spring and camped in tepees, or skin tents. By Butterfly's winter count, I know they began building earth lodges the next winter. I was too young to remember much of this.

5

Two years after we came to Like-a-fishhook bend, smallpox again visited my tribe; and my mother, Want-to-be-a-woman, and Corn Sucker, died of it. Red Blossom and Strikes-many-women survived, whom I now called my mothers. Otter and old Turtle lived with us; I was taught to call them my grandmothers.

Clearing Fields

Soon after they came to Like-a-fishhook bend, the families of my tribe began to clear fields, for gardens, like those they had at Five Villages. Rich black soil was to be found in the timbered bottom lands of the Missouri. Most of the work of clearing was done by the women.

In old times we Hidatsas never made our gardens on the untimbered prairie land, because the soil there is too hard and dry. In the bottom lands of the Missouri, the soil is soft and easy to work.

My mothers and my two grandmothers worked at clearing our family's garden. It lay east of the village at a place where many other families were clearing fields.

I was too small to note very much at first. But I remember that my father set boundary marks——whether wooden stakes or little mounds of earth or stones, I do not now remember——at the corners of the field we claimed. My mothers and my two grandmothers began at one end of this field and worked forward. All had heavy iron hoes, except Turtle, who used an old fashioned wooden digging stick.

With their hoes, my mothers cut the long grass that covered much of the field, and bore it off the line, to be burned. With the same implements, they next dug and softened the soil in places for the corn hills, which were laid off in rows. These hills they planted. Then all summer they worked with their hoes, clearing and breaking the ground between the hills.

Trees and bushes I know must have been cut off with iron axes; but I remember little of this, because I was only four years old when the clearing was begun.

I have heard that in very old times, when clearing a new field, my people first dug the corn hills with digging sticks; and afterwards, like my mothers, worked between the hills, with bone hoes. My father told me this.

Whether stone axes were used in old times to cut the trees and undergrowths, I do not know. I think fields were never then laid out on ground that had large trees on it.

Dispute and Its Settlement

About two years after the first ground was broken in our field, a dispute, I remember, arose between my mothers and two of their neighbors, Lone Woman and Goes-to-next-timber.

These two women were clearing fields adjoining that of my mothers; as will be seen by the accompanying map (figure 1), the three fields met at a corner. I have said that my father, to set up claim to his field, had placed marks, one of them in the corner at which met the fields of Lone Woman and Goes-to-next-timber; but while my mothers were busy clearing and digging up the other end of their field, their two neighbors invaded this marked-off corner; Lone Woman had even dug up a small part before she was discovered.

However, when they were shown the mark my father had placed, the two women yielded and accepted payment for any rights they might have.

It was our Indian rule to keep our fields very sacred. We did not like to quarrel about our garden lands. One's title to a field once set up, no one ever thought of disputing it; for if one were selfish and quarrelsome, and tried to seize land belonging to another, we thought some evil would come upon him, as that some one of his family would die. There is a story of a black bear who got into a pit that was not his own, and had his mind taken away from him for doing so!

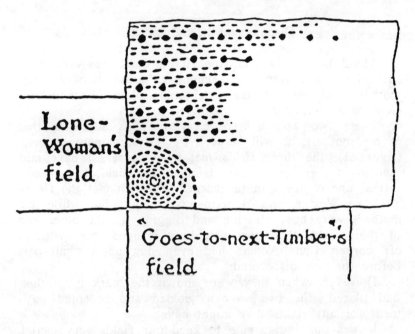

Figure 1. Map of newly broken field

Turtle Breaking Soil

Lone Woman and Goes-to-next-timber having withdrawn, my grandmother, Turtle, volunteered to break the soil of the corner that had been in dispute. She was an industrious woman. Often, when my mothers were busy in the earth lodge, she would go out to work in the garden, taking me with her for company. I was six years old then, I think, quite too little to help her any, but I liked to watch my grandmother work.

With her digging stick, she dug up a little round place in the center of the corner (figure 1); and circling around this from day to day, she gradually enlarged the dug-up space. The point of her digging stick she forced into the soft earth to a depth equal to the length of my hand, and pried up the soil. The clods she struck smartly with her digging stick, sometimes with one end, sometimes with the other. Roots of coarse grass, weeds, small brush and the like, she took in her hand and shook, or struck them against the ground, to knock off the loose earth clinging to them; she then cast them into a little pile to dry.

In this way she accumulated little piles, scattered rather irregularly over the dug-up ground, averaging, perhaps, four feet, one from the other. In a few days these little piles had dried; and Turtle gathered them up into a heap, about four feet high, and burned them, sometimes within the cleared ground, sometimes a little way outside.

In the corner that had been in dispute, and in other parts of the field, my grandmother worked all summer. I do not remember how big our garden was at the end of her summer's work, nor how many piles of roots she burned; but I remember distinctly how she put the roots of weeds and grass and brush into little piles to dry, which she then gathered into heaps and burned. She did not attempt to burn over the whole ground, only the heaps.

Afterwards, we increased our garden from year to year until it was as large as we needed. I remember seeing my grandmother digging along the edges of the garden with her digging stick, to enlarge the field and make the edges even and straight.

I remember also, that as Turtle dug up a little space, she would wait until the next season to plant it. Thus, additional ground dug up in the summer or fall would be planted by her the next spring.

There were two or three elm trees in the garden; these my grandmother left standing.

It must not be supposed that upon Turtle fell all the work of clearing land to enlarge our garden; but she liked to have me with her when she worked, and I remember best what I saw her do. As I was a little girl then, I have forgotten much that she did; but this that I have told, I remember distinctly.

Turtle's Primitive Tools

In breaking ground for our garden, Turtle always used an ash digging stick (figure 2); and when hoeing time came, she hoed the corn with a bone hoe (figure 3). Digging sticks are still used in my tribe for digging wild turnips; but even in my grandmother's lifetime, digging sticks and bone hoes, as garden tools, had all but given place to iron hoes and axes.

My grandmother was one of the last women of my tribe to cling to these old-fashioned implements. Two other women, I remember, owned bone hoes when I was a little girl; but Turtle, I think, was the very last one in the tribe who actually worked in her garden with one.

This hoe my grandmother kept in the lodge, under her bed; and when any of the children of the household tried to get it out to look at it, she would cry, "Let that hoe alone; you will break it!"

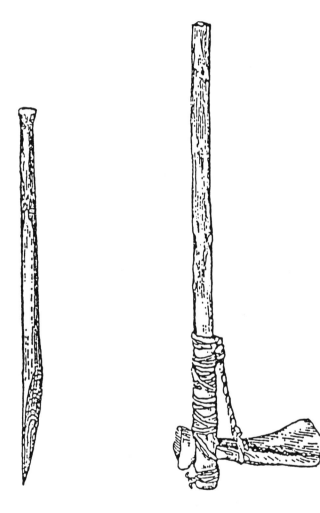

Figure 2. Ash digging stick   Figure 3. Bone hoe

Beginning a Field in Later Times

As I grew up, I learned to work in the garden, as every Hidatsa woman was expected to learn; but iron axes and hoes, bought of the traders, were now used by everybody, and the work of clearing and breaking a new field was less difficult than it had been in our grandfathers' times. A family had also greater freedom in choosing where they should have their garden, since with iron axes they could more easily cut down any small trees and bushes that might be on the land. However, to avoid having to cut down big trees, a rather open place was usually chosen.

A family, then, having chosen a place for a field, cleared off the ground as much as they could, cutting down small trees and bushes in such a way that the trees fell all in one direction. Some of the timber that was fit might be taken home for firewood; the rest was let lie to dry until spring, when it was fired. The object of felling the trees in one direction was to make them cover the ground as much as possible, since firing them softened the soil and left it loose and mellow for planting. We sought always to burn over all the ground, if we could.

Before firing, the family carefully raked off the dry grass and leaves from the edge of the field, and cut down any brush wood. This was done that the fire might not spread to the surrounding timber, nor out on the prairie. Prairie fires and forest fires are even yet not unknown on our reservation.

Planting season having come, the women of the household planted the field in corn. The hills were in rows, and about four feet or a little less apart. They were rather irregularly placed the first year. It was easy to make a hill in the ashes where a brush heap had been fired, or in soil that was free of roots and stumps; but there were many stumps in the field, left over from the previous summer's clearing. If the planter found a stump stood where a hill should be, she placed the hill on this side of the stump or beyond it, no matter how close this brought the hill to the next in the row. Thus, the corn hills did not stand at even distances in the row the first year; but the rows were always kept even and straight.

While the corn was coming up, the women worked at clearing out the roots and smaller stumps between the hills; but a stump of any considerable size was left to rot, especially if it stood midway between two corn hills, where it did not interfere with their cultivation. My mothers and I used to labor in a similar way to enlarge our fields. With our iron hoes we made hills along the edge of the field and planted corn; then, as we had opportunity, we worked with our hoes between the corn hills to loosen up the soil.

Although our tribe now had iron axes and hoes from the traders, they still used their native-made rakes. These were of wood (figure 4), or of the antler of a black-tailed deer (figure 5). It was with such rakes that the edges of a newly opened field were cleaned of leaves for the firing of the brush, in the spring.

Trees in the Garden

Trees were not left standing in the garden, except perhaps one to shade the watchers' stage. If a tree stood in the field, it shaded the corn; and that on the north side of the tree never grew up strong, and the stalks would be yellow. Cottonwood trees were apt to grow up in the field, unless the young shoots were plucked up as they appeared.

Our West Field

The field which Turtle helped to clear, lay, I have said, east of the village. I was about nineteen years old, I think, when my mothers determined to clear ground for a second field, west of the village.

There were five of us who undertook the work, my father, my two mothers, Red Blossom and Strikes-many-women, my sister, Cold Medicine, and myself. We began in the fall, after harvesting the corn from our east garden, so that we had leisure for the work; we had been too busy to begin earlier in the season.

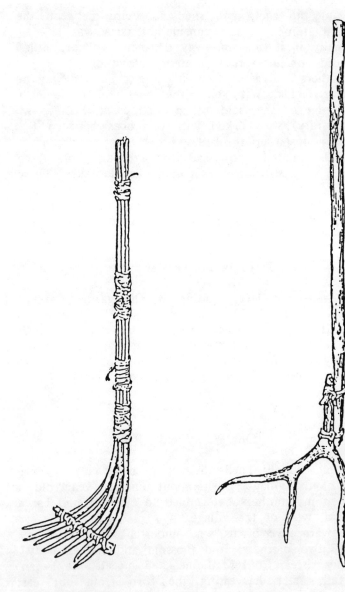

Figure 4.

Native-made rake (wood)

Figure 5.

Native-made rake (antler)

We chose a place down in the bottoms, overgrown with willows; and with our axes we cut the willows close to the ground, letting them lie as they fell.

I do not know how many days we worked; but we stopped when we had cleared a field of about seventy-five by one hundred yards, perhaps. In our east, or yellow corn field, we counted nine rows of corn to one *na'xu;* and I remember that when we came to plant our new field, it had nine *na'xu.*

Burning Over the Field

The next spring my father, his two wives, my sister, and I went out and burned the felled willows and brush which the spring sun had dried. We did not burn them every day; only when the weather was fine. We would go out after breakfast, burn until tired of the work, and come home.

We sought to burn over the whole field, for we knew that this left a good, loose soil. We did not pile the willows in heaps, but loosened them from the ground or scattered them loosely but evenly over the soil. In some places the ground was quite bare of willows; but we collected dry grass and weeds and dead willows, and strewed them over these bare places, so that the fire would run over the whole area of the field.

It took us about four days to burn over the field.

It was well known in my tribe that burning over new ground left the soil soft and easy to work, and for this reason we thought it a wise thing to do. . . .

How We Got Potatoes and Other Vegetables

The government has changed our old way of cultivating corn and our other vegetables, and has brought us seeds of many new vegetables and grains, and taught us their use. We Hidatsas and our friends, the Mandans, have also been removed from our village at Like-a-fishhook bend, and made to take our land in allotments; so that our old agriculture has in a measure fallen into disuse.

I was thirty-three years old when the government first plowed up fields for us; two big fields were broken, one between the village and the agency, and another on the farther side of the agency.

New kinds of seeds were issued to us, oats and wheat; and we were made to plant them in these newly plowed fields. Another field was plowed for us down in the bottom land along the Missouri; and here we were taught to plant potatoes. Each family was given a certain number of rows to plant and cultivate.

At first we Hidatsas did not like potatoes, because they smelled so strongly! Then we sometimes dug up our potatoes and took them into our earth lodges; and when cold weather came, the potatoes were frozen, and spoiled. For these reasons we did not take much interest in potatoes, and often left them in the ground, not bothering to dig them.

Other seeds were issued to us, of watermelons, big squashes, onions, turnips, and other vegetables. Some of these we tried to eat, but did not like them very well; even the turnips and big squashes, we thought not so good as our own squashes and our wild prairie turnips. Moreover, we did not know how to dry these new vegetables for winter; so we often did not trouble even to harvest them.

The government was eager to teach the Indians to raise potatoes; and to get us women to cultivate them, paid as much as two dollars and a half a day for planting them in the plowed field. I remember I was paid that sum for planting them. After three or four years, finding the Indians did not have much taste for potatoes and rather seldom ate them, our agent made a big cache pit——a root cellar you say it was——and bought our potato crop of us. After this he would issue seed potatoes to us in the spring, and in the fall we would sell our crop to him. Thus, handling potatoes each year, we learned little by little to eat them.

The New Cultivation

The government also broke up big fields of prairie ground, and had us plant corn in them; but these fields on the prairie near the hills I do not think are so good as our old fields down in the timber lands along the Missouri. The prairie fields get dry easily and the soil is harder and more difficult to work.

Then I think our old way of raising corn is better than the new way taught us by white men. Last year, 1911, our agent held an agricultural fair on this reservation; and we Indians competed for prizes for the best corn. The corn which I sent to the fair took the first prize. I raised it on new ground; the ground had been plowed, but aside from that, I cultivated the corn exactly as in old times, with a hoe.

Life on Long Prairie
Charlotte Ouisconsin Van Cleve

Charlotte Ouisconsin Van Cleve published her autobiography when she was 69 years old. During her lifetime she saw the midwestern wilderness undergo a dramatic transformation. When she lived at Fort Snelling as a child in the early 1800's, the population consisted mostly of Indians, fur traders, and soldiers. By the time she wrote her book, farms and towns had sprung up along the banks of the Mississippi River. Nearby, the city of Minneapolis, where Charlotte lived, had become a major center of trade, industry, and education.

Charlotte was born in 1819 at Prairie du Chien, Wisconsin, where her father's regiment was located. She spent her early years at Fort Snelling and then, as a young girl, was sent to a girl's school in Connecticut. She returned to the midwest and married Mr. Van Cleve who, shortly after their marriage, resigned from the military and became a teacher. They lived in Ohio, Missouri, and Michigan. In 1856, because of poor health, they decided to join an emigration company settling in Long Prairie, Minnesota. The selection below describes the family's ordeals during their first winter on the frontier. Charlotte attributes their survival to two factors: love of family and faith in God.

Source:
Charlotte Ouisconsin Van Cleve. "Three Score Years and Ten": Life-Long Memories of Fort Snelling, Minnesota, and Other Parts of the West. *Minneapolis: Harrison & Smith, 1888.*

In the autumn of 1856 our family removed to Long Prairie, Todd County, Minnesota, as the nucleus of a colony which was to settle and develop a large tract of land, purchased from the government by a company, some members of which were our friends and relatives. The weather was very pleasant when we left our Michigan home, but at the Mississippi river the *squaw winter*, immediately preceding *Indian summer*, came upon us with unusual sharpness, and lasted through the remainder of our journey. We were to cross the river at a little hamlet called "Swan River," and our plan was to hire conveyances there which should take us the remaining distance. But on arriving at this point we found a young friend who had come West for his health, and was acting as agent for my brother, one of the owners of the purchase. He was on a business errand and not well prepared to take us back with him, but as we learned that it would be impossible to procure transportation for two or three days, and were extremely anxious to reach the end of our journey, he decided to make the attempt. We made the transit in small skiffs amidst huge cakes of floating ice, which threatened to swamp us before we reached the western shore, and our fears well nigh got the better of some of us, but taking a lesson from the implicit confidence our dear children reposed in us, we rested in our Heavenly Father's love and care, and so passed safely and trustingly over. At 4 P.M., we struck out into the wilderness, but the roads being rough and our load heavy, we made very slow progress. By 9 o'clock we had not reached the halfway mark, but by way of encouragement to the horses, and in consideration of the tired, hungry children, we came to a halt and improvised a nocturnal picnic. It was cold, very cold, there was no shelter, no light but the camp-fire, and yet there was an attempt at cheerfulness, and the entertainment passed off with some degree of merriment.

After an hour's rest we resumed our journey, and, although our conveyance was an open wagon, so crowded as to be very uncomfortable, especially for the children, yet we did the best we could, and the little emigrants bore the journey bravely for some hours longer. But within six miles of our destination, just beside a deserted Indian encampment, our horses fairly gave out and would not pull another inch. So a large camp-fire was made; a sort of shelter constructed of branches of trees; a Buffalo robe laid on the ground, and the weary travelers found a temporary resting place, while our young friend, above alluded to, started with the used-up team to bring us help, if he could reach the prairie. I had chosen to pass the hours of waiting in the wagon, feeling that I could better protect my dear little baby in this way. So when all the tired ones were still, and the silence only broken by the crackling of the burning fagots, the occasional falling of a dry twig or branch from the bare, ghostly looking trees about us, the hooting of an owl, the dismal howlings of the wolves in the forest, I sat there looking at the weary forms so illy protected from the cold, thinking of the little white beds in which my dear ones were wont to slumber peacefully and comfortably, the friends who we had left, whom might even now be dreaming of us, of some of the farewell tea drinkings by cheerful firesides in dear old Ann Arbor, where tender words had been spoken, and our prospects in a far western home been discussed over delicate, tempting viands, prepared by loving hands; and these thoughts kept my *heart* warmed and comforted, albeit I shivered with external cold; but hugging my baby closer, and committing all to the care of Him who never slumbers nor sleeps, I was just sinking into unconsciousness when a voice, not heard for a year and a half, broke the deep

stillness with: "How! Nitchie!" and there by the flickering
light of the fire, I saw our eldest son, who had left us,
for a trip with his uncle to the Rocky Mountains a mere
boy, and now stood before us in size a man. As his
father rose to his feet, he exclaimed in an agony of joy:
"Oh! Father, is it you?" and he fell upon his father's
neck and wept, and his father wept upon his neck. Then,
as in a dream, I heard, "Where's Mother?" In an instant
he stood beside me, and I was sobbing in the arms of
my first-born, my well-beloved son.

Our messenger had told him that the horses had given
out just beside an Indian encampment, and that, unless all
haste was made, the load might be carried off. So the
boy, without a moment's delay, took his horses and came
at full speed to save the goods. Hence his first salutation,
greeting, as he supposed, a party of Chippewas.

The little camp was all alive with surprise and joyful
excitement, and with a hearty appreciation of this very
good practical joke, we were soon in motion again,
wending our way, with lightened hearts, to our journey's
end, which we reached without further let or hindrance.
After a brief, but much needed rest, we opened our eyes
on a calm fair Sabbath morning, and our new home, in
the soft hazy light of an Indian summer sunrise was very
lovely. It required no very vivid imagination to fancy
ourselves in the happy valley of "Rasselas, Prince of
Abyssinia," and it seemed to me impossible that any one
could ever desire, like that discontented youth, to leave so
charming a spot. The term prairie is a misnomer in this
case; instead we found a beautiful fruitful valley lying
between two low ranges of hills, interspersed with groves
of trees and picturesque lakes, and watered by a river
winding gracefully through its whole length. It had been
the seat of the Winnebago Agency, and there were, still
standing, in pretty good order, a large number of houses.
These buildings, empty though they were, gave the idea
of a settlement, dispelling every thing like a feeling of
loneliness or isolation. On our way to our new home, we
had purchased, at Dubuque, ample supplies for a year,
but (the steamboats at that season being much crowded)
were obliged to leave them with our household goods to

follow, as we were assured in the next boat. Resting in this assurance and being supplied for the present, we had no anxiety for the future; we knew not what was before us. God tenderly "shaded our eyes," and we were very happy and full of hope. Prairie hens and pheasants were abundant beyond belief. Our boys, standing in the kitchen door, could frequently shoot as many as we needed from the trees in the dooryard, while the numerous lakes in the vicinity afforded us most excellent fish, such as an epicure might have envied us. Some of our family, enfeebled by malarial fevers, and the ills resulting from them, imbibed fresh draughts of health and life with every breath, the weak lungs and tender irritable throats healed rapidly in the kindly strengthening atmosphere, and hearts that had been sore at parting with dear friends and a beloved home, were filled with gratitude to Him who had led us to so fair and lovely a resting place, and we mark that time with a white stone in memory of His loving kindness in thus preparing us for what was to come.

Early in December, winter came upon us in earnest; snow fell to such a depth that we were fairly shut out from the whole world, and so suddenly as to find us unprepared. It was difficult and almost impossible, on account of the deep snow, to procure wood sufficient to keep up the constant fires necessary on account of the intense cold. We had no mail, no telegraph, no news from our supplies. Yet we hoped and made the best of our situation. Our children, who had read *Robinson Crusoe* and *Swiss Family Robinson*, thoroughly enjoyed this entirely new experience, and, every day explored the various empty houses, returning from their expeditions with different household articles left by the former occupants as worthless, but which served us a purpose in furnishing our table and kitchen. But day by day our temporary supplies lessened, and with all the faith we could call to our aid, we could not but feel somewhat anxious. A crop of wheat raised on the place the preceding summer had been stored, unthreshed, in some of the empty buildings, and this, at last, came to be our only dependence. The mill on the property had, of course, been frozen up, and only after hours of hard work, could my husband and the boys so far clear it of ice, as to succeed in making flour, and such flour! I have always regretted that we did not preserve a specimen for exhibition and chemical analysis, for verily the like was never seen before, and I defy any one of our great Minneapolis mills to produce an imitation of it. The wheat was very smutty, and having no machinery to remedy this evil, all efforts to cleanse it proved unsatisfactory, but the compound prepared from it which we called *bread,* was so rarely obtainable, as to be looked upon as a luxury. Our daily "staff of life" was unground wheat.

A large number of Chippewa Indians were encamped about us most of the time, and not being able to hunt successfully, on account of the very deep snow, were driven to great extremity, and sometimes, acting on the well established principle, that "self-preservation is the first law of nature," broke in the windows of our extemporized granaries, and helped themselves to grain. They were welcome to it under the circumstances, but in obtaining it they had broken in the windows, and had mixed glass with it to such an extent that it was unsafe for food until we had picked it all over, grain by grain. This process was our daily occupation and amusement. I distinctly recall the scene in our dining-room, when all the available members of the family were seated around a long pine table, with a little pile of wheat before each, replenished from time to time from the large heap in the center, working away industriously, conversing cheerfully, telling interesting and amusing stories, singing songs, never complaining, but all manifesting a feeling of gratitude that we still saw before us what would support life, for, at least, a while longer; and taking heart and strength to endure, in the hope that before this, our last resource was exhausted, we should receive our long expected supplies, which were somewhere on the way to us. This wheat was boiled, and eaten with salt, the only seasoning of any kind we had; no butter, no milk, no meat, nothing, and yet we never can forget the intense relish with which our children partook of it, one of them remarking, on one occasion, "Mother, how good this wheat is; I wish you would write to Ann Arbor and tell the boys there of it; I don't believe they know." A little child was teaching us, and the amount of strength and comfort imparted to us by such a manifestation of perfect contentment, gratitude and trust can never be computed in words. We realized in those days, as never before, the full force and beauty of the Icelandic custom: living in the midst of dangers seen and unseen, these people, we are told, every morning open the outer door, and looking reverently up to Heaven, thank God they are still alive. So when with each returning day we saw our children safe and well, our first feeling was, gratitude that the Eternal God, who was our only refuge, had not removed from underneath us His everlasting arms.

The nearest settlement of any kind was "Swan River," on the Mississippi, but we were so completely blockaded with snow, that no team could possibly get through. Two or three times during that memorable winter, our oldest son, a boy of eighteen years, made the trip on snow-shoes, at the risk of his life, to get our mail, and learn, if possible, something of our supplies. The round trip was a three days' journey, and there being no stopping place or house of any kind on the route, he, of course, was obliged to camp out one night. Our anxiety during his absence was terrible, and we remember vividly our overpowering sense of relief, when, at the close of the third day, long before his form was discernible, some familiar song in his clear ringing tones, broke on the still night air, to assure the dear home folks he was safe and well. Like the man whose business was so urgent he could not stop to rest, but now and then picked up a stone and carried it some distance, then threw it down, and went on relieved and encouraged, so we, when we laid down this burden of anxiety felt rested and better able to bear our daily trials.

It is due to our only neighbors, the Indians, to say that they were by no means troublesome, that our inter-course with them was pleasant, and to some of them we became much attached. A great chief's wife was a frequent visitor at our house, her little son, of perhaps eight winters being her invariable attendant. On one occasion having missed a small case-knife of rather peculiar formation, which was in daily use, I ventured to ask her if the little lad had taken it to their wigwam, it occurred to me he might have done so, innocently, to show some of his family, in whose honesty I had implicit faith. The old woman drew herself up to her full height, and with a grace and dignity which would have done honor to the mother of the Gracchi, said, in all the expressiveness of her native tongue: *"The son of Ne-ba-quum cannot steal!"* In real admiration and reverent contrition, I laid my hand on the injured mother's shoulder, and explained my meaning. She accepted my apology fully and graciously, giving me her hand, in token that my error was condoned, and you will readily believe it was never repeated. Through all the years of our residence at Long Prairie she and her family were always welcome guests at our house, when in their wanderings they came that way, and when, during our late war, her brave, loyal husband's offers to assist us in our struggle, were contemptuously scorned by one of our Generals, and the mortified, broken-hearted old chieftain, unable to bear under such an insult, went to the "happy hunting grounds," we sincerely mourned the loss of our staunch and honored friend, Ne-ba-quum.

Some time in January, our five year old boy was very suddenly seized with pleurisy in its most violent form, and for hours he seemed in mortal agony. We had no efficient remedies, no doctor within thirty, perhaps fifty miles, and to complicate matters, I had lain down sick for the first time, thoroughly vanquished by fatigue and unusual exposure. But that sickness of mine had to be postponed, and we fought all that night with the fearful disease, using vigorously all the external remedies within our reach, cupping the dear child with inexperienced hands, but prayerful hearts, leaning entirely upon God, who, when we cried unto Him in our distress, heard and mercifully regarded our cries. The acute and agonizing symptoms of the attack were subdued, but lung fever supervened, and for four weeks our dear boy lay very near death. His form wasted, his hands, through extreme attenuation, became almost translucent, and we could only watch and pray, and use all the means in our power to alleviate his sufferings. I recall the seasons of family worship around the sick bed, when we were drawn so near the All-pitying Father that we could talk with Him, as a man talketh with his friend, when the loving Savior made us feel that He was near us to sympathize with us, and the Blessed Comforter brooded over us, and spoke peace to our sorrowing hearts, so that we could say, "Thy will be done," and from our hearts could sing:

> "*Ill* that God blesses is our *good*,
>   And unblest *good* is ill;
> And all is right, that seems most wrong,
>   If it be His dear will.

> "When obstacles and trials seem
>   Like prison walls to be
> We'll do the little we can do,
>   And leave the rest to Thee."

During this trying time, our stock of candles was nearly exhausted, and our weary watchings were only lighted by a sense of God's presence. So with our hand on the dear sufferer, and our ear attentive to his breathing, his father and I sat beside him, lighting our candle only when absolutely necessary, and felt as none can feel until they have tested it, the sustaining grace and Infinite love of the Blessed Watcher, who never slumbers nor sleeps. He granted us sweet thoughts of His love and precious promises, which were to us as songs in the night, and under the shadow of His wings, our hearts were kept in perfect peace. Thanks to the Great Healer, a change for the better came, and then occurred a strange thing, that has always seemed to me directly Providential.

During a bitter wind and blinding snow storm, some snow birds took refuge in our wood-shed and were caught by the Indian boys. At the suggestion of our oldest son, who had read somewhere the story of a sick child and her Canaries, these little refugees were brought into the nursery and soon became perfectly tame, flying all about the sick boy's head, lighting on his hands, and amusing and resting him wonderfully. For several days the storm continued, and we sheltered the little creatures, our invalid growing better so rapidly as to excite our surprise. But at last there came a mild bright day, and we turned them out to find their companions. Why was it that they flew only a few rods and then fell dead? To us it seemed that these little winged messengers had been driven to us in our extremity by the fury of the storm as healing agents, and had given their lives for our child's. The question now arose, where shall we find suitable food for our convalescent? There seemed no possible help for us, but we believed it would come. One morning as I sat wondering how this would be brought about, my dear brother came in, and handing me a fresh laid egg, said: "I did not know there was a fowl on the place, but it seems that an old superannuated hen, who doubtless has lived in the wheat all winter has suddenly been aroused to a sense of her duty, and this is the result." Had the golden egg, famous in fable, been presented in his other hand for my choice, it would have been to me no better than a chip, but the treasure he brought me was of priceless value, and I received it gratefully as a gift from God. It furnished a whole day's nourishment for our exhausted, feeble little boy, and for three days he was supplied in the same way; then, just as he was more hungry than ever, and when it was evident he never could regain his strength without nourishment, the supply ceased. We waited and trusted, and in a day or two our son found a fine pheasant, which had evidently lost its way, sitting in the snow, wondering, perhaps, where all its companions were, and why the berries were all gone. Where it came from we never knew, but we do know that there never was so delicious a bird eaten. It was reserved for the sick child, but a small piece was given to each of the other children, and not one of them will ever forget the taste of that precious morsel. By the time this nutritious supply was exhausted, our invalid was so much better as to be able to do his share of picking over wheat, and of eating this simple but very healthful diet.

Soon after this the wheat ran low, the long hard winter had told upon us all, and we seemed to need more substantial food as we had never needed it before. Day after day we managed to prepare something that sustained life, but I had a nursing child, and supporting myself and him too, almost solely upon a wheat diet, had been hard on me and I was much exhausted. We did not lose faith; the spirit was willing, but the flesh was growing weak. I sat one morning after our simple breakfast, with my precious baby in my lap, wondering on what I should feed the dear ones at noon, as scarcely anything remained. The children were full of glee in their unconscious ignorance, and I must not, by a word of repining, shake their sweet trust and faith. Our eldest son sat near me, reading my thoughts, but saying nothing, only conveying by a loving look his sympathy, when, suddenly, a shadow darkened the window; he looked up quickly, and said: "Mother, look there!" I looked, and directly at our door were two sleds heavily laden with our long-looked for supplies! Then came the first tears I had shed that winter. I could not speak, but my over-wrought feelings found most salutary relief in those blessed, grateful tears. There was danger that the powerful reaction would overcome me entirely, but very soon every member of the little colony knew that relief had come, and the work of unloading the sleds, opening boxes, and unheading barrels, was carried on with such ardor, as to leave no chance for such a result, especially as we learned that the teamsters had had no breakfast, that they had been three days coming 28 miles; had been obliged to shovel their way through great drifts, a few rods at a time, and had reached us thoroughly worn out and exhausted. Then came the preparation of that wonderful breakfast. No need that a priest should burn frankincense and myrrh, sending up our orisons in the smoke thereof. The odor of that frying pork, the aroma of that delicious coffee, the perfume of that fragrant tea went up to heaven, full freighted with thanksgiving and praise. No need that a President or Governor should proclaim a day when we should return thanks in view of God's great goodness; it proclaimed itself, and every human being within our reach was bidden to our thanksgiving feast.

Our supplies were ample and varied, and 3 o'clock found a large company seated around a table loaded with excellent, well-cooked food, of which all partook with a gusto most flattering and gratifying to the cook, who was glad to retire to her room with her baby, when the meal was over and rest on her laurels, while the young people danced and made merry in very gladness of heart.

Night closed around a little settlement of thoroughly grateful, happy human beings. What if it was still cold, and there must yet be many stormy days? No fear of suffering or starvation. God had not forgotten us, and we should never cease to trust Him. I could not sleep for very joy, and the delicious sense of relief from anxiety on the score of providing for the daily meals. I seemed to see in the darkness, in illuminated letters, "Jehovah *Fireh*," and felt He had abundantly verified his blessed promise.

In due time the days grew longer and warmer; the snow melted. Large flocks of wild geese passing northward over our heads assured us, with their unmusical but most welcome notes, that the long winter of '56 and '57 was over and gone. The ground was broken up, crops were planted, and everything gave promise of a favorable season. Our home, in its lovely, fresh robes of green, was enchanting, and we felt that the lines had indeed fallen unto us in pleasant places. But as we take pleasant walks through our happy valley, what means this unusual sound that arrests our footsteps? It is like the pattering of gentle summer rain, and yet the sky is clear and cloudless; no drops fall. What can it be? Ah! see that moving in the grass! We stoop to examine, and find myriads of strange-looking insects hardly larger than fleas. They must be——yes, they are, *young grasshopers*. And now may God help us! for we are powerless to arrest their depredations. Day by day they grew and increased, until they covered everything; fields of wheat which promised a bountiful harvest were eaten up so completely that not a green blade or leaf was left; gardens were entirely demolished; screens of cloth put over hot-beds for protection were eaten as greedily as the plants themselves, and the rapidity with which they did their destructive work was amazing. So faded away all our hopes of raising anything available that year, and we watched and waited. But one bright June morning there was a movement and an unusual sound. We rushed to see the cause, and beheld our dire enemy rising in masses, like a great army with banners! They passed over us, making our home for a time the "land shadowing with wings," and finally disappeared in the south. With lightened hearts and willing hands we went to work, replanted some things, and labored thankfully, hopefully and successfully to provide for the next winter.

The experience of the past had taught us much. We felt our hearts stronger and richer for its lessons, and we all look back on that memorable time as something we would not willingly have missed out of our lives, for we learned that one may be reduced to great straits, may have few or no external comforts, and yet be very happy, with that satisfying, independent happiness which outward circumstances cannot affect.

"God Was Good to His Immigrants"
Melissa Genett Moore

The Moore family emigrated to Kansas in 1857 and settled on "broad prairie" five miles from LeRoy. Moore's account includes typical homesteading situations. She describes two families (fifteen members living in one room), running out of provisions during a blizzard, the drought and the grasshoppers; the mother making the children's shoes from the men's old boots, the variety of preachers passing through—Dunkards, Campbellites, and Methodists. When Melissa's father decided their homestead was not a good one, they moved to Allen County. Melissa married at a young age (probably at the age of fifteen), and she and her husband took out a claim on a homestead. Melissa is one of the few writers who discusses politics; she homesteaded in Kansas when the debate was hot between "free state" men and those who were pro-slavery. Of particular interest is her account of 200 Osage Indians who lived nearby and provided the family with protection.

Source:
Melissa Genett Moore. The Story of a Kansas Pioneer, Being the Autobiography of Melissa Genett Anderson. *Intro. Melvin Gillison Rigg. Mt. Vernon, Ohio: Manufacturing Printers Co., 1924. 22-46.*

The first of March, 1857, found us saying good-bye to our neighbors and life-long friends and to my dear old grandmother, Mary Cramer Jeffrey. The greatest sorrow that ever came to my childish heart was leaving Grandmother behind, and all alone. If I could have had my choice, I would have stayed with her.

A good neighbor took us in his wagon to Richmond, fourteen miles away. There we took the railroad to Indianapolis, and then on to Kokomo. From Kokomo we went by wagon to Greentown, Indiana, where one of my mother's sisters lived. It was not for the purpose of making them a visit, as much as we enjoyed that, but so that Uncle and his family could join us in the trip to Kansas.

We found our aunt in delicate health; so it was decided that Mother and we children should remain a few months with her while Father and Uncle should go to Kansas, get located, stake out their claims, and build a house. Uncle would then return for both families.

They took adjoining claims of 160 acres each out on the broad prairie, five miles from LeRoy, in Coffey County. On the side where the claims joined, a plot of 20 acres, 10 acres in each claim, was fenced. Father then went to Missouri, where he bought two yoke of oxen and an ox wagon, for all the timber for improvements had to be hauled from the Neosho River, three miles distant. Uncle now returned to Indiana for the families, leaving Father to get the timber cut and the logs hauled for a house.

It was August before enough logs were on the ground. Then the neighbors were all invited to the house raising. That was the custom--everyone helped everyone else raise his house. But alas! August was the month the ague set in. No one was exempt. Any man, woman, or child was likely to be prostrated between nine o'clock in the morning and noon. The attack might come any minute. The person would be very sick until, sometime in the night, his fever would go. Then in the morning he could work for a while. By the time Father's house was four rounds high, the men, one after the other, had been attacked by the ague. It took three raisings to get the walls up, and on account of the "fever and chills," as the ague was sometimes called, that was as far as the house got before the families arrived.

Uncle returned to Indiana, settled some business, and then we all started to Kansas. Besides the two families, the party included a young man, the son of Uncle's former partner in a store at Greentown. My older sister, Harriet, was fifteen years of age at this time, and this young man's companions took advantage of the opportunity to tease him about her.

"I know what you are going to Kansas for," they would say. "You are going after that Anderson girl."

"No, I'm not," was the reply. "If I'd take either, I'd take the little one." This was myself, twelve years old.

We went by railroad to St. Louis, where we were to take a boat up the Missouri River. When we arrived at St. Louis, we found a boat that would start in an hour. There was also a new boat starting the next morning on its first trip. We wanted very much to take the new boat, but with our numerous family thought it best not to wait. The next afternoon we saw the new boat coming with flags flying. Men were waving hats; women, handkerchiefs. Our boat fired up and we ran side by side for an hour. Then the new boat steamed ahead with great shouting and rejoicing. The next afternoon we passed the new boat again. This time there was no waving of banners or any other sign of life. The bare top was out of the water. It had sunk in the night, we learned, and although no lives had been lost, there had been no time to save property.

We were five days and five nights on the river, being installed two nights on a sand bar. Our family seemed to attract quite a little attention on the boat, I suppose on account of its size. While Mother was in Greentown, a baby was born to her, making her seven children. Then there were all of Uncle's family and the young man from Greentown. He was evidently regarded as one of Mother's children, for he was frequently asked for introductions to his "sister" (Harriet). My oldest brother, who was ten years old at the time, one day overheard a conversation. "There is a Mormon on board this boat," the man was saying. "He has two wives and seventeen children. There stands one of the boys now." The speaker pointed at my brother.

We left the boat at Westport Landing, near Kansas City. Father met us here with two yoke of oxen and an ox wagon. We had brought very little besides our bedding and clothing, but it was necessary to pile box on top of box. We left room in front for Mother and for the eight children under seven years of age. The rest walked the hundred miles to the Neosho Valley. We were two weeks making the trip. The oxen were slow; we were heavily loaded; and when it rained we would not break camp.

Sometime in October or November of 1857 we reached our claim, and stretched our tent in the yard. It rained all night and most of the next day. There was no prospect of getting breakfast, but about ten o'clock three neighbors came to see how we were making it, and took us into their homes until the rain stopped. Father was sick, and the little two-months-old baby died. Uncle and the young man that came with us soon covered the house with clapboards, which Father had prepared by splitting oak chunks three feet long. They then cut out a door, built a fireplace in one end, and painted the cracks between the logs with mud. There was no floor except that of Mother Earth.

We were then ready to move in. The next thing to consider was furniture. A goods box was made into a table. Bedsteads presented a harder problem, but a tidy mother like mine could not make her beds on the floor, especially when that was nature's soil. She got some fence posts, smoothed them off, and bored a two-inch auger hole through them for the bed rail to rest in. Smaller holes were bored every eight or ten inches apart around the bed, and a strong cord, called a bed cord, was run lengthwise and crosswise and was drawn tight. This made a comfortable bed. Seats, if not chairs, were made by splitting logs of various lengths and attaching legs. Our goods boxes were made into cupboard and shelves. We cooked at the fireplace, baking bread in a skillet. Thus was our home furnished. And it was as good as anything belonging to our neighbors, who were taking claims at the time, and whose little log houses were dotting the prairie for miles around us.

We had a warm and pleasant winter. We could not get lonesome with fifteen in the family. By January 1, however, Uncle had his house ready and moved out. This left us reduced to eight.

Provisions were high and scarce. Flour, which had to be hauled from Missouri, was twelve dollars a hundred pounds. But we fared much better than the immigrants that had come in the fall before. Cabins had been few and far between then. Two men had left for Missouri to get provisions, expecting to be gone two weeks. Their families had supplies for only that length of time. But a snow storm caught them in Missouri, and they were four weeks on the trip. One family had a sack of wheat for sowing, which they boiled and lived on for the two weeks. The other family lived on hickory nuts.

And yet God was good to His immigrants. Long before the white man knew anything about this beautiful Kansas, He was making it ready. Along the grand Neosho River were large hickory, walnut, and pecan trees, loaded with their rich nuts. The plum and the wild grape were also to be found; and along the smaller streams the blackberry, dewberry, gooseberry, and persimmon were plentiful: all planted and tended by His loving hand.

We were too late for the fruit the first year, but I remember that we found about a peck of hazel nuts in a hollow tree, placed there no doubt by squirrels. The only meat we had this first winter was a wild hog which Uncle and our Greentown friend killed. The bacon was, however, too thin to fry and had to be boiled. We were not reduced to straits such as those experienced by the settlers of the previous winter, but many days found us with only bread to eat and coffee, which was without cream or sugar.

In the winter of '57 a preacher came from Missouri. He was planning to come once a month, he said. The second time he came we were to have a Sunday school. But a Sunday school without a library was not to be thought of for a minute; so a collection was taken. The minister was to bring the books on his next visit. But he never came again. He was not censured; times were too grave.

The free state men were pouring in, determined to make Kansas a free state. The proslavery forces were just as determined that it should be a slave state. Men were shot down if they differed in politics. Many an old grudge was settled with a bullet on some lonely highway.

By spring, Father's health was much improved; so he took one yoke of oxen and the wagon and made a trip to Missouri. He brought back two milch cows, two bushels of seed potatoes, and a few other necessary articles. And when Mother got out her large bag of garden seeds which she had brought with her, it did seem that our hard times would soon be over. How good the potatoes looked! But every one was to be planted. Oh, we did have a mess or two out of the hearts after the precious eyes were cut away.

Then came the planting and the waiting. But oh! the soil! The first year's sod dried out so quickly. Rain did not come. So not one potato set on the vines. The rest of the garden withered and died. Father got very much discouraged with his high prairie claim, and decided to sell the first opportunity. But there were the cows. We were that much better off than we had been the winter before.

And we had good neighbors all around. It made no difference whether they were Yanks, Buckeyes, Hoosiers, Missourians, or what not--we were neighbors. And we all used the English language, even if our expressions were sometimes different. The Yank went out to pail a ke-ow. The Missourian would take a bucket and milk a cow.

This difference in pronunciation had been made use of in the early rush to the territory. In 1856 on every Missouri road leading to Kansas, a cow would be tied. Each immigrant would be asked, "What animal is that?" If he said "cow," he was allowed to pass, but if he made it a "ke-ow," he was searched, all his firearms were taken from him, and he was turned back. This was the Missourian's way of preventing Kansas from becoming a free state.

I remember one day when I was learning to milk, and was milking in a tin cup. A little Yank came along and made fun of me, asking why I did not run to the house and get a tablespoon to milk in. Milk was too precious to waste, or I would have thrown it on him.

A saw mill was now running at LeRoy, and we had a floor in our cabin. LeRoy also had a general store. One could buy a pound of coffee, a bottle of quinine, a smoothing iron, a yard of cloth, or a plug of tobacco. I walked the five miles more than once to get Father his plug of tobacco. The post office was in one corner of the general store.

The second winter, 1858-1859, found us without shoes, and with no prospect of getting them. Here Mother's ingenuity came into play. The men all wore boots. They would wear the feet out, and throw them away. Mother gathered up the old boots, ripped them, soaked them soft, and pounded them on a smooth surface. She then fitted every child with a last, which she made herself. She made pegs by sawing off rounds of an oak limb the length she wanted the pegs. There were no barefooted children in our family that winter, as there were in many other families.

My brother, James Watson, was born this winter, March 3, 1859. When quite a small boy, he got the nickname of "Dot," which clung to him as long as he lived.

I have mentioned previously that a young man, Philip Marshall Moore by name, had joined our party at Greentown, Indiana, and had come to Kansas with us. He lived part of the first winter in our house, and then took a claim about three miles from Father's. In the spring of

1859 we became very good friends. I was fourteen years old on May 20 of that year. On the tenth of the following August he was twenty-four, and that day we became engaged. He asked me how long he would have to wait. "One year, at least," I replied. It was written in his memorandum that a year from that day we would be married. He was very kind and good to his little girl fiancee. He knew we were planning to move to a new neighborhood; so he told me that I would meet new people, and that I should go out with the young people, and have a good time. He also said that if I found anyone I would rather walk through life with, to let him know.

In September, 1859, Father sold his high prairie claim and bought a second bottom claim in Allen County between Iola and Humboldt. It was three miles from Iola, the county seat of Allen County. I bade good-bye to my fiance and left for our new location. I had no reason to change my mind, although I met a goodly number of young people that winter and had a good time.

Our new home was a box house, the boards running perpendicular. Here we had a fine truck patch, containing pumpkins, squashes, watermelons and turnips. We made good use of these. Two loads of pumpkins were allowed to freeze. They were soft when frozen, and were put into a press. The juice obtained was boiled down to a syrup. Another load of pumpkins had been put under a haystack where they could not freeze. These were stewed and used to thicken the syrup, the mixture being boiled in an old-fashioned copper kettle. This made twenty gallons of fine butter. We also made watermelon rind preserves by cooking the rinds in a syrup made from the juice of the melons. The preserves and butter make good substitutes for sugar.

In the fall of '59 the little school house began to make its appearance. Also the itinerant preacher was seen oftener. Where there were school houses, meetings were held in them. Where there were none, services were held in homes.

Weeks went by after our moving without my hearing anything from my fiance. I was expecting him to walk in

any day, yet I realized that sixteen miles was a long walk
and consequently was not worried by the delay. Finally,
after three months had passed, he came. The reason he
had not come before was that he had gone with two
other men on a buffalo hunt. They went as far as the
present site of Wichita before they found any buffalo.
There they camped until they were loaded. But just as
they were ready to start for home, a terrible blizzard
struck them. They were unprepared to meet it and all
night long fought for their lives. When hope was about
gone, the Indians found them and covered them with
buffalo robes, under which they slept all the next day.
But they were sick for several weeks after their return
home because of the exposure.

The ox was still the beast of burden. The horse could
not live and work without grain. The faithful ox would
plow all day, turning over the prairie of sod, and at
night he could be turned out on the grass where he
would eat his fill, lie down and rest, and be ready for
another day. It was not until the spring of 1862 that the
ox began to be supplanted by the horse. Consequently,
sixteen miles was a long journey. The choice lay between
walking and riding in a lumber wagon hitched to a yoke
of oxen. And if the oxen were not well trained, someone
must walk to drive them. But Moore's oxen were well
trained. The second time he came he hitched the oxen to
the back wheels of a wagon. He had a board nailed on
for a seat. Here he would sit and crack his whip,
holloaing "Gee!" "Haw!" This kept them in the road and
they trotted along three miles an hour, which was fast
time for oxen.

This winter was cold enough to freeze the ponds over,
so one day Father asked me to go fishing with him. He
took his axe and a two bushel sack. The large buffalo
fish could be seen lying under the ice. Father would
strike a hard blow over the fish's head, and then cut a
hole in the ice. I held the sack, which was soon filled
with fine fish.

This was also the year of drought. No rain or snow
fell to moisten the groud. Corn planted that spring dried
up in the field. Sometime in July our first rain came

with the fury of a downpour. Two boards had been knocked off the north side of our house, but left so that they could be put back readily. Father, seeing the black cloud, rushed to get them back, but before he finished the storm broke. The house was shaking, and we were told to run to a log house near. We made poor headway and soon discovered that the log house had been blown down. Our house stood because the planks on the side which the storm struck ran into the ground. But many things inside had been blown away. We had only one picture on our walls, the portrait of Andrew Jackson. Poor Andrew! We never heard of him again. A man living two miles away came bringing my brother's hat.

August the tenth was approaching but, consulting the almanac, we found that the tenth came on Friday. So my wedding was postponed two days. On Sunday, August 12, 1860, in our little box house on the farm, I was married to Philip Marshall Moore.

III.

My husband's claim was a timbered one on the Neosho River. It was in Woodson County, two and one-half miles from Neosho Falls, and three miles from Father's first claim in Coffey County.

My husband's house was much larger than any around us because a New Yorker had come out and erected it as a hotel. It contained three rooms. The first was a room twelve by fourteen feet. There was a second room above it, which could be reached by a ladder in one corner. There was space for one bed in the center, and it was only in the center of this room that one could stand upright, for the roof slanted down to cover an addition. This addition, fourteen feet square, intended as a dining room, was the third room of the house. The New Yorker had gone back East to get his family, but they had refused to come to such a wild country to keep a hotel. He remained away for more than six months, and his claim became "jumpable." My husband decided to jump the claim and consequently built a small house of his own, ten by twelve, on the land and made the necessary legal records. There was a great deal of jumping going on. Many persons were taking claims and then deserting them, just as the New Yorker had done, and the claims would be taken by others. The government office was at Fort Scott, fifty miles away, but the road was kept clear of grass.

My husband did not interfere with the New Yorker's house with its padlocked door. He had batched in his little ten by twelve for nearly ten months when the New Yorker returned--without his family. But he came back with a gun and with the threat to "get" the man who had jumped his claim. My husband had thought it best to keep out of his way and so went to Uncle's to live until the trouble should blow over. He left his own cabin padlocked. This padlock was promptly broken by the New Yorker, a thing that he had no right to do. Finally Uncle went to Fort Scott on business. Possibly the New Yorker thought Uncle had gone to have him arrested. At any rate, he must have known that he had absolutely no legal rights in the land. One day he met my husband in LeRoy and, stalking up, inquired, "Be you the man that jumped my claim?" My husband admitted the charge--a brave thing to do. "Well, here are the keys to my house," the New Yorker added, "I suppose you might as well go over and take possession."

My husband had been on this claim almost three years when we were married, and he brought me to this "hotel" to live. He had furnished it for me the best he could. Somewhere he had found a little cookstove called a step stove. There were first two lids, then a raise of six or eight inches with two more lids and an oven, which would hold only one pie. But it was a stove, and there were few of them in Kansas at that time. Another marvel was the possession of two chairs, which a man away out on the prairie had manufactured. The demand was so great that a person could get only one or two, but we had our two. We also had some good stools. Our table and bedsteads were home made.

Whenever there was the privilege of church, everyone for miles around would yoke up the oxen and go. We often went three miles for night meeting, and would find ox teams standing all around the school house. In October, 1869, there was a camp meeting on Spring Creek, about three miles away. We planned to go Saturday and stay till Monday. A neighbor and his wife were going with us, and for some reason they did not get over till after dark. We started anyway, hoping that we would get there before the evening services were over. The road went straight for one mile, then wound around quite a large pond, and then went straight in the same direction. All four of us were riding in the wagon. Presently we heard the oxen splashing in the water, apparently having decided to go through the pond instead of around it. The men had to get out and start them again. It was very dark and we had no kind of light. We went on till we thought we were surely about at the camp. Then the oxen stopped. The men got out again, and found that the oxen were standing in front of the bars at the entrance to our own barnyard. But we were not to be disappointed, so we turned around and made the second start. We got into camp just as the people were retiring, but we were ready for the Sunday services.

At the time of our marriage my husband had only a claim to his farm. Land for miles along the Neosho River belonged to the New York Indians. It had been traded to them for land in New York state. The Indians had come to Kansas but had been so severely attacked by the ague that they returned to New York. Land tenures were consequently in a very unsatisfactory condition. We were all expecting the land to be "opened for settlement" and there were at least two false rumors to that effect. Each time such a rumor came everyone would lay a foundation of four logs and post a notice that the land in question was taken. Every quarter section had houses already built but they did not count. The new foundation and notice would, however, hold the land for thirty days, and before the thirty days had expired we would know whether the rumor was false or true. During the winter of 1860 the government offered to every New York Indian who would return within six months 320 acres of land. Not one returned and the land was "opened for settlement," this time in earnest. Settlers who had been on their claims for six months were allowed to "prove them up." We preempted our land at this time, or purchased it from the government, for $1.25 an acre.

We had a pleasant winter. Everyone within five miles was our neighbor. It was not at all strange to have a wagon load of people drive up to stay all day, entirely without warning. People did not wait to be invited. They would just come, and then fly in to help get dinner.

One guest whom I had the great pleasure of having in my home many weeks at a time was my grandmother. The second year after we came to Kansas, she followed us. She had stood the loneliness in Indiana as long as she could. She liked Kansas and remained till her death, which occurred in November, 1866. It was my hands that prepared her body for its last resting place, after God had said, "It is enough, come up higher!" Her body sleeps in the old Logue Cemetery in Coffey County, Kansas, which now holds so many of her loved ones.

In the spring of 1861, when we were expecting the sun to shine, and peace and quiet to reign over our new territory, which had seen nothing but bloodshed, murder, and war since it had been opened for settlement, a big black cloud was gathering which was to break and engulf the whole United States. It was in the midst of all this trouble that our eldest daughter, Viola, was born, on July 21, 1861.

The citizens of Kansas were like the Minute Men of old, ready to grab the musket, shotgun, or anything at hand for the protection of their homes. The fall of 1861 found three companies of men at Iola. They could hardly be called soldiers, as they were not mustered in until the following spring. Father enlisted in the company of Captain Coleman of Allen County. My husband enlisted with Captain Goss of Woodson County. The other captain's name I have forgotten. They served all winter without pay or uniform. It is hard to realize how remote Kansas was at that time from the more thickly settled portions of the country. Our nearest railroad was then at Jefferson City, Missouri.

Scouts were sent out but were told to take no prisoners. There was no place to keep these, and the men did not want the enemy to know their weakness. One day the scouts passed themselves off as Rebel soldiers and for a little while took prisoner an old Indian. They asked him if he thought they could take Humboldt.

"Yes! Take Humboldt."

Then they asked him if they could take Iola.

"No! Keep soldiers at Iola."

If it had not been for these volunteers, no doubt we should have had to leave our homes. Early in the fall of '61, Humboldt, only a few miles from Iola, was taken and burned. Later on, it was burned again. The refugees were passing day and night.

My husband was out one night on picket duty in a cold, drizzling rain and came into camp shaking. This brought on an attack of pneumonia, and he was brought home in a spring wagon. The next day a runner came for him. The mustering officer had arrived, but he could not go. The company was mustered in and went away without him. One man with only one foot was in the company. A boot was nailed to his wooden leg, and he passed. He was a good harness maker, and the boys wanted him along to keep their saddles in repair. My husband, however, was compelled to remain in bed for days, and then he was left with a cough that unfitted him for service.

South of us were the Osage Indians, who took the side of the North. They were a great protection to us against the murderous bands who infested our border. The Osage insisted that when an Indian shot a man and cut off his head, he was really dead. The white soldiers, however, tried to restrain the Indians from this savage practice. On the Fourth of July, 1862, there was a celebration at Humboldt. An old chief in blanket and feathers was asked to speak. Through an interpreter he tried to convince the people that the Indian's way was best. "White man shoot a man; go away; leave him for dead," he said. "Indian shoot a man; cut off head; go leave him sure enough dead." He thought he undoubtedly had the best of the argument.

There were a few Southern sympathizers in the neighborhood. At a time when it was still uncertain which side would be victorious, one of these named his son Lee. At about the same time, he acquired a new dog, which he called Jeff Davis. A post station not far away sent out a squad to investigate, and the man was spared the rope only through the intercession of several of his neighbors. Poor Jeff, however, was born under an ill-fated star. He managed to get his head caught in an old tea kettle which was used to hold meat scraps, and was found dead. This fate seemed to us at the time prophetic of what might happen to the other Jeff, but milder measures, fortunately, were taken.

The Indians in Indian Territory divided, a large number going with the South and driving the rest out of their country. The refugees came pouring into Kansas, reaching the Verdigris River in the dead of winter in a suffering condition. There the government met them with wagons, and conveyed the sick, aged, and children to Le-Roy, where headquarters were established. So many had been dying that on the night they reached LeRoy a woman was hanged as a witch. This hideous practice was later stopped by government order. From LeRoy as headquarters, the Indians were scattered along the Neosho River for about ten miles. There were possibly ten thousand of them, mostly old men, women, and children. All the young, able-bodied men had enlisted in the service. They stayed with us until the war closed, and the government took them back home.

For two years about two hundred of them were always camping on our farm. They were organized into villages which kept moving from place to place. Rarely would a village stay in the same location for more than two weeks. They would move early in the morning, but usually before nightfall I could look out of my window and see another village on the site. Some villages were clean, while others were dirty. Some entertained themselves every night with grotesque Indian dancing, accompanied by weird, unearthly cries. Other villages would have religious meetings. I attended some of these and was interested in distinguishing certain Hebrew proper names in a sermon, otherwise unintelligible to me.

The Indians had their own government, with some curious laws and customs. Whenever I saw a woman with streaming hair, I knew she was a widow, for a woman was not allowed to comb her hair for a year after the death of her husband. She could not remarry for three years. I once noticed a very pretty woman who always wore a shawl around her head. I learned that she had remarried too soon and that her ears had been cut off in punishment. These barbarous punishments were not uncommon; I saw one woman whose nose had been cut off.

They got their water at our well, drawing it up by means of windlass, rope and bucket. That bucket was going up and down from early morning until twelve at night, and there was always a line waiting to use it. The women usually carried a pail in each hand and one on the head.

They were great traders. The government issued to the women eight yards of cloth for a dress, but they would manage to save about a yard and a quarter from each piece and would come wanting to barter the remnant for roasting ears. I have had my house full of these remnants. Fortunately, the government had little regard for individuality in dress, and many of the pieces were from the same pattern. They also sold nuts and wild fruit of all kinds. They had a way of ripening some of these artificially before their season.

They made a soup from cornmeal, which they pounded out with mortar and pestle. Soup, however, could apparently be made out of anything. A squaw once bought a green pumpkin from me for soup. They would gather about the big pot and pass a large spoon around the circle, each helping himself in turn. Their knowledge of the conditions of public health can be surmised. What medical treatment they gave was largely a matter of charms.

The worst trouble we had was that they did not want to bury their dead. It was less work to put the body inside a hollow log or tree. My husband was down in a timbered pasture one day and noticed a strip of bark tied around a tree. He thought the Indians had hidden something. His axe was in his hand and he hacked the bark

away. A large chip fell out. He stuck his head in the
opening and found a corpse! He came home about as
white as a corpse himself. He went immediately to the
Indian Agent and said that if they did not bury their
dead, they must move off his place. But there were too
many dying to watch them all. One morning before
sunrise my husband found two men with a corpse tied to
a board coming through the gate into the pasture hunting
a tree. As a rule, however, they began to bury their
dead. The women would often sit on my steps and visit
with one another. One day two of them seemed to be in
trouble. I could see tears in their eyes, and asked a little
girl who spoke English what the trouble was. I was told
that the baby of one of them had died the night before
and the other Indians wanted to put it in a hollow log.
But she wanted it buried--if she had a shovel she would
dig the grave herself. They still believed in helping their
dead in the Happy Hunting Grounds. I have stood by
and have seen them put a pipe, tobacco, herbs, a pocket
knife, and various other things in the grave.

But they were not bad neighbors. They never stole
anything, not even a watermelon. One day I saw a girl
thumping watermelons in my patch. I yelled at her to
keep her from hurting them. The next day an old man
came leading the girl to the house to ask me if she had
been trying to steal my melons. He told me he had not
"raised her to be a thief." I was sorry then that I had
paid any attention to her.

They were very kind to the little white woman, as
they called me, and loved my little baby girl, my "hook-
tu-chee." They would take her to their tents and keep her
by the hour. But more interesting to them was the birth
of our oldest son, Charles Edgar, which occurred February
8, 1864. Many of them would come to the house, look at
the baby and inquire smilingly, "che-by-no-see?" And
they were tremendously pleased when we answered that
he was indeed a "che-by-no-see," or a boy.

The Kansas soldier saw some fighting and had many
hardships. At one time salt was so scarce that a level
spoonful sold for a dollar. Once in a while a joke relieved the sad incidents of the war. When there was great

excitement over the report that General Price was marching to Kansas with the special intent of destroying Fort Scott, every able-bodied man was ordered out. A big German was made corporal and told to take a sentinel out and put him on duty. When the two men reached the assigned place, the corporal turned to the sentinel with the query, "Now I know not vat mine duty iss. Can you tell me?"

"Yes," came the ready answer, "I will lie down here and sleep. You are to stand guard and wake me when you see a Rebel."

A soldier's life was too hard for Father. After eighteen months, part of which was spent in a hospital, he was mustered out and came home. He was never well again. He sold his Allen County farm and bought one in Woodson County, three miles from Neosho Falls, and within half a mile of us. He lingered along until August 29, 1875, when he died, leaving his widow and nine children. He was at that time 59 years and eight months old. He lies buried in the Logue Cemetery.

IV.

In 1886 a school house was built on the corner of our farm, and was always referred to as the "Phil Moore" school house. For three years we had been having a six months term of school, taught in an old log house. But now that we had a school house, we could have church as well as school. A Methodist circuit rider passed through once a month. He would baptize either by immersion or sprinkling, just as was preferred. A Dunkard came once a month also. But he preached that you must go under the water three times, face foremost. The Dunkard men wore their hair bobbed and parted in the middle, and both men and women had their distinctive dress. They practised foot washing, and when meeting saluted with a kiss, men kissing men and women kissing women. My son Charles was four or five years old at this time, and admired the Dunkard preacher very much.

He would stand before the mirror, part his hair in the middle, and sleek it behind his ears in imitation. I would sometimes ask him what he was going to be when he grew up. "Be a Dunkard preacher," he would reply. Then we had a local preacher who held afternoon meetings once a month. He was known as a "Campbellite." I do not think anyone sent him; he just came. He had one great trouble--he never knew when to stop. He was preaching along one afternoon when the sun was getting low. In those days the men took one side of the house and the women the other. It would have been considered a great breach of etiquette to do otherwise. Finally my husband arose from his seat on the other side of the room and went out. He reached a place where he was in view of myself, but not of the preacher, and motioned for me to follow. I did not think it was right to leave while the man was preaching at the top of his voice, but the motions were repeated until I got up and left.

"What is the trouble?" I asked.

"Trouble!" he answered, "It will be dark now before I can get the cows milked."

The next day he was going with his hired man past the same school house. Both were driving teams. The hired man was ahead and had just come even with the building when my husband called out, "Jim! Stop and go to the school house door!" Jim got down to carry out the order. Then my husband continued, "Look in and see if Moody is still preaching!"

There was one circuit rider who often took his wife and little girl with him. It was hard and tiresome for the child. One day, looking up into her mother's face, she said, "Oh! I wish my papa was not a circus rider!"

But it made no difference who preached, or what he preached, or when he preached, we all went and got, I trust, some good from each meeting.

Of course no account of early Kansas would be complete without mention of the grasshoppers. Their first visit to us was sometime in the sixties, I do not remember the exact year. On one bright, sunshiny afternoon we noticed that the sun was growing dim, and found that the air as high as we could see was alive with flying insects coming nearer and nearer to the ground. Before we could think, grasshoppers were devouring everything green. I looked out at my fine cabbage patch, all nicely headed out--only the bare stalks remained. After they had eaten everything in sight, the grasshoppers did have the good manners to rise and fly away.

This was not true on their second visit. My memory fails me again in regard to the exact year, but I think it was in the fall of 1874. We first knew of their arrival when we noticed our orchard standing as in the dead of winter, stripped of all foliage. Later, the trees came out in full bloom, and our next year's crop was gone.

This time the grasshoppers deposited immense numbers of eggs in every acre of cultivated land. Corn planted the next spring got a few inches high when the grasshoppers began to hatch, and they soon made away with it. A little later the fields were replanted in the hope that by the time the corn was up, the grasshoppers' wings would be grown and they would fly away. But they ate up this second planting. The fields were planted a third time, and the grasshoppers were gone, but it was the first of July. Although the corn grew rapidly and made fine, large ears, when it was in the milk, frost took it. My husband had 115 acres in corn, but not an ear fit to feed a horse. There were also twenty acres in wheat. The grasshoppers let it alone until it headed out; then promptly devoured it. There were hard times for Kansas!

And yet conditions were gradually improving. How many conveniences the young bride of today has that we of 1860 never dreamed of! Because we had never dreamed of them, we were contented with what we had, and as each new help came to us, it was an added joy. My mother had had to dip her candles, but I had a candle mould. I could mould four at once. My first coal oil lamp my husband carried from Fort Scott fifty miles on horseback. It was the only lamp in the neighborhood. Of course I knew nothing about the care of a lamp. I was admiring it, but noticed a speck on the flue. I took a damp cloth to remove it, and the flue broke, the pieces flying in every direction. Everyone in the room except myself was wondering why it broke. I did not try to clean any more hot flues with a wet cloth.

I had heard of the sewing machine, but it was 1867 before I ever saw one. In 1869 I got my first one, a little thing that had to be fastened to the table with clamps, but oh! it would sew. It immediately became a neighborhood machine. No matter what I had planned for the day, I would see a neighbor coming with a big roll in her arms, and I knew at once she was coming to sew. My work was at once slipped away, and a happy woman left for her home that day with more sewing accomplished than she could have done in a week by hand. I felt it no hardship; I was happy I could help her. Neighbors meant something in those frontier days. After we moved into our new house on the farm, I had a larger sewing machine.

When Charles was seven years old, his father took him to town and ordered him a tailor-made suit: coat, vest, and long trousers. He also was fitted with some red-topped boots. But the boots did not last long. He had seen men oil their boots, so of course his must be oiled. Taking a cup of coon oil, he began the task, pouring the oil on them and holding them in the fire. Suddenly I heard the oil sputtering and frying, and the boots were burned up.

In 1876 we went over near the Missouri line to visit a brother of my husband. After leaving Mound City we saw, out on that beautiful prairie, a peculiar new house. Every window and every door were covered with wire screening. That took my husband's eye, and he examined it carefully. Soon after we got home our house was the wonder of the neighborhood, all screened in. It did not seem possible that flies could be kept out. And oh! what a pest they used to be. In the evenings the ceilings would be black with them, and in the early mornings such a buzzing as they did make! There was no napping after they began. Whenever we began to set the table, someone had to take a brush to keep them off. But the fly has been conquered. If one gets into the house today, it is so lonely it cannot sing, but sits ready for the swatter, which it is sure to get.

Our oldest children, Viola, Charles, Effie, and Ada, were all born in the log house. We later moved into a new frame house on the farm. Here our baby Pearl was born, October 20, 1876. She died November 30 of the same year, and is buried in the Logue Cemetery. It was in this house also that our son Arthur was born, April 13, 1878.

Viola, our oldest daughter, had a beautiful, happy childhood. When she was twelve years old, we got her a little melodeon, which brought joy and sunshine to her and to the rest of the family. On May 5, 1878, Viola was married to Park Vannordstrand. But on July 21, 1879, her eighteenth birthday, we had to see her go. Though our hearts were broken, we could not keep her. She lies in the Logue Cemetery.

We lived on the same "claim" for twenty-three years, in 1883 moving to Greenwood County. On October 5 of that year, Arthur, too, left us. He is buried in the Greenwood Cemetery. Our youngest son, Roy, was born about one mile from Eureka. We later moved into town, and here, on April 18, 1890, my mother passed away. She lies with Arthur in the Greenwood Cemetery.

"Well, We Stuck"
Jennie Stoughton Osborn

At the age of 87 Jennie Osborn was just learning to use her new typewriter when she recorded her memories. She demonstrated that adventurous young women on the frontier had a wide range of options: she taught school, she tried the millinery business for awhile, she hauled young fruit trees to Texas—sometimes teaching part of the year and hauling trees in the summer. The excerpt below begins with her marriage in 1874 and delineates the ups and downs of farming over three decades. The Osborns were continuously plagued with problems: they tried raising sheep but that venture failed; they tried raising wheat and that too failed. Because they were always "starting over," she said "It seems to me that I was nearly always a pioneer." This is her message: "All this I have written may not be interesting to some who may chance to read it in the years to come, but it is a part of the memories stored away in my brain for over eighty years, and for what purpose, I do not know. Perhaps it is to show that, with good health and energy, we can conquer most any hardship if we have the stick-to-it-iveness in our constitution. This is required. Well, we stuck. We could not have left without sacrificing what little we had, so we determined not to yield, but to conquer "hardship." (42)

Source:
Jennie Osborn Stoughton. Memories. *Medicine Lodge, Kansas: Barber County Index, 1935. 40-56.*

Mr. Osborn, the clerk of the school board, and I had planned to be married the first of March, but the closing of school for two weeks changed our plans. Instead of putting off our wedding day, we were married in February, at the time of the forced vacation, and that left the way clear for our other plans. My sister and her family, the Whitmans, had moved into the district; and I was staying with them at that time; so we just boarded with them until school closed. Then commenced the "tug of war" to get the folks who were living in Mr. Osborn's house out, so that we could move in.

The house was made of cedar logs from the canons [sic] south of Cedar Creek. They were hewed smooth on each side and built up, making a nice sized room and a small room or garret above. There was not room for a bedstead, so Mr. Osborn made a swinging bed, which he hung to the rafters in the garret for himself when he had a tenant living in the lower room. The cracks between the logs were plastered with gypsum, home burned and ground. They had to go to the hills for the gypsum rock, burn it in a home-made kiln, pulverize it; and then, it was ready to be mixed with the ever ready sand and water.

It was not an easy task to build a house in those early, settler days because there was nothing but native material that the people could afford to use. John Easley built a sawmill four miles west of the Lodge. Most of the lumber sawed was cotton-wood, which warped and twisted so it could hardly hold the nails securely. But it seems to be a very lasting timber, for there is a board of it out at the farm (or there was a short time ago). It is 55 years old, or near it, and has stood the out-door weather for over fifty years. When I saw it last, a year or so ago, it was still quite sound.

Mr. Osborn had taken the claim after giving a man 50 cents and his watch for it. He built the house in the fall after the "Indian Raid of 1874." Three different families had lived in it with him for a while, when they first came to the county. The last family, being so obstinate, Mr. Osborn thought that perhaps if I would come and stay with him, they might take the hint that we really did want them to move out. We had some hens among her chickens, and when I came down, I told her that I wanted to gather some eggs to set a hen, so that we could have early fries. I did not get any eggs, for every time a hen cackled, she ran to get the egg. This scared the hens so much that they would not become broody. They were not like the English lady's hens. She did not know what ailed them and complained that they would just "sit and sit and wouldn't lie at all."

Mr. Osborn liked the man and did not want to force them out of the house. He helped them find another place, and then they moved out. In the meantime, I went back to my sister's and stayed until they were gone. Then we fumigated everything and plastered every crack and crevice we could in the old logs, so we could live in it for a couple of months until we could build a new house. I helped to make the garden and fed and petted the hens until they would eat out of my hands, and they hatched out a lot of chickens for me. But they were not all to be fries. One day when the girl staying with me and I were alone a heavy hail and rainstorm came up suddenly. We could not get out to rescue the chickens. We could see hens trying to cover their brood, but the hail pelted them so that they would have to stand up; and their poor little chicks would get killed. After the storm we gathered up three buckets full of limp chickens. About one bucketful revived. The rest had to be buried. That was almost everybody's luck in those days before we had adequate buildings to protect them.

Just as soon as the spring crop was planted, Mr. Osborn drove down the river toward Kiowa to a mill to get the dimension lumber for the new house. He had to sell a yoke of oxen to get the money to pay for it. Then he went to Wichita for siding, flooring and finishing lumber. I think the sheeting came from the mill down the river. He hauled buffalo bones and cedar posts to Wichita to pay for the pine lumber. When he took his last load of posts, he had to drive on to Newton to get the shingles, doors and windows, for there were none in Wichita. My brother built the house with two rooms below and two above, and we painted it white. The inside was not entirely finished, but we moved in, anyway. Our house and one down the river toward the Lodge were the only frame houses between the Lodge and Lake City, but that was 56 years ago. People coming now could not imagine the picture as it looked then. People missed the fruit they had been used to, but they soon found the healthfulness of the fruit that God had planted in the valleys and canons [sic] of the Medicine Lodge River, especially the abundance of wild grapes and plums.

All this I have written may not be interesting to some who may chance to read it in the years to come, but it is a part of the memories stored away in my brain for over eighty years, and for what purpose, I do not know. Perhaps it is to show that, with good health and energy, we can conquer most any hardship if we have the stick-to-it-iveness in our constitution. This is required. Well, we stuck. We could not have left without sacrificing what little we had, so we determined not to yield, but to conquer "hardship."

Chapter XII

Living in the clean, new house was much nicer with new things but the inside was unfinished. In the fall, when the crop was gathered and the feed stored away for the stock in the winter, the roads were too bad to go to Wichita to get the lath so we could plaster the walls of the rooms. There was a brick-kiln in the Lodge, we decided on buying brick and building it up between the studding to plaster over it. This made our rooms warm if not beautiful. With the thought of Indians still haunting my dreams, there was another horror which presented itself too frequently to be pleasant. It was the knowledge of being on the opposite side of a river, without a bridge and away from a doctor in case of sickness. Our first year was a busy one, with our crops and the building of the house. Our first anniversary came February 12th, 1880. Our guest that day was our wee baby son, Leon L. It was a cold and stormy day. I do not remember very much about that winter; I must have been too busy taking care of the baby. But I do remember one beautiful warm day that winter when we drove up Cedar Creek to see Mr. and Mrs. Parker and over the hills to Dick's Peak and across the river to Father and Mother's claim. We had only filed on the claim. Our intentions were to buy the land, and the time was coming soon when we would have to "prove up," as it was called, and to pay $1.25 per acre for it. That made the settler have to raise $200 which not many had. There was a depression on then, at least for the settlers here, and the government extended the time six months. The government also made a ruling which gave the settler the privilege to leave his claim to go anywhere he could find work to earn enough money to "prove up." No one was allowed to "jump it" while he was gone.

We did not have any money, but since we could leave the claim this time in safety, Mr. Osborn concluded to go out and earn it. We turned the milk cows with their calves out on the range with the other stock, got someone to come each day to look after the chickens and pigs; and then we drove to Hutchinson. He sent baby and I on the train to Kansas City for a few weeks' visit. He was to haul freight from Hutchinson and Wichita to Medicine Lodge while we were gone. Only a few years before this, I had been on the same road with a bird cage and a guitar. I had had many offers of help at that time, but this time with the baby, a pillow, and a small grip no one offered to help me; so I trudged along with my burdensome load into the station and dropped down into the nearest seat.

As the people were getting off the train, I noticed a man and woman walking along, scanning the crowd. They passed me in the waiting room, but went on after giving me a mere glance. I never did find out whether they were expecting to see a society lady, holding her dog's chain and the nurse holding the baby, or just a plain country woman and baby. Anyway, they couldn't find another baby and came back to me. They were my husband's brother and wife. They took us to my sister's in Kansas City, Kansas. My sister's husband had gone to meet me, but his streetcar had been blocked by a drove of cattle crossing the track and he could not get there in time.

I had a nice visit of two weeks with the two families of relatives. The time was up to go to Garnett to visit with the rest of my new kinfolk. But I was not to get away without some more experience. We sent the trunk over to the station with a neighbor in the morning, and we followed later. Again there was delay by cattle being driven across the streetcar track. When we got to the station, the train was just pulling away from it, and we went back to my sister's home. The next day we came over again, and I checked my trunk, or one that looked exactly like mine. Baby and I got on the train and were just nicely settled when in came the baggage-man, who told me that a lady had claimed my trunk and had even identified it. He wanted me to come to help find my trunk. I left baby and went with him.

The baggage man and I hunted among all the trunks, but could not find it. Then to stir me up a little more, the conductor came rushing toward me saying, "The train is about to start. You'd better get your baby off and hunt for your trunk later. I did and boarded a streetcar back to my sister's home again. I was looking out of the window as we passed the opposite end of the depot from the baggage-room, when standing on the end of the platform I saw my big old Saratoga. I had the conductor let me off. Then trudged back with my luggage, found the baggage man and saw that my trunk was safely in the baggage-room and checked. I got to the streetcar again and went back to sister's to be ready for another start

the next day. The third trial was the "charm," for we
arrived safely in Garnett where Mr. Osborn was to meet
us.

He arrived on time, too, and we visited around there
for a couple of weeks. Then we took the things out of
my big trunk and tied them in a roll to strap to the
back of the seat of the buggy. We filled the trunk with
apples and shipped it home by rail. Then we were ready
for the start home. We were jogging along within a short
distance of Eureka when, "Snap!" went something; and we
were almost pitched out of the buggy. We got it patched
up some way, so we could drive into Eureka, where we
stayed that night. Next day we got nearly to Wichita, and
our next night we were close to Kingman, a night we
never forgot. The lady who took us in was alone and
said that she had been housecleaning, but we could stay.
She had only one bed up yet; but baby and I could sleep
with her, she said. She made a bed on the floor for Mr.
Osborn. The baby was so tired that we thought we would
just have to stay. Mr. Osborn could not sleep for some
reason, so he lighted a lamp to investigate. He saw the
little red varmints coming from every direction. They
looked so lean and lank that they reminded him of a
hungry pack of wolves. He got up and went out to
finish the night in the buggy.

It was so dry that summer that our grain did not
mature but we had fodder and sorghum hay and took in
some cattle to feed through the winter. This gave us
money to go ahead with our improvements. As I had
finally received my school wages, we were able to prove
up our land. Our second anniversary came on a bitter
cold day with the ice on the river a foot thick. One of
our neighbors, Mrs. Horn, was buried that day. There
was a piercing, cold wind and only a few men could go
with the body to the cemetery. There was quite a snow
on the ground, and when they came to the river crossing,
the ice was too slick for the horses to pull the wagon
across. The men unhitched the team, skidded the wagon
across and led the horses. It took so much time that they
were nearly frozen before they got back, and our wedding [second anniversary] dinner was served rather late
that time.

There was free range for stock when farmers first began to take pre-emption claims in the county. The stockmen, who were holding large bodies of land with a great number of cattle, did not like them and annoyed the settlers because the settlers encroached on their free range. For a few years ranchmen could run their stock all winter without feed excepting the green grass in canons [sic] and along the streams and the cured buffalo grass on the prairies. But when the climate changed, they were glad to be able to procure the grain and fodder the farmers raised, especially when a heavy snow was on the ground. Many large ranches were acquired by the cattlemen through inducing cowboys to prove up on quarter sections included in their ranch holding. They secured many acres of land in Barber County for but little over the government price of it. I think that, among my old tax receipts, I hold one of the very first given in the county.

December, with its lean holidays, had come and gone again. But when February 12th, 1883, came, we had our anniversary dinner as usual. We had as guests that day, Mr. and Mrs. Williams, neighbors, and our first little daughter Cecile, who was about three months old. That was not a happy day, for one of our nearest neighbors, Mrs. Wm. Dole, was lying very near to death from tuberculosis. I was weary, too, from sitting up nights, helping care for her. Settlers of this county in the "seventies" and the "eighties" were kind to each other; they had to be kind because they had to depend on neighbors in emergencies. There was no undertaker here, so the women took care of a woman who passed away and prepared her for burial. The men took charge of a man and usually had to dig the graves for those who died and to bury the body also. Some may think pioneers had an easy time, living on the frontier; but I can assure anyone who wants to know that it was hard work and hard to stick to it. It seems to me that I was nearly always a pioneer. I was a first baby; surely that was beginning early. Then, I was with my parents in Oakwoods while they were clearing off a new farm; and as a pioneer teacher in two different states; and lastly a Barber County, Kansas Pioneer.

Chapter XIII

This morning of 1935 and the 15th of January, I sit here at the typewriter in a quandary, wondering whether or not I should make a trip to Baldwin. Somewhere between Berkeley, California, and Baldwin, Kansas, the body of Ida M. Price, my sister-in-law, is on its way to Baldwin to be buried beside her husband, Rev. John Price, in the cemetery of that city. The sun is shining brightly most of the time, but it is hard to guess what the morrow will be.

However, I am not ready just yet to "bury the dead past," so I must go on with "My Memories." Some of them are very sweet to me yet, even if some of them were born during the hardship of pioneer days. We did have many, many difficulties to overcome in those days. Poor crops, as I remember, were the worst of our troubles; for we usually had good health. It was well we did keep well because the doctors here were all such old men, and it had been so long since they had been in college. Dr. Riggs and Dr. Johnson were young, but they did not stay here long. If you are hunting for names of the old settlers, the best place to find most of them is in the cemetery. The ones left will soon have to travel the same road.

It was in the early "Seventies" when the first settlers began to locate in Barber County, but many left after the Indian raid of 1874 and never returned. Many of the children who were here in those days are getting to be quite old men and women, even though they would rather not admit it. In a few years, when the memory of the Indian raid became dim, more people came to this county to become in love with its everlasting hills and canons [sic]. But the everlasting crops were few and far apart because of drought and hot, boiling winds, coming from off the sandy desert in New Mexico. Sometimes when the corn was in the roasting ear stage, a hot wind would come and strike it. It did not take very many hours to cook the blades until they could be pulverized. The corn shriveled on the cob, and the crop was a failure. Still we lived and thrived in health, if not in wealth.

We were impatient and wanted a little wealth also. So we went into the sheep raising business. In the spring of 1882 we took 500 head of ewes, selling our best horse to buy the males. But we thought we were going to be rich in a few years. Our neighbor, Mr. Williams, bought 300 ewes while we took ours on the share plan, of half of the lambs. Mr. Williams lost his farm by the venture, and we lost a year's labor. We had 200 lambs and half of the wool for our share. Out of the price of the lambs there was the feed, the herding, dipping and clipping to be paid. The price of wool at that time was so low that there was nothing left after returning the sheep to the owner.

We then tried raising wheat for a few years. The chinch-bugs ate the wheat, and not being fully satisfied with it, they would march over the dry ground into the cornfield and attack the corn. When farmers began to see the futility of trying to raise grain crops, they turned to hay and fodder, to feed cattle. We would take a bunch of cattle to feed through the winter but never received the money for it until the stock was turned over in the spring to the owner. And our larder was often nearly empty.

Time waits for none of us to catch up. If we have fallen behind, it is lost to us forever. We can only gain some knowledge through it. We were gaining knowledge, if not wealth, and determined to stay with our land. We could raise feed for stock in spite of drought and hot winds. It was not all the loss of crops that bothered us. There were cattle rustlers here, and the Texas fever that killed many cattle in hot dry summers. It was brought into the county by herds of Texan cattle driven through here from Texas. Some dishonest person, driving a bunch of cattle by the farm, would often drive off a cow or a calf. It was up to the owner to follow the thief to get it back. One incident of that kind happened one morning before our milking time. A man moving from Medicine Lodge to western Kansas with a small bunch of cattle passed our place that morning. The calves were outside, and when Mr. Osborn went out to turn them in with the cows, one calf was missing. He felt quite certain about where it had gone, so he saddled a horse and rode after the moving outfit. He caught up with them where they had camped at night and pointed out the calf; but they claimed that it belonged to them and would not let him have it. He told them to stay where they were until he could go bring the cow to prove it was her calf, and if they wouldn't wait, he would send the sheriff. When he came back, he turned old Kelly out of the corral. She didn't hesitate for a minute to take up the road west. When she came in sight of the cattle, she mooed long and loud until the calf rushed out to meet her to get its refreshments. "Kelly" seems like a queer name for a cow, but we used to buy some calves, and if one was a heifer, we named it for the man from whom we got it. That is why this cow's name was "Kelly."

Old Kelly had an experience all her own sometime later. Some rustler kidnapped her and drove her to Comanche County. It was nearly a year before we found her. She was still wearing our brand but the calf she brought home with her had the rustler's brand on it. Such things occurred frequently, and we began to believe that it was just the cowboys who did it on purpose to get a little fee for finding the strays. They needed it to fill up on their joy rides to Medicine Lodge.

Time moved on and we with it; but there came a time when things changed until we were not so hard pressed for the money to purchase the things we really needed in our business. Farmers needed machinery, but it took money to get it. Some mortgaged their farms to buy the needed machinery, and frequently they lost their farms by doing it, and the machinery also. Good crops were less frequent in the "eighties" and the "nineties" than in the last twenty or more years because the soil was newer. The drought of '33 and '34 was only a prolonged duplication of many droughts in the early settlement of this county.

Drought and hot winds did not seem to retard the crop of children that grew up here in those early days. They flourished like the Russian Thistles of today. Doctors made a slim living by their practice. I think, perhaps, they often had to take butter and eggs, or maybe potatoes. I am sure I do not know how they collected their bills. I do know that there was not much loose money lying around. But still, the people were blest with good health.

February 12th, 1884, was quite a cold day although the winter, as a whole, was a mild, open winter. We had Mother Osborn with us for that anniversary dinner. While she was there we took her with us to get the little cedar trees that have grown into such large ones, standing so tall and friendly in the front lawn of the old homestead. Some were so small that they were pulled out of the ground by hand. They have stood there at this time forty years. The two old bunches of lilacs by the house we brought in little oyster cans from Garnett, Kansas, in the summer of 1880. The elm trees in the yard were about three inches high when I pulled them up and planted them the first "Arbor Day" in Kansas. They all link me with the past that I can never forget, the time when we were struggling to hold on and to keep up our courage to subdue the hardships of frontier life that confronted us in the early settlement of this county.

It was very discouraging to plant the crops spring after spring, and probably, not have any harvest of grain. But there was seldom a failure of a fodder crop. That suited the cattlemen because they could get it to feed their cattle, and the money for the feed helped to feed the farmers' families. Those with enough "grit" struggled on until times grew better. As I remember now, about the only exciting thing that happened was the bank-robbery and the killing of the bankers, Payne and Geppert, that spring. I remember when the man came who was gathering up the crowd to help get the robbers out of the canon where they were barricaded, and how excited I was when he said that Payne and Geppert had been killed. They wanted Mr. Osborn to go to help to dislodge them. I didn't want him to go, but he did anyway and went on to town with them when they had captured the robbers, although he did not stay for the hanging. There was a great deal of excitement in the Lodge that evening, he said, while he was there. One old man was dragging a rope around and calling on the

"Powers Above" to help them, and said, "But they must die." Mr. Osborn thought he knew what was going to happen, so he came home. A man who attended the affair dropped dead the next day while he was in a store. It had been too much for him.

We had quite good crops the year of 1884. We thought we were entitled to another visit. We did not want our farm life to become monotonous because we would be dissatisfied with it. A man and his wife were engaged to come in to our house, to do the house-work and the farm work while we were gone. We had them drive us and the two children to Harper, then the end of the Santa Fe. Our route was by way of Winfield, Cherryvale, and Iola to Bronson—to visit a few days with brother Worth Osborn and family. From Bronson to Iola we rode in the caboose of a freight train to catch the passenger train. The freight was so slow that the dogs chased it nearly all the way. We went from Iola to Garnett to visit a few days with Mother Osborn. Then we went to Kansas City to see Mr. Osborn's brother, Wick, and my sister, Mrs. Lowerre. We were there a week, during which time we saw the parade celebrating the anticipated election of Grover Cleveland to the presidency of our country. It was a fiery parade; the Infernal Region could not have looked more fierce than the parade did as it passed by us. That same evening of the parade, as we came up from the old depot on the old horse-drawn streetcars, the horses could hardly pull the car up the hill, it was so loaded full of men in the inside and hanging on the outside, wherever they could get hold of the car. When our time was up for our return home, we came back to Garnett for a day or so. When we arrived at Harper again, our man was there with the team to meet us and to bring us home. We had enjoyed the recreation of the trip and were ready with more zest to take up again the duties of farm life.

The winter 1885 I had Miss Lizzie Steel staying with us to help with the work. On the morning of our 5th anniversary word came to us that our neighbor Anderson Hayes' horse had come home without him, and he was not in town. There was a thin coat of ice on the river where the men hunted for him, but not finding him there, they hunted each side of the river for some distance and finally succeeded in finding him a mile or so down the river, crouched in a depression of the ground, frozen to death. It was supposed that the horse did not like being forced into the icy water and dumped his rider into it. It was late in the evening when Mr. Osborn came home, and our dinner was late. We had one guest, a lonely old man that we had invited to eat with us that time. It was not a happy evening for us because of our nearest neighbor, who was lying a corpse, the victim of the liquor traffic.

March the 11th, 1885, was another event not easily to be forgotten, because the stork visited us again and left a little bundle that proved to be another little girl. We had some trouble in naming her, as her daddy thought it was his turn and proposed Magenta, saying that it would match her color. But I objected and said that since he wanted to name her for a color, I'd give her a white name, and he could give her a second name. I named her "Ermine"; he gave her the name "Lucille."

Later in the same spring, we had a flood that drowned a number of people along the Medicine Lodge River and its tributaries. Five persons (campers) were drowned near the Lodge. Their bodies rest in the cemetery here, marked by a monument contributed by the citizens of the town. That flood was the most serious one known to residents of this county. We were greatly worried that day as we were on the south side of the river and knew that somewhere on the north side brother Worth Osborn was moving his family and stock to Barber County and might have been caught in the flood that night. Just as soon as a horse could swim the river, Mr. Osborn started on a hunt for him. He found that they had crossed the last river before the flood and were safe on high ground. 1885 was a good crop year for us, and our corn-bins were full. There was no drought that season. We kept a man busy that fall and most of the winter husking corn.

Chapter XIV

1886 came in cold and stormy. The thermometer dropped to zero weather frequently during January. Uncle Worthington Hooker of Portland, Oregon, came to visit us and insisted on helping Mr. Osborn feed the cattle. The men wore mustaches, and their breath froze on it. When they came into the house, they had to stand near the fire to melt it enough to break it off. The water in the river was frozen to the sand, and teams crossed it every day. My mother had fallen in the autumn of 1885 and was injured so severely that before she recovered she developed typhoid fever and was an invalid the rest of her life. All that cold weather we had to cross the cold, icy river to go to Mingona four miles west, every two or three days.

February was a warmer month. The temperature was 54 above zero on the 12th. When spring came and the ice broke up from a rise in the river, caused by melting snow and rain, it piled the ice up on each side of the bank so perfectly symmetrical that it looked like a piece of masonry. We had our anniversary alone that day with our three children. Later, my sisters, Mrs. Kate Whitman and Mrs. Elizabeth Lowerre, came to be with Mother for a while. When they were gone, brother Harry Osborn came and then, my nephew, Tom Hagan, from Monett, Missouri, and another nephew, John S. Whitman, of Pierce City, Missouri. We usually called him "Stote" when we wanted his attention. One day in mid summer he came to our house and said, "Aunt Jennie, I'm sick." I told him to go upstairs and to get into bed, which he did. Just as soon as I could, I went up to see him; I found that he had a high fever and that he was delirious. We sent for a doctor who said that he had typhoid fever. Then we knew we were in for a siege of several weeks' sickness in our own home, and Mother was still sick in her home a few miles away. Besides the medicine the doctor gave the boy I gave him a cup of chicken-broth once a day and a cup of sweet milk three times a day. When the fever left him at the end of three weeks, he lay like a dead person for twenty-four hours. We could hardly see that he breathed, and we thought our effort to save him was a failure; but when the doctor came, he told us, "The danger is over." Two days later, while we sat at dinner, he shocked us by coming down the stairway fully dressed. He said, "I want some of that boiled cabbage. I smelled it cooking." We told him that he must not eat cabbage yet, for it might kill him. He helped himself to it. The doctor said that the reason he got up so strong was the way I had fed him.

The years sped on as they always do, with snow and rain and the morning dew, and with it, another milestone of married life to be crossed. It was a nice, warm day; and we spent our anniversary very happily with Brother Worth and his family, who were with us for dinner that day. If we could have seen ahead any distance, we might not have had many happy days. My father had a neighbor in whom he was interested. The man was a "drunkard," and father was anxious to reform him. He worked with him faithfully, counseling him to quit his habit of drinking liquor. He was finally converted in a Baptist meeting and wanted to be baptized. According to their "rite" there was no place to immerse him but in the river. He was a large man and the preacher small. The preacher laid him down, but was too light to lift him up again. Father rushed into the cold water to help lift him, and to get him out to the bank. That night father had a chill, and it was followed by pneumonia. He lived but eleven days; then he fared forth on his winged journey, March 16th, 1887. He had given his life for his friend.

We took mother to our home, where we could take better care of her, and her granddaughter, Maud Hagan, who had been living with them. We added another room to our house for mother, so we could keep her on the first floor. We were very busy that summer and could not attend church as regularly as we had been attending, both church and Sunday school. Another reason was that the stork was on duty those days, same as he is at present. On August 28th, the bird brought another baby girl to us, and we named her "Nellis." We thought that our family was increasing rather rapidly for our means of taking care of a family of six persons. Our crops were fairly good that year. Everything moved along as usual and time rolled on. Then, when time rung out the year, 1887, it rang in 1888 with a cold storm, riding on the wings of the wind from the northern border of our country.

Mother became worse rapidly and "crossed the bar" on January 3rd. She had been with us in our own home nearly a year, and we missed her tired, patient smile. She loved baby Nellis so dearly that she would often say, "You will never raise her, for she is just too sweet to live." We laid mother in the cemetery beside father and in eight months little Nellis joined her. We placed her beside her grandmother.

We had some rain the summer of '88, and had a wonderful crop of peaches. Harry, Blanche and Sarah Osborn were here in peach harvest. They helped us to take care of some of the fruit. In October Mother Osborn came to visit with the two Osborn families for a few weeks. We always enjoyed their visits with us. We thought they all came that fall to cheer us over the loss of our little Nellis.

During the winter of '89 both of our two older children were in school. We had never boarded a teacher, but we were persuaded to take a young man four days of each week during the school term. Most people, some time in their life, know what it is to be in love. Well this young chap became in love with one of his pupils; but sadder still, our hired man was in love with her too. He had been going with her all summer and did not like the idea of a rival in his love affair. The teacher sang her praises to me each day he came from school, and the other fellow glared at him. We began to fear that there might be a delicate situation approaching us. The teacher won and married the girl, but the other poor chap left for his home in another state; and we lost a good farm hand. But we were consoled when June 19th came, bringing us another little son, George Elliot. We thought perhaps the time would come when we would not need a hired man. But we were mistaken, for neither of our sons chose farm life.

In the fall of '89 there seemed to be considerable unrest politically among the farmers. But the most of our unrest was caused by whooping cough when the children caught it from other school children. It was followed by a scourge of "lagripe" among the adult population, and continued its "grip" on the people most of the winter of 1890. We had our anniversary dinner this winter, but I failed to keep a record of it for the first time. I was so busy most of the time that I dropped the record, but not the dinner, guest or no guest.

The winter of 1890 was unusually cold, and the snow was often piled high in drifts, making a serious condition for stockmen. Cattle sometime drifted with the wind into canons [sic] or against a fence and were covered with snow where they were often frozen or tramped to death, causing a heavy loss to the owner. We had a niece, teaching out among the hills that winter, and when we asked her how she got through the drifts, she said she had just lain down and rolled over them.

When the old log schoolhouse burned, a new frame house had been built, making it more comfortable for the school children. We were not very well satisfied with the progress our children were making, and we thought they might do better in the town school. We had a family move on to the farm, and we moved into town. After we were settled in town, the farm work finished for that season, Mr. Osborn said, "Now it is your time for a visit in Kansas City with your sister while I am not busy." As he could be with the children, I could go and not be the least uneasy, although our little boy was only three. When I arrived at the old Union Station, Wick Osborn was there with his horse and buggy. The streets were covered with ice, but the horse was sharp shod, and his hooves clicked as he lightly tripped over the icy pavement. The weather was not very nice for a visit; however, I enjoyed it hugely. When I came home, I found everything all right but our baby boy. He seemed to have forgotten that he had a mother.

It was about that time that the Populist party was organized, and the Populists, headed by Jerry Simpson, were "rampant." They were so furious toward the other political parties that they frightened some folks. Several women who lived in town said to me, "I'm really afraid the farmers intend to kill all the town people." My niece, Maud Hagan, was also living in town at this time. She had been married to Jo Zimmerman two years before, and there was a young baby at their home. It was now my turn to be of some help to her, and I was quite busy most of the winter.

The Prohibition Law of Kansas had been enacted in 1880, and we had a W. C. T. U. Association of which I was a member. In March, 1892, the Reverend Anna Shaw, of New York City, came with other women from the East to organize an Equal Suffrage Association of which I became a member. We kept it alive until the men voters gave the women "equal suffrage." The WCTU closed its eyes when Congress passed the Eighteenth Amendment. It slept serenely in full belief that it would never again hear the midnight brawls of the old saloon days, making the night hideous with drunken carousal.

While I was kept quite busy the three years we lived in town, it was not the drudgery like caring for the milk and butter and the poultry end of the business; and I had leisure to do things occasionally more to my taste. I attended the Teachers' Institute whenever it was in session as I had always enjoyed it as a teacher. Political meetings were numerous, and speeches bitter against the opposite party. At that time it was between the Republican and Populist parties. The Democrats had silently slipped into the "New Party." They hated the Republican Party and saw a chance to defeat it (at least in Kansas).

Chester I. Long and Jerry Simpson were opponents. Some of the Republican women conceived the idea of having a number of their party women go to a meeting at Kiowa in costume of yellow cape and cap as a boosting group for Long. I do not remember the number of women; however, there was a goodly number of them. They proudly marched up Main St. Then they marched down to the railroad station, a laughing, joshing group of women, with their captain gaily leading them. As we were marching up Kiowa's Main Street there were many heads sticking out of business houses to see us. One man

called to another, "Oh, did you ever see such feet?" We
supposed that he meant "big feet" and were not much
flattered. The funny part of the whole affair was when
the Populists were celebrating the election of Simpson;
they had at the head of their parade a girl, riding on a
mule; and she was wearing a yellow cape and cap.

After moving into town, we bought a house, expecting to remain in the Lodge most of the time while the
children were in school. But we discovered that no other
person would take care of our stock as we wanted them
to do it. We lost several head of cows by the tenant's
carelessness. They would leave the gates swinging open,
and the cattle, getting into the fields, died from over
eating. Mr. Osborn discharged the tenant and undertook to
do the work himself, driving to the farm and back to
town each day. It was so lonesome at the farm that even
the dog would pick up the cat and come to the gate to
meet him.

We knew we were losing money by not attending
strictly to our business, even if it was only a farm. The
two older children were old enough to drive to school in
town, and the other two could attend the home district
school; so we decided to move back to the farm. It was
not an easy task, that we could see, as soon as we
inspected the house. The first thing to do, we concluded,
was to fumigate, paint, and paper, which we did and
moved in. We soon had things on the farm going to suit
us. The young folks were doing all right in school.
Occasionally we would raise a wheat crop and receive a
fair price for it, but when we wanted a visit, we
generally went one at a time, as we saw the need of
close attention to business. Many changes took place in a
few years, but that has been always so since the world
began rolling on its axis.

Her Father's Right-Hand Man
Adele Orpen

In the opening pages of her book, Memories of the Old Emigrant Days in Kansas, 1862-1865, *"Doaty" Orpen asks the question, "What did we seek?" Most pioneers would say they were looking for better land, greater independence, a better standard of living. Orpen, looking back several decades, answers the question in philosophical rather than economic terms: "What did we seek? The unknown, the strange, the new, and because unknown and strange and new, therefore desirable." But Orpen, like most who recorded their memories, is less interested in a sociological analysis than in describing every day experiences. She also shows how the Civil War affected the lives of new settlers in Kansas. Her reminiscences are most interesting, perhaps, because she records the story of a girl's life on the prairie homestead and the challenges she faced. Orpen writes: "But if a little girl from whatever combination of circumstances found herself turned into a boy, or rather her father's right-hand man, at the age of eight years, she would acquire a sense of personal importance and responsibility that then and there her childishness would fall away from her like a worn-out garment." Doaty and "Auntie" accompanied Mr. Orpen to Kansas in 1862 when Doaty was seven years old. Doaty's mother and baby brother had died three years earlier, and Mr. Orpen believed the Kansas prairies would be a healthier place to live than in Virginia. Mr. Orpen clearly had a great deal of money to invest in the homesteading venture; in addition, he worked as an engineer for the railroad. His work and other activities consumed much of his time, so that Doaty and Auntie were frequently left in* charge of the homestead. Mr. Orpen gave his daughter knives and taught her how to use them. He also taught her "how to turn screws, drive nails, and whittle sticks." He refused to support Auntie's attempts to teach Doaty grammar, arguing that she was a bright child and would use correct grammar if she heard correct grammar.

The family left Kansas in 1865. While Doaty and Auntie thrived on the prairie, Mr. Orpen's health failed after he developed ague.

Source:

Mrs. Orpen. Memories of the Old Emigrant Days in Kansas, 1862-1865. Edinburgh & London: William Blackwood, 1926. 56-65, 79-85, 141-47, 209-12.

It must have been in this first spring of our emigrant life that Auntie resolutely took my education in hand. She determined to lay it on a firm foundation, so she began with grammar. Ye gods! what a thing to offer a wild prairie child of eight. But she kept firmly on, and very soon I was completely lost in a thicket of nouns and adjectives, and of subjects and predicates, with here and there articles, adverbs, and pronouns to trip me up at every step. I could find no trail anywhere, and was reduced to the wildest of expedients to make my way out into light and clear understanding. Some days I did better than others, and therefore I made a mental table of days for my own behoof, and searched for adjectives on Mondays, while Tuesdays were devoted to predicates—as many as I could find,—and so I floundered on, not understanding in the smallest degree what I was at, any more than a South Sea islander could understand the laws of harmony if set to study them as a preliminary to learning an English song. Pretty soon disaster followed and then punishment, and then my father took notice of things. I do not know what he said, but I remember overhearing this remark, "She is very imitative, and if she hears nothing but good English spoken, you need not worry about the rest." Though I did not know what "imitative" meant, I knew from the sound of his voice that I was reprieved from the punishment of grammar.

Anyway, I hated being a little girl. All a girl's duties were irksome to me, and, be it remembered, I had none of an ordinary girl's pleasures into which personal vanity

so largely enters. On the other hand, a boy's work exactly
suited me, and though I could not distinguish an adverb
from an adjective in my grammar puzzles, I was unerring
in finding a new-born calf hidden by its mother in the
wide-stretching prairie. That is to say, Nellie, Pluto, and
I could find it. We were completely equipped in our
three selves for the solution of many baffling puzzles
where animals were concerned. Our cattle used to range at
large over the open prairie, and when a cow calved she
would hide the calf, and then some two days later
present herself along with the rest at milking-time. Then
would come the order to me to "find the calf." The plan
of campaign was as follows: Pluto was at once summoned,
and came with joyous yelps, and Nellie was caught and
saddled. Nellie lived in her twenty-acre pasture field, so
as to be always on hand for emergencies such as this.
But the catching of a wild Indian pony by a very small
girl would seem to the uninitiated a very ticklish operation. A handful of salt, however, did it. Animals grazing
two thousand miles from the ocean are always rabidly
eager for salt. Therefore when Nellie was wanted I had
only to hold my two brown paws out to her and call her
to come to me. She would begin by making wide circles
around me, and then by degrees coming nearer and nearer
she would finally commence to lick salt in my hand. I
would then put the reins over her neck, and as soon as
she had licked up every grain I could bridle her. Of
course, it goes without saying that one must never cheat
an animal. They never forget or forgive a trick. But if
this commandment be obeyed one's horses and dogs will
trust one completely.

To resume our proceedings. Nellie, Pluto, and I, thus
assembled, would take the newly calved cow as the centre
of our circle, and gallop with wild whoops and barks
straight away from her towards the north a short distance, under a quarter of mile. We would then stop and
look at the cow. If she showed no interest in our ma-
noeuvers, we would come slowly back to her and repeat
the operation in a southerly direction. Again, if that
failed we would direct our course towards the west, when
assuredly the cow would begin to follow. The calf,

therefore, was somewhere towards the west, and by zigzagging in front of the cow we would eventually reach the neighbourhood of the calf's hiding-place, sometimes as much as three or four miles away. Now a cow has two bugle-calls in her register: one meaning "lie low," which is soft and smooth; and the other meaning "jump and run," which is sharp, quick, and hard. Both are always implicitly obeyed by the new-born calf. As soon as we get near the hidden calf the first bugle-call sounds continuously, and Pluto ranges back and forth through the low cotton-wood scrub, while I sit motionless on my little saddle awaiting the inevitable denouement. Pluto gets to within a few paces of the calf, and then the second bugle-call rings out. The calf has never heard the sound before, but the knowledge of its meaning has mysteriously come into his mind with the first breath he ever drew, and he obeys. With a raucous cry and one bound he is beside his mother. We all three return home in triumph with our captives amid the acclamations of those at home. Could the finding of a dozen predicates compare in excitement and glory with the finding of a single calf?

Corn-planting and Dish-washing

Not all the boy's work which devolved upon this little prairie girl was as exhilarating as the finding of a hidden calf. By no means. Some of it was deadly dogged work: corn-planting, for instance. This was well within my powers, and I did a lot of it on the occasion of our first planting season. The corn, of course, was maize, and it is planted in little holes three feet apart every way. To accomplish this, drills are opened by the plough three feet apart, and then cross drills are made at the same distance. Then at each intersection of these drills three seeds of maize, no less and no more, are dropped. It is quite simple and seems very easy, but nothing is easy when inexorably repeated for five hours at a stretch on a hot prairie field. The drills themselves produced a sense of giddiness from the chess-board like recurrence of the squares. At the end of a day's work I began to be unable to drop the seeds steadily, and stooping down to pick up the wrong ones made matters worse. It was only the direst need that sent me into the field to plant corn, but no one else was to be had. The war had begun to drain men away from the land. . . .

However, the corn got planted and began to grow. Soon it got over my head, but that was only 4 feet 2 inches, and then it hid my father's head also, and then rose gloriously into the air and blossomed at 7 or 8 feet. A fairy-land it became to me. The path to the spring went through it, and I dawdled so long on my trips to fetch spring-water for dinner that I was often punished by being mulcted of my Sunday maple-sugar. How could any child pass through such a wonderland without dawdling! The corn-stalks were round and smooth, very similar to bamboos, and the long ribbony leaves had only one drawback: they possessed saw-edges which prevented me from tying them round my neck, but the silk was all joy. The silk, so called, was in reality the numerous thread-like styles hanging like a long tassel out of the shuck which closely enveloped the young seeds. The flower with the pollen was on the top of the plant like the white mop of the pampas grass, only it was yellow in colour. On a windy day in July there used to be a cloud hanging over the corn-field which was caused by the pollen flying. The silk was brilliant in colour—yellow, pale green, or vivid crimson; and as it was borne low down on the stalk, it was easily within my reach. It came in great handfuls, six to ten inches beyond the end of the seed envelope. Of course, I had to pull the tassel out and hang it over my ears and around Pluto's neck. No child could pass it, so tempting was the soft clinging, shining thing; and thus it was that I used often to be late with the spring-water for dinner. Of course, I soon peopled the corn-field with creatures of my imagination. These were not fairies. I knew nothing whatever of fairies or fairy tales. I never saw a picture of one of these little fanciful creatures, and never heard the name. Living as I did always with grown-up people, I had learned only their ideas, very much distorted, of course, through my ignorance and inability to understand what the grown-ups said, but my ideas were on the same lines as theirs. My fancies were more or less a multiplication of myself projected into various situations more or less difficult, out of which I would emerge rather more than less triumphantly. I used to declaim my ideas to Pluto and Nellie, and I noticed how whole-heartedly Pluto entered into the excitement of the proceedings, which largely consisted of riding desperately after or from something or somebody. Nellie, on the other hand, took no interest whatsoever in what I said, although she never interrupted me, being a lady of excellent manners. In after-years when it came to be my destiny to address in drawing-rooms audiences of ladies with their best gloves on, I was sometimes reminded of Nellie listening to me, without any overt sign of interest, as I shouted my stories to her while I sat on the prairie grass in far-away Kansas.

I have said that I hated girl's work. So I did—all of it—but there were, of course, degrees of detestation, and I think washing-up after meals took the first place. I simply loathed it. It must be remembered that for two years we were short of water. What a multitude of petty miseries does that brief expression bring to my recollection! Still among these remains one bright one that stands forth clearly above all the others—one supreme dishwashing that I recall as if it were but yesterday. A subsequent knowledge of history tells me that this dishwashing must have occurred in the summer of 1863. A young cavalry soldier had stopped at our house for dinner. He had dined well off one of Auntie's famous pemmican ragouts, which she could get ready in an hour. Talk followed, with canned peaches, which also were one of Auntie's miracles of food not found elsewhere than in our house in the old emigrant days. Auntie and the young soldier retired to her room to talk, while I was left to wash-up. The water and the soap were duly in the dish-tub, which was placed on a stool, but when I raised my hands to put in the pile of plates I somehow hit something, and over went the show—that is, the dish-tub of hot water,—for I still held the plates in my hands.

It did not need my scream of dismay to fetch them out of the next room. They were both out before the water had run a quarter of the way over the floor. Auntie's temper was ever like good pie-crust—very short. She raised her hand to box my ears, but quick as she was that young soldier was quicker still. A very large hand came from behind her and caught her wrist, and a very loud cheery voice said, "No, no, you mustn't! The poor little Siss, she wasn't tall enough to reach over the tub." Then everything happened together, as they say in novels in the thrilling moments. Through the magnifying and multiplying lenses of my tears the floor seemed covered with arms, and hands, and legs, and boots, and spurs, and shiny buttons, and the ceiling rang with Homeric laughter as that soldier man mopped up the water and wrung out the dish-cloth and cleaned up the floor in a twinkling. Then he jumped to his feet and clicked his spurs and chucked me under the chin and said, "No more tears, Siss; I'll wash up your dishes for you." And he did—while he whistled and whooped and sang soldiers' songs, clattering his boots to the time of them, till the very harness on the walls trembled with joy. After that he kept me by his knee telling me stories. Then he mounted his horse and rode away, flourishing his cap high over his head and yohoing to me. We never knew his name nor whence he came, nor whither he went, but the bright vision of his kindness never faded from the memory of a deeply mortified little girl whom he had restored to complete happiness and cheery pleasure in his visit. . . .

Cattle Lore

I was always with men, my father first of all and those he had with him as workmen. One was a University man, another was a farmer "from 'way East," another man whose large family had one time and another furnished us with servants. Negroes sometimes appeared spasmodically, but to these I never was to speak except in the house, when I was too busily engaged feeding

them to speak to any. Then I had my outside work,
cattle hunting on the prairie, where there was never any
one except myself with Nellie and Pluto. Later on there
came other people, and then soldiers, for the war swept
up our way, and my cattle-ranging was instantly stopped.
This sort of training produced an unlooked for result. I
became very grave. I believe I never laughed, and did not
play as children should. I walked about looking after my
hens and chickens, or else mounted my pony, and,
whistling to Pluto, rode away into the vast and measure-
less prairie. Was I lonely? Not a bit of it. I simply did
not know what loneliness meant. I was full of my duties
and my pleasures. The day was never long enough for
me, unless, of course, it contained grammar and dishwashing to an objectionable extent, when I would simply
remain mentally quiescent. Auntie was horrified. She said
I was nothing but a little savage, and I suspect she was
right. My father said, "She might be worse; I am content
for her to be as she is. I've seen enough of civilisation
and its effects to welcome a little healthy savagery." What
Auntie meant when she said I was a little savage was
that I knew so much that most girls never knew, and
nothing at all of what all girls should know. At nine
years of age I could not spell my name, for example, but
I was able to remember correctly all the cattle I had seen
for the past week and exactly whose they were and
which way they were heading. I was therefore in great
request among the settlers around us.

A man would ride up to our bars (gate) and hail the
household. Nine times out of ten I answered the hail, but
if not, then immediately would come the question——

"Whar's your little gal? I want to ask her if she's seen
my stock?"

And the little gal would promptly reply, "Yes, I saw
them two days back. They were on the north side of
Little Sugar Creek, two miles east of Adam's Mound. The
sun was three hours high. They were heading towards the
Big Sugar Creek. The white cow with the broken horn
leading."

This was information accurate and precise as an
Admiralty wireless. From it any frontiersman could easily

gauge where to hunt for the animals within a few miles.
Cattle, unlike human beings, follow their own laws and
obey their own rules implicitly. Thus they stay in herds.
No man's herd will split up and join on to another
family, or run away from home, as it is called when
humans do it. Each herd follows its leader, always the
oldest and steadiest cow. This is quite contrary to human
practice. They never change their minds about their food,
but graze steadily ahead at the rate of five or seven
miles a day, so if the direction and the leader is known,
then their place on the prairie can be calculated. The time
was always taken from the sun. "Three hours high" may
sound vague, perhaps, to the uninitiated, but it should be
remembered the sun was always on hand, winter and
summer, on the prairies. It also was steady in its course.
Latitude 38 makes the sun rise in the East, set in the
West, and be overhead at noon, approximately at least.
One's life was thus regulated with much decorum. One
got up a little before the sun did, one went to bed just
after he had set the example, and one had dinner when
one's head cast no shadow worth noticing. . . .

My Absence Cattle-hunting Causes Alarm

Now although I could do such foolhardy things and
yet not be found out, I was in reality kept very carefully
under observation. This was accomplished by means of
two forces working in combination—namely, my habit of
the strictest obedience to the orders given by my father,
and Auntie's extraordinary long sight. When giving her
mind to it she could see farther than any one I ever
knew, and when not giving her mind to it she saw less
than any human being not completely blind. Here is an
example of how anxiously I was looked after.

It was sometime late in May. The corn was up and
was being tilled by the two-horse cultivator. I was told to
take our bunch of cattle to the spring and water them,
and I was not to go farther than the spring, but to bring
them straight home again to the pasture field. That was
all very well for me, but the cattle were not told any-

thing. As soon as the first half-dozen had drunk, taking their time over it according to the habit of cattle, the younger ones found this very tedious and immediately set off down the trail towards the river. Pluto and I, on the alert, raced around and headed them back. This we accomplished satisfactorily for the moment, but if cattle imagine there is any fun on hand in which there is a chance of getting the better of a human being, they immediately become possessed of the devil. No sooner did I get the half-dozen deserters back to the spring than the others looked for a chance of mischief, and soon the whole herd (about twenty-five) laid its nose to the ground and stampeded. Now Pluto and I, left behind, knew that once those animals got among the brushwood of the creek and had drunk their fill, they would skulk there in hiding for days and maybe weeks. The grass was tall and luscious down in the bottom lands. There was nothing for it but to gather them up while still drinking. Therefore behold Pluto, Nellie, and me in swift and relentless pursuit! The creek was two miles away. However, we were not far behind, and in we splashed, shouting, barking, and slashing. The cattle, many of them sedate mothers who knew they were setting a bad example, came swiftly back to a sense of decorum and started for home, up the rocky trail we had just come down in such fiery haste. All this took time, far beyond what was allowed to me to water the cattle at the spring.

Meanwhile my father came home to dinner and was told that I had gone to the spring and had not returned, nor could I be seen anywhere from the observation platform at the end of the house. Auntie had been up to look for me again and again. My father leaped on the bare back of the younger of his two horses and set off at a gallop towards the eastern side of the farm to ask at the Weddells' house had they seen me. He was just on the crest of the little rise of prairie that separated our farm from theirs when I emerged from the bottom land and saw him. I saw the flash of the chain-traces as they banged against the horse's flanks, and the wild sweep of his straw hat as my father beat the horse desperately with that fast disintegrating piece of head-gear. I knew at

once what it meant. He was afraid that some accident
had happened to me. I had been so long gone; in fact, I
did not know how long. My father's horse even in his
wild rush had caught sight of me and my cattle. Down
they bore rapidly on me, my father's face, even under
the tan, greenish-white. Was it anger? I was frightened,
but I said as steadily as I could—

"They ran away from me, and I had to follow them
to the creek before I could get them under control."

"Are you all right?" he asked brokenly, and a shudder
seemed to pass over him.

"Yes, quite all right. Was it wrong to follow the
cattle? I never could have found them if I had let them
scatter in the bottom land."

"Yes, yes, but I could not think what had happened,"
he said hurriedly.

Auntie had got a bed ready and hot water and things
in case I was brought in hurt. My father did not go
back to work that day in the cornfield. He did not feel
equal to it. Auntie afterwards told me never to follow the
cattle again, but to let them go anywhere rather than be
out after I was told to be back. I did not at the time
understand why; my decision to bring home the cattle
had seemed so sound to me.

It must be remembered that I was only nine years
old, with a mind of the same age, and a memory that
held only two images of my mother: the one of her
dressing my doll for my birthday, and the other, a few
days later, of her lying in her coffin with the little
waxen baby on her arm. I did not realise that my poor
father was ever haunted by the fear that I, too, should
be taken from him. I was a fairly healthy child, but he
could not trust to that. The others had seemed very
healthy also, yet my little brother had died of scarlet
fever, and my mother and my infant sister had died of
diptheria, a new disease of which no one had ever heard
before. I was all that remained to him of his small
world, and in the wild life of Kansas he was trying to
keep me from danger of infection, while fortifying me
against any possibly inherited weakness of constitution. . .

Some of My Duties

Although I paid no heed to the flying years, it was far otherwise with those in authority. Talk began to reach me of going East, of school, of seeing people again whom I only faintly remembered. The young girl whom I had so alarmingly driven ahead of the thunderstorm had already gone, along with her mother and two sisters. I did not, of course, realise in the faintest degree what it would mean to me. I was still full of my duties as they came to me out of my life on the plains. Chickens there were to rear, and in this my last year I raised one hundred and thirty-five, all to my lone hand. It says a great deal for the real healthiness of Kansas that I could do it at all. But we were disease-free as far as chickens were concerned. We had no chicken cholera, no pip, no gapes, no dying in the shell. Let the chicken-rearers of to-day think enviously of our luck. All eggs hatched out except those broken by rude hens fighting over their families. There was an ample henhouse, as yet quite free from infection, and there were two storeys to it, with separate entrances for the laying hens and the hatching mothers, each one of which attended strictly to its own affairs. Though we had foxes of sorts about, they had not yet learned to attack henhouses, and anyway a few shots let off at night kept them at a distance. This was chicken-rearing in Kansas in the first years of my life.

As a contrast, let me give the numbers of my last attempt at chicken-rearing. Eight dozen eggs, bought from two chicken stations advertising as members of the Poultry Society, and keeping only one pure-bred stock, hatched out 50 percent of scandalous mongrels, showing traces of a dozen different mixtures in cross-breeding. Of those hatched, 20 per cent did not survive to produce wing feathers. Of the remainder, ten birds were killed by a homicidal cat that invaded the brooder by night. At the end of the season I had twelve indifferent chickens, thin, undersized, and hopelessly behindhand in the race for the dinner-table, and this after six months constant attention in feeding and care.

The other night, being wakeful and impatient with the weariness bred of long illness and slow recovery, I reached out again and again a languid finger and pushed a button. Instantly the room was flooded with light, a light so vivid and searching that it sought out every crack and crevice on the wall, and showed up each picture and print hanging thereon. Of course, it was the electric light I turned on and off according to my sick whim. Then there flitted across my memory the light of other days. What sort of light did we have in Kansas? Just tallow candles, and I had to make them. It was a job I sincerely loathed, from the boiling of the fat to the extracting of the finished candle out of its mould, scalding my fingers and scratching them with jagged tin every step of the way. There was not a redeeming feature in the whole business, except that we had a twelve-candle mould, and since for a least six months in the year we got up at sunrise and went to bed at sunset, we did not require very many candles for that period. During the rest of the year candles were brought in with ceremony, and used with discretion. I, for example, was never entrusted with a match during the whole time I was in Kansas; they were too dangerous. There are no rules for deciding what is dangerous for children. Some things are dangerous to some children and some are not, and there's an end of it. Only you have got to remember what sort of child it is you are dealing with.

Thus I was permitted to go alone into the stable, feed the horses, climb up and over and under and around them any way I chose, so as to get their harness on and buckle it tight, to bring them out and put them to the wagon, single-handed. No one paid the slightest heed to me, well knowing that no matter how many times I fell off the pole when trying to sling the housing over Bess's big back, I would eventually bring the wagon and the two horses correctly harnessed to the door, and myself, hot and angry maybe, victoriously seated aloft, reins in hand and whip securely deposited at my feet. That was well within my power; but to strike a match and light a candle was quite a different thing. I was supposed not to be capable of doing it safely until after I was twelve years old. Such is the force of early training, however, that there remains with me to this day a feeling of anxiety when anybody else is lighting lamps and candles, so that if I am talking at the moment, the words hang on my lips, and I begin to watch the process of match-striking to be certain it is safely accomplished before I continue my remarks. I suppose one never forgets the things one really learned in childhood, hence the vividness with which I recall the four years of my emigrant life.

"I Want to Write About My Days of a Slower Progress"
Alice Dahlin Lund

Alice Dahlin's family were among the first settlers in the Wisconsin community of West Sweden. The rough, heavily wooded land was cleared and the settlement was begun in the 1860s; in 1875 Alice's father was elected to the first town council. Also in 1875, the town built a new school, one and one-half miles from the Dahlin farm, large enough to hold the expanding enrollment and to provide space for social gatherings and church services.

Alice married John Lund in 1888 and had ten children, two of whom died in infancy. In 1944, at the age of seventy-five, she began to write her memories of her youth in West Sweden. She addresses her writing directly to her children and grandchildren and includes, at random intervals, many of her favorite hymns and prayers. Her memoirs are personal—"One day, who should I see coming down the hill? It was my Swede [her future husband]. 'Oh,' I thought, 'he looks like a real American.'" And sometimes she is poetic—"One night the moon lit up the snow like silver."

Her positive creative spirit shines through her accounts of overwhelming responsibility, hard work and danger. She states that her mother-in-law ordered her to stop embroidering on aprons and baby clothes, and do something useful. "But," says Alice, "I thought there was time for both.

Alice's ninety-six page manuscript covers her life from her trip to West Sweden as an infant to the birth of her children. The following selection focuses on her early childhood and early adulthood.

Source:
Alice Dahlin Lund. "Tender Memories Dedicated to My Children and Their Families." Unpublished manuscript. Minnesota Historical Society Archives, 1945.

As I sit here and watch the children of this age and think back about seventy years or so, for that is as far back as I am able to remember, for I am now seventy-five years old. My parents and another family came from Sweden in 1868, settling on a homestead in a wild forest in Wisconsin in the year of 1870. The closest neighbors were then about seven miles from our homestead.

My parents had four children of which I was the youngest. The other family had one little boy. Our homesteads joined and they built the log cabins as close together as they could to make it convenient for water, mutual aid and the joy and comfort of close fellowship.

I wish I could take time to describe in an elaborate way this beautiful country that was to become our home for many years. It was a very beautiful country. There was a big creek running through our land. This was a big advantage to us as well as beautifying our property.

There were many Indians living in our neighborhood. There were also all sorts of wild animals such as bears, wildcats, wolves and panthers. At night the wolves would come so close to our cabin and howl so loudly that we could not sleep. My parents then would take a torch and lantern and go out to try to scare them away. The wolves were afraid of fire. In the meantime, we children would sit up in bed and howl almost as loudly as the wolves for fear the wolves would kill our parents. We were lucky for they always came back safely to us.

One night, I remember I was very worried. My parents and our neighbors went out and killed a wildcat.

The next morning we all went out to look at it. I remember I was afraid even though it was dead. I ran to my mother and wrapped her skirts around me. The skirts in those days were not like the skirts of today. Then they had to have eight or ten yards to make a dress. That is more than twice as much as is needed for a dress for a lady today.

In Sweden my mother was considered quite well-to-do. After she married my father and heard so much about America and what a wonderful country it was, she made up her mind to leave her homeland and go to this new land with him. I do not think their journey was a very pleasant one for I heard they came over in a sail boat and it took them four weeks to cross the ocean.

They had friends in Marine-On-St.-Croix, Minnesota, so they spent two years there before they came to their homesteads in Polk County, Wisconsin. They later named this new locality West Sweden, a name that is till used for a township and also a small town consisting of a school, church, store, creamery, and a blacksmith shop.

How do you suppose we got there? There were no trucks in those days, and no one had horses. This is how it was done. Each person carried as much as possible. Cows and young stock were loaded like pack mules. The two families had two wheelbarrows to push. The trip was made on foot. It was a bit difficult as the distance to our homesteads was about fifty-five miles and the last seven miles had no road at all. We had to wind our way through the woods the best way we could. Of course, the men had been there before and had marked the trees so they could find their way to their homesteads and cabins, which they had built. We at least had a roof over our heads when we reached our destination. I think it took about three days to make the trip.

There were no beds with springs and innerspring mattresses for them to rest on when they arrived there. Oh, no! they had to fill their bed ticks with hay cut from the meadow and put that down on the floor for a bed.

The cows and chickens had to be watched so the wild animals wouldn't come and take them. My father and our friend, Anders, fixed up a saw rig so they sawed all their lumber by hand that was to be used for doors, window-frames and floors. They made beds, benches and chairs. My father also made drop-leaf tables and a folding bed from this lumber. We used it for a couch in the daytime and a bed at night. It was fixed so that we put all the bedding in it during the daytime. It was real handy.

There was much to do for the land had to be broken up for garden and grain so we could raise wheat for flour, and corn and oats for growing stock. The first year or so enough ground was broken up with a grub axe, hoe and spade so we could plant corn, potatoes, and other vegetables.

We could not go to the grocery store every day as we do now. The nearest trading place was thirty miles away and the only way we could get our merchandise home was to walk and wheel it on a wheelbarrow which took three days. We not only had to bring groceries in this way but we also had to bring garden tools, hay rakes, chains, window lights, scythes and all kinds of things including yard goods for clothing.

When the young steers grew up so they were big enough to put a yoke on their necks, they were trained to work. Wagons and sleds also had to be made or bought. Roads had to be built so they could drive. As time went on more people moved into the neighborhood, making it easier for Father and Anders. They got help to open the roads and put up a building which served as a church, school and town hall.

A cemetery was also dedicated. The first burial that took place there was that of a small baby that died while its parents were on their way to their homestead.

It was not long before we had a pastor for our community. At first he came to our church about every third Sunday. Every one went to church, it seems. Some people walked six miles or more to attend this little log church on the hill. Folks seemed to love getting together.

Now, don't think that people did not take pride in their clothing or manners. The ladies wore full skirts, over-skirts and hoop-skirts. The men wore long coats

with a slit in the back. My father had four different
styles of coats that he wore on different occasions. He
even had a white vest! They wore stiff bosom shirts and
used stiff paper collars. During hot weather they caused
the men a bit of grief as they wilted and wrinkled when
the men perspired. Because of this they did not put the
collars on at home but would put them in their pockets
until they came close to the church when they would stop
and help each other put them on. They wore big black
neckties with elastic attached to them and were buttoned
around the neck. The ladies were used to going barefoot
and found it difficult to wear shoes when they went out
on special occasions. When they went to church they
would carry their shoes and stockings. While the men put
on their collars the ladies would dress their feet. I can
see the funny side of it, but don't think anything seemed
funny to them. They were in earnest and came into the
church sober-faced with a prayer on their lips and bowed
their heads in silent prayer holding their hats before their
faces. Of course we children went barefoot everywhere
during the warm weather. We were taught manners and
we knew our place. We never dared whisper or make any
kind of noise in church no matter how long the sermon
lasted.

When I was nine years old I was expected to remember the text chosen by the pastor for the day, what he
read in the Bible and the songs that were sung. I was
expected to be able to repeat all this when I got home. I
could even remember it during the week. . . .

Chapter Two

As I sit here alone with my hand-work, my thoughts
go back to my childhood and my home in the wild
forest. I well remember one fall when the weather was
cold enough to keep the doors closed. Many Indians often
came to see us but they did not know how to get in the
house. They walked around the house and stopped and
looked in the windows but they were not able to figure
out how to open the door. My father and mother

laughed, but I was too young, at the time, to see any fun in it. After a little while my father opened the door. He beckoned for them to come in. They did not need coaxing! They came right in. There were so many of them, they filled the entire kitchen. They were interested in the cookstove and held their hands over it. Mother went over to show them how it worked. They talked between themselves and finally they started to go out so my father showed them how to open the door.

The next time they came, they just walked right into the house, so my father told them to go out again. He went with them and motioned for them to take notice. Father knocked on the door and waited for someone to say, "Come in," or to come and open the door. Then they went in. He got them pretty well trained so they really knew enough to rap on the door when they came again.

I remember once some braves came just as my mother was taking bread out of the oven. They looked at the bread and talked to each other so mother cut some bread and gave it to them without butter or anything else spread upon it. They ate it and seemed very much pleased with it. She cut up almost two loaves for them. They did not have any sort of an errand. They just made a social call. They left before they were through eating.

The squaws used to come and visit, bringing their papooses along. Mother very often made coffee for them. They could not talk to each other. They always seemed to enjoy the visit. Mother and our neighbor lady always returned their calls and of course we children always went along. We would go from one wigwam to the other, but we favored two families, so we spent more time at their places. Mother showed interest in their handwork and also the way they did their cooking. One afternoon the squaws gave us a treat. One of them took a tin pan and spoon and scoured it until it shone like new and then washed the pan, filling it about half full of maple sugar and offered us to eat. She pointed to the spoon and held up one finger, meaning it was all she had. We sat there a long time enjoying our treat because sweets were not plentiful.

We went to visit them when a papoose was sick. We called to see how it was. It was much better. The mother was preparing the evening meal. She had a kettle hanging over the fire filled with a big chunk of pork, rice and plenty of water. She kept stirring in it with a wooden ladle. I am sure it looked good to a hungry brave coming home from a hunt in the woods. The squaw was making bread also. She had a hole in the ground lined with rocks. This served as an oven. Filling it with wood she made a fire to heat the rocks. She was heating some others at the same time. When the oven was hot she swept out the cinders and put some of the bread dough in it, covering it with earth and putting the other rocks on top of that. Perhaps it is hard to believe, but when the baking time was up the bread was just as brown as if it had been baked in one of our own ovens.

Mother and father went to see them to learn to prepare a turtle for turtle soup. They cooked the soup once but did not like it. The neighbors did not relish it either. I believe they had a little too much of other meat to bother. . . .

The early settlers had to depend almost entirely on their women for most of their material for clothing as they wove cloth as well as spinning yarn for scarves, mittens and stockings and a long time all the sewing was done by hand.

It was fun to watch the squaws trying to make yarn. We had a spinning wheel and also wool cards with which we carded wool, preparing it for spinning. One day, when the squaws came to see us, they thought they would like to learn how to card and spin. They did learn to do the carding, but when they tried to spin, it did not work so good no matter how hard they tried. The wool, it seems, would slip out of their fingers before they caught on to the twist of it, so they gave up trying. They had some good laughs anyway.

The Indians liked to smoke. The squaws liked to smoke as much as the braves did but they had a substitute for tobacco. It was a shrub called Kinnikinic. They scraped bark off this shrub and dried it. The squaws as well as the braves would fill up their pipes and smoke.

We called this bark Indian Tobacco. Not long ago, while I was listening to the radio, contestants on a Quiz Program were asked to define Kinnikinic, but not one of the contestants knew what it was. It amused me for I knew plenty about it. . . .

The Indians were really sympathetic. I recall when my sister's baby passed away, they came to offer sympathy before the funeral. They petted my sister to express as much as possible how they felt. They could not speak English. We showed them the baby and they looked at it; large tears rolled down their cheeks. Really, they made us feel good, too, as we appreciated their friendship more than any of you might think. There were four squaws and two or three Indian maidens. The oldest of the group beckoned to the others. They all knelt on their knees while the oldest squaw said a prayer. We all knelt also as we knew what they meant, and we also knew they were sincere in their desire to comfort my sister in her grief.

Chapter Three

Now I believe we will let our Indians rest for a little while and go back again to farming. By this time we had enough of our ground broken up so we raised enough wheat to take to the mill to have it made into flour. A great deal of work was required before they got the wheat ready to put into sacks.

They had to cut it by hand, using a scythe or cradle to tie it into bundles. When it was tied, it had to be threshed. That was also done by hand. They made a flail out of two sticks of wood tied together so the shortest stick would be able to swing easily striking the wheat so the kernels fell out of the straw. We built a granary for this purpose. Next the wheat kernels had to be separated from the chaffs. They used wooden shovels with short handles and threw the grain very swiftly across the big floor. In that way the wheat fell in one place on the floor and the chaffs fell in another place. They used this method instead of a fanning mill. After this was done the grain was finally ready for the mill, which was thirty

miles away. We had progressed enough now to have a
yoke of oxen, so it was not bad at all. That was considered very good. On one of their trips to the mill my
father brought home a four-poster bed that I am sure I
will never forget as it seemed to be the cause of my
first grief and deep sorrow. A young couple came to visit
us. The lady's name was Inga. She wore a white print
dress with some very tiny red flowers on it. After she
had left, I made a new doll. My mother gave me some
white cloth and I made a dress for it. I picked some red
berries and somehow made little red flowers in this
material with the berries. I named this doll Inga. I had
other dolls too, but Inga was best.

I had a brother that was a year and a half younger.
We played many games together. This particular time we
played "Dolls." One day two of the dolls became sick.
They got worse and worse until at last they died! We had
heard that good children went to Heaven but the bad
ones did not. One of these dolls was good but the other
was not so we chose the highest place for the good doll
and the lowest for the bad doll. My brother climbed
upon the bed and put the dolls in their places. Of course,
it was not long before we took them down again. Sad as
it was, one day Inga became sick and died and we had a
burial for her. We put her down in the ground and
placed a marker on her little grave. In a short time we
went back to get her. We meant to put her on the high
poster, but we could not find her. The marker was there
but the doll was gone! Finally I asked my mother if dolls
went to Heaven. "No, my dear child," she said, "Dolls do
not have souls." "Yes, but I put my doll in the ground
and now I can't find her." "Listen, dear, when you do
bury something you don't go back and dig it up. Dolls
are not alive like we are, when we die our soul goes to
Heaven if we are good but our body is buried in the
ground, and we never see the bodies again." I felt worse
than anyone can understand. That such fate came to Inga
was almost a little too much for me to stand. I lost all
interest in playing with dolls for quite a long time. As I
grew older, of course, I understood that my mother had
taken Inga just to give me a lesson which was a wise
thing for her to do.

It seems children are always up to something. A few days later we asked my mother if we could go down and play in the water. "Yes," she said, "but don't go beyond the beaver dam." There were beavers a little below our house. They had built a dam across the creek, extending into a meadow. It filled up with water there making a very nice swimming pool. The water was not very deep. Mother let us have a brass lamp to play with. She had taken the top part off so we filled it with water and emptied it over our heads. Suddenly we saw some frogs and what did we do but pick one after another putting them in the lamp. They slipped into the lamp so easily but when we got tired and were going to take them out we could not do it and we had to bring the lamp back. We realized we had done something wrong; the only thing we could do was to go in and tell mother about it. Well——We went in but with fear in our hearts. Mother took the lamp and went along. She stuck the lamp under the water and tipped it on the side. The little frogs came swimming out one after the other. I was still waiting to be punished, but mother went into the house without saying a word. I was so glad I could have thanked her but I did not say a word for fear she might change her mind. I could never be too sure.

My parents were God-fearing people. I remember that right after breakfast every morning Father read a chapter in the Bible and we got down on our knees and had prayer. Many of the neighbors did the same as we did.

One morning, real early, I had to go to a neighbor that lived about three miles away on an errand. I walked through the woods on an old Indian path about a mile. I did not meet any wild animals on this trip but I had a scare anyway. I can laugh now when I think of it. How my heart went pit-a-pat! I got out on the big road at the top of a big hill and looking down below I saw a big lake where the water came up on both wheel tracks. Oh! I did not know what to do—for if I ran across there I might fall and if I did fall I might roll into the lake and drown. That is what flashed through my mind. I did not dare go back. This is what I did. I got down on my little hands and knees and crawled across. I got to the

place where I was going safely. Their door was standing
wide open and they were all on their knees in prayer so
I tiptoed in and knelt down beside one of their children.
When the prayer was over, I said, "Good Morning," and
related my errand. They were nice to me and I was quite
happy. The lady gave me some lunch. I remember I
wanted to stay and play very much, but I had to go
home as I had been told to go right back home. I was
not afraid when I went back for when I got to the lake,
I did the same as I did before. I got down on my knees
again. Just think! I was only seven years old and had to
go those six miles all alone. I did not meet anybody and
I did not pass any houses. I had to go through the wild
woods all the way. I was not afraid—I had been taught
that God takes care of his children wherever they are and
I had faith. . . .

Chapter Four

One year a young man came to our neighborhood and
took a homestead that joined our land and stayed at our
place while he built his cabin. After that was done he
moved into his own home. He was single and had to do
his own cooking and all his housework. One day, he
came to our house to grind some wheat as we owned a
big coffee mill and all of the neighbors around there
used to come to grind some wheat. They used that flour
for making coarse bread and muffins and for cereals for
mush which we used for our evening meal. If any of it
was left we fried it for breakfast. It was very good
served with butter.

While he was grinding something must have gone
wrong for he said something that we had never heard
before for our father never used profane language. After
he had left we asked mother what Gustav meant when he
said that. She told us it was a naughty word and we
should never say it. "If you do," she said, "you will be
punished. If I am not around to hear you, God will hear
you even if you whisper." It did not have any effect on

me but my brother was terribly tempted. I was afraid he would say it as I did not know just what would happen to him if he did.

One day he made up his mind he was going to use this strange word. We were sitting on a trunk right under the coffee mill. I tried to persuade him not to do so, but—— All of a sudden he said, "I am going to say it—right now—and out loud." "FAN"—rang out that dreaded word (meaning devil). What happened do you say? Mother came and lifted him right off the trunk and he got his little seat warmed (then and there!)

It was early summer and the fragrance of the flowers filled the air. The bright moonlight evenings were very beautiful, but little chance for romance for Gustav. So it seemed little Cupid was on the watch for him so eventually Gustav got a wife. A neighbor who lived close by had a sister that came to visit them and whisperings went around that she surely would be the one who would make a good mate for Gustav. It so happened that a party was given and they were both invited and were properly introduced. Some time later we saw Gustav going past our place all dressed up in his Sunday best. He was on his way to see this girl. Oh, to be sure, she thought he was all right for it was not long preparations were being made for their wedding. This was the first wedding in our community. His sweetheart came over and helped fix up the cabin. White curtains were hung up and tables and benches were scrubbed so white they fairly shown. It was a nice wedding, but when the big day was over, their lives and duties became like those of the other families—working and planning for something better.

I used to like to go up to their home on an errand for mother. About a year or so later I was called upon to go there to take care of a little baby that the stork had left there on his travels through the country. My mother made me a sunbonnet and an apron of the same goods. They always let me go home on Sundays. One Sunday I came running home, my mother and another lady were walking around in the garden. When I came up to her she said, "Why didn't you wear your apron?" (Well kids are kids, I guess) I did not stop to think that this other lady was Tilda's sister-in-law. I just said I could not as Tilda had used it for a diaper for the baby and it was not clean any longer. Mother was quite put out about it and the lady visiting mother thought it was an awful trick to do, too. I forgave her as she was so very kind to me. She never scolded me. . . .

One night as we lay in our peaceful slumber, a man on horseback rode up to our door and rapped on the window pane calling out as loudly as he could saying, "Get up and get ready as fast as you can to go out and fight the Sioux Indians. They are on their way out here and they will burn and kill everything. See that the women and children hide some place. The men will meet at the schoolhouse corner."

We got into our clothes as fast as we could. I happened to be at the home of our friend Gustav at the time. I only got half dressed and my teeth chattered so that I was unable to talk. Gustav took his gun; we ran as fast as we could to my home. My folks had already received the news so they had gone over to our next door neighbors who were only a short distance away.

It was decided that the children and women would go to my home and stay there and if they heard any startling news, to use their own judgment as to what to do and where to run and hide.

By this time more men had arrived and they started out prepared to fight against the Sioux Indians. One man in our community became so frightened that he committed suicide.

People were really afraid, and no wonder. The time that I am speaking of now was at the time of the terrible Indian Massacre in the State of Minnesota. The situation looked very grave. We knew that we were in great danger. The news of the Minnesota Massacre where such a large number of white people had been killed by the savages had instilled fear in the hearts of the white settlers as well as in the friendly Indians who were of another tribe.

Morning came at last and nothing had happened. Most of the men returned. Some men, on horseback, had gone

on to find out all they could about the reason for the
alarm that had been given. A message came to us about
three days later explaining everything. We were not alone
in our fear for the Governor of Wisconsin had been
notified by the county board who had telegraphed the
alarm. Two army officials were sent to investigate the
Indians at Wood Lake, Wisconsin. The Indians had been
having a powwow, and had danced around the Indian
Mound nearby. Two settlers could speak the Chippewa
Indian language. One man was married to an Indian
squaw. The other man was Trader Carlson from Trade
Lake who had traded with Indians for many years. These
men acted as interpreters.

So as to show their friendliness, the Indians offered
the Peace Pipe to the men, who, together with the Army
officials, willingly smoked them to show that their
friendship was accepted. These Indians assured the men
that there was no danger from their tribe and were sorry
that their powwow, which was only a celebration, had
been mistaken as the beginning of another possible
massacre.

The Indians around our homes were also questioned.
They said they knew nothing at all about this celebration
for this was another tribe and the Chippewa tribe was as
much afraid of the Sioux Indians as we were. . . .

We were three farmers living close together and we all
had sheep. We did not have any pasture for them and we
did not dare let them go into the woods alone so in the
evenings after supper we used to go together and watch
them until about ten o'clock at night. We could tell
readily if there were any wild animals near for the sheep
would come running to us for protection, and the dog
would bark to let us know. This night I know the sheep
had not had their fill of grass, but came running up to
us in fear. The rams were now stamping their feet in the
ground and the dog was growling so we hurried them
home as fast as we could. After we got the sheep in
their place safely, we all started for our homes. When we
came to our gate we saw a bear down by the creek just
a little ways from us. We invited our neighbors to come
in and spend the night with us for they had to cross the

creek right where the bear had been standing in order to get to their home.

A few nights later just as my brother and I left our house to join the others we heard a blood-curdling scream. We hurried to the place as fast as we could. Our other neighbors were already there. We were all excited to learn what it was all about.

Two boys had gone out ahead and built a fire. They were only eight or ten years old. The youngest heard something close to him but thought it was his brother and kept right on talking but when he looked up instead of his brother it was a big black bear standing on his hind legs looking at the fire.

His brother had gone to gather some more firewood. When the older brother came running the bear got down on all four feet and ran away. We all got there in a few minutes but the bear did not return. The poor little boy became so hoarse from fright and screaming that he could not talk out loud all evening.

You may wonder why the men did not do this work. They had to rest for they got up at four o'clock in the morning to start their farm-work and we children enjoyed the evenings bears or no bears. While the mothers sat by the fire visiting we children played games and had all kinds of fun. We were not out in open fields, Oh, no! We were right out in the thick forest with large trees with open spaces here and there where the sheep found plenty of good grass to eat.

I will tell you another little incident that I think is kind of cute. One of the farmers who lived about three miles away from our home was plenty puzzled about the disappearing of their milk. Since we did not have ice houses or creameries then, cellars were made in a side hill. They were fixed up nicely with crude shelves and tables. In those we kept our milk, butter, meat, and all kinds of food. Milk was strained in pans of tin and earthenware. We made our butter in a churn with a dasher and packed it in earthen crocks. We also made all our cheese.

For some time when the farmer's wife came to the cellar to skim the cream off the milk, she found the pans empty and turned upside down on the shelf. At first they thought of Indians, but Indians were never seen roaming around at night and further more they could have milk by merely asking for it, so there would be no reason for them to steal it. The men got together and took their guns with them. The first night nothing happened. They went again the next night. They moved very quietly. About midnight who do you suppose came walking down the path to the cellar? A big black bear! He raised up on his hind legs and pushed the door open, went in and had his drink of milk and turned the pan upside down. The poor bear had a sad surprise when he came out this time. The hunters all fired at him. They had caught the thief this time.

I had a frightening experience myself after I was married and raising a family, but living in the same neighborhood. My husband and his brother were running a sawmill. My sister and I had married two brothers and at the time were making our home together. We had four cows and my sister and I took turns in bringing them home and milking them. This was my turn to go so I took my little nephew with me for company. For some reason I did not care to have a dog with me when I went to look for the cows. This time they were not in the pasture but I could hear the bell and when we came there we found the cows were acting wild. It was impossible to get them started toward home. I was worried as it was getting dark. "Come dear," I said to my little nephew, "We will leave the cows and go home while it is light enough so we can see the path." "Look, Auntie, the dog is coming! Look!" My heart just about stopped for it was not a dog at all. It was not only one bear cub, it was actually two of them. I heard the mother bear on our trail. I did not dare to run or scream. My hair seemed to stand up straight. I just did not dare to tell the child for fear he would cry out. We started home, and when we were almost there my husband and his brother met us. I told them what had happened. They laughingly teased me saying it might have been raccoons or a couple of skunks. However, the next day the people at the post office were telling about the big bear with two cubs that had walked through the wheat fields the morning following our little scare. They believed me then and stopped teasing me about getting the cows.

I knew a lady who became a widow through an unusual accident. Her husband was hauling hay on a low sled. The neighbor's ox went mad and jumped upon the sled and fatally wounded the man with his horns. He left a wife and a family of six children to face a problem of pioneer life. The youngest child was still an infant. Later she married her husband's bachelor brother and moved to his homestead about six miles away. She still kept her homestead which had some valuable cranberry marshes on the shore of a rather large lake. The country was very wild and full of lynx, panthers, wildcats as well as wolves and bears. There were many Indians who would come to this lake to harvest wild rice. They were not at all interested in the cranberries. The white settlers would steal the cranberries and ruin the vines so someone had to keep watch over the marshes as in their hurry to gather the berries with their box-like rakes, they forgot that there would be a poor crop following year.

Two of her sons, about eight and ten years old, would go up to their old homestead to watch these marshes. The Indians were very friendly and the boys did not mind sleeping in the old log house. They rather liked it, camping there with their own food supplies, feeling quite grown-up. One night the younger boy, who was a light sleeper, was awakened by a scratching noise on the door. He could not rouse his sleepy brother so he lay there in the dark wondering just what might happen. The scratching ceased and in the morning they discovered bear tracks and large grooves in the plank door. A bear had almost made his way through the door.

Years later, about in 1914, the boy who was an infant when his father was killed, went deer hunting with some of his friends. He set his gun by a stump and did some exploring. A hole in the ground interested him. He got down on his knees and peered into the hole. He now began to wonder if a bear could possibly be hibernating there. He soon found out. He saw two shiny eyes and heard and felt a growl that almost blew his cap off. The young man ran for his gun and shot the bear right between his eyes. The bear was slow and sleepy or this bear story might never have been told. This bear measured about seven feet and was made into a beautiful rug. . . .

Chapter Six

It is not good for man to live alone. Two of our friends found that out. They were two very fine and honest men. They bought farms, but found it hard to do both the farm work and the house work too. Since there were no girls in our community, they decided to advertise for girls. In a short time they had a reply to their advertisement and they started to correspond with them. The girls liked the letters and decided to come up and look things over. One of the young men lived only a mile from our place.

One day father went up to see him about something. He had been washing clothes and had an axe lying on the stove heating. Father asked him what he was doing with the axe. "Oh," he replied, "I have no flat iron so I thought I could iron my shirt with an axe. If I could just get the cuffs and collar ironed I could wear my coat so that the rest would not show." Father told him to bundle up his clothes and he would take them home and have his wife do them up extra nice.

Eric got his shirts and they were starched and ironed beautifully. He told father the girls were coming on the next stage, which was the following week. The girls came and they also married the men. The homes that those two girls moved into were simple log cabins consisting of one room, but they never complained. They went to work on the farm and worked just as hard as their husbands. They cleared and burned brush piles and helped grub stumps and cut and stacked hay and grain. In a few years they built new houses and barns.

Shortly after they were married we had a big community picnic. I think it was the fourth of July. The men got together the day before the picnic and cleared a picnic ground and put up tables and seats. The big day came and men, women and children gathered from all around bringing large baskets of food. The newlyweds were there too. Of course, everybody was glad to meet the new brides.

My father was speaker for the day. We children had to sit very quiet during father's speech and the singing but we did not listen to the speech very much. Our little minds were too busy thinking about all the good food we were going to have to eat. This was the first picnic in this community so it seemed to be a big affair. After this we got together more often. We had Sunday school picnics, get-together parties as well as ladies aids and camp meetings.

In the spring we used to go together and shear the sheep. We came in the morning and spent all day. Those who had many sheep had to invite many ladies for they usually did all the work. The lady who gave the party had her hands full doing the cooking. We served lunch consisting of coffee, lump sugar, and sweet rusks and cookies. At noon we had a big dinner. In the afternoon we were served lunch again. We even had our supper before we left in the evening. Children were allowed to go to those parties too, and it was fun for all, old and young. The work was completed and they had a good visit.

After all the sheep in the neighborhood were sheared then came the soap-making. Most of the ladies did that work alone. At home my mother made the soap, with the help of our closest neighbor lady, who would come over. They would work together and divide the soap. My father made a soap-cooking rig. He made a big barrel out of a big hollow log. This was for the ashes which was used in making the lye for the soap. He then made a large trough for the lye. One end was made solid for the barrel to stand on and grooves were made in that so the lye could run down into the trough. First we placed twigs in the bottom of the barrel, putting straw on the twigs. We filled the barrel with nice wood ashes, adding water from time to time until we had as much lye as needed. When the lye was strong enough to float an egg or a potato it was ready for making soap so they hung up a large iron kettle over the fire and put the lye in it with tallow or other fats that they had saved during the winter. When the soap started to thicken the kettle had to be watched very closely or it would boil over. When the soap had been cooked enough, it was stirred over and over again. It was beaten until it became white. The more it was beaten the more white the soap became. It was then put into kegs, crocks or whatever utensil they had and was then put away in the cellar or the granary.

Well, during the summer each one was busy with their own work. The women helped with the outdoor work, gardening, haying, and all sorts of chores. They did anything they could to help. They even grubbed stumps.

The farmers did not have enough milk cows of their own to make a supply of cheese for their families so they would all get together, bringing their fresh milk to one home and spend the day there making cheese, visiting, eating, and all in all having a good time talking over many things. Another day they would gather in the same manner in another home, rotating until all had a nice supply of good cheese. These gatherings were far from dull, for old and young feasted and had a jolly good time. They usually made the cheese for the pastor and his family and would always make them as big and nice as they could.

They brought their milk in milk cans or other large utensils. The milk, with rennet added to it, was heated until a soft gummy cheese appeared at the top of each vessel. A clean soft white cloth was placed inside of some forms that had holes in the bottom. This soft gummy cheese would then be poured inside of the cloth and the whey would then be allowed to run out of these holes. It required a lot of hard pressing by hand. It was a really big job. The cheese would then be put away in a clean place with a heavy plate or other weight and left to age. Some added certain seed to flavor some of the cheese, and others made a sandy cheese out of the whey that had a sweet burnt taste.

Let me tell you about rennet. It is now bought in tablets or powder form but it might interest you to know that rennet is really the inner membrane of a calf's stomach and is used in coagulating milk. The pioneers made their own rennet. I remember well when my mother made it. It required a lot of work. Right after the birth, a calf was placed in a clean pen. My mother washed this pen every day and the calf was fed only fresh clean milk. Just before butchering they would give it a gallon of fresh milk that would curdle in its stomach. Just how it was done, I do not know, but his stomach was removed, and it and the contents were preserved in a cloth bag and was hung up to dry. All this might seem funny to the present age but I think you will find that rennet is still important in making cheese.

Father tanned hides from animals for shoes, boots and harnesses. The sheepskin was used for vests and robes. Every family had one or more of these robes. The winters were cold and the robes had many uses.

Then too, we used to have quilting bees. Father made a quilt frame that could be rolled up on either side with a crank. Everyone in the neighborhood used to borrow it and also our spinning wheel, which was brought to this country from Sweden. Quilting bees were as a rule attended by the women and some of their children, but you could bet they had their coffee with sugar lumps and something good to eat. The quilts were made of good wool filling and were covered with quilting material, or more likely a top for the quilt had been made previously and had been saved for this purpose. During spare time the good housewives would make these tops out of scraps of material left over when making aprons, dresses, shirts, and even trousers. Our homes were simple and we lacked may conveniences but we prided ourselves in many things. The ladies were proud of their lovely new quilts and would try to add some more each year or to cover some of the old ones. We made warm quilts out of old but clean woolen materials. We tied and quilted them by hand. Once in a while we bought new material for quilt covers but we were more proud of our quilts that were made from salvaged material, as we were proud of being economical. Within the last ten years I have enjoyed making many quilts for myself, my children, grand children and great grand children. I want you to know that each of the million little stitches represents my love and well wishes for all my loved ones.

Brooms were made from willows that we used for everyday sweeping. They sorted out the slender branches with fine twigs for the best brooms, using the heavier ones for the granary or outdoors. Our scrubbing brushes were made of twisted hay tied together in a rope-like fashion; instead of rags we used white moss. Two pails of water were used in scrubbing floors; one for scrubbing and the other for rinsing, so don't think our homes were not clean. The floors and woodwork of our homes were unpainted so they had to be scrubbed clean. Saturday was the day for cleaning thoroughly. During the winter we were expected to remove our shoes before entering the house. We were barefoot in the summertime.

One day when my mother was making some brooms a little neighbor boy named Emil came over. Mother asked him if he had an errand. He said he just came over to play. He was five months older than I and I was always glad when he came as I liked to play with him. We started to play but in a few minutes his mother came running into our house through one door as he ran out the other. As she went through she called, "Good morning," stooped down to pick up a soft willow switch and ran after him. I almost cried, for I did know what a switch meant. The next day I ran over to the saw-rig for that was midway to his home and we were allowed to meet and play there. When Emil came there I asked him if he got a whipping, but he carelessly answered, "No, I got home before she did." "Oh," I said, "my mother would not do that, and I don't dare run away as I then get it all the worse." I pouted a little as I felt my sympathy for him had been wasted but it was all forgotten when we started playing.

We also made egg beaters but we used birch wood for that as the wood did not give off any taste. We picked the branches in the spring and scraped the bark off. The smaller ones were used for beating eggs and cream. First

we would dip them in hot water to soften them, and
then we put them in cold water. We beat eggs and cream
for frosting or similar food. The more heavy ones were
used in stirring mush, porridge and other foods thickened
with flour. We used spruce branches for door mats as
they were nice for that purpose.

Father also made his own tar. He made it of pine,
but just exactly how, I do not know. I remember when
he brought the tar in it was thick and black. I also
remember him using a funnel shaped thing made of sheet
iron. It was round and quite large. . . .

Chapter Ten

Somehow, this evening reminds me of an evening on
the old homestead when I was a small child. The same
sun was then, as now, trying to spread its last rays on
the tree tops before settling for the night. We children
were playing in the rather small yard. We dared not stray
far away or the great trees would swallow us from sight.

With the exception of our close neighbors, we seldom
saw white people. We were more used to the Indians than
we were the white settlers.

We could hear a sound at a distance and glanced up
in that direction to see what could be coming. We saw a
man and woman dressed in black, carrying a baby. They
were coming down the hill toward us. . . . [We thought]
they were not Indians because they wore black clothing.
The Indians wore colored blankets wrapped around them
or buckskin clothing. Father and mother came out to
look, almost as bewildered as we. Suddenly mother called
out to father, "Do you suppose it could be Maya and
Johanes and their child?" Father exclaimed, "I believe that
is just who it is!" So saying they ran to meet them and
gave them a hearty welcome. These people proved to be
father's sister, Maya, her husband, Johanes, and little
Charlotta, whom every one called Lotta, thereafter. It was
a happy occasion to have folks from Sweden, their
homeland.

Father and Maya had a brother, who had built a cabin on his homestead, nearby. He often went away to work; as he was a single man, the homestead laws did not require him to live there continuously. The newcomers from Sweden stayed with us for a while, but when Uncle moved to work elsewhere, they moved into his little home and stayed there a few years. My uncle never returned. Father last heard from him in Canada years ago.

The couple began to stock up their place with a cow, chickens, a white Indian pony and other farm necessities. The youngsters would watch eagerly to see him get on his little pony for he was a tall man and we expected his feet to touch the ground. We were disappointed for they were quite a way from touching the ground.

Johanes would often help Father with the haying. Father had once written to his parents in Sweden, telling them about the tall wild grass that grew in his meadow, saying it was so tall a man could easily get lost in it. They did not believe him at all. One time when Johanes offered to help, father told him to go down into the meadow to get a foundation for a haystack, thinking to himself, "Now I will have a little fun and prove to the folks at home how tall my grass really is." Johanes willingly went in search of the foundation and father fixed a pole for the haystack. He could not find his way back and was soon calling, "Yo Hooo!" Dad did not answer at first but kept walking toward the foundation and Johanes and waited until he called out again. Father was so close to him he could almost touch him. "Well, what is the matter?" he said. "Are you lost?" "Well, I never saw such a nest. A fellow can't see what direction he is going." "Well," said Dad, "Now it is your turn to write to the folks back home and tell them how tall the grass is, and that you actually got lost in my meadow."

Johanes was a home-loving man, and though he went out occasionally to earn some money, he never stayed as long as the other men would. I was very small, but I do remember that his family stayed with us once when he was out working so they would not have to be alone. He was gone a short time only, about six weeks, when my aunt looked out and started to cry, as she saw him coming. She knew it required more money to run their household than that. She and my mother talked in low tones but I could not understand how anyone could cry when Johanes came, and ran as fast as I could to meet him. All the children loved him as long as he lived, I think. . . .

There was a serious diptheria epidemic that claimed many lives in eighteen eighty-two or so. Wherever there was help need Maya and Johanes would be found. They labored endlessly without thought of pay, night and day. They nursed the sick and dressed the little dead bodies. Some families lost as many as five children, one after the other. Uncle dug graves and hauled the dead to the cemetery. This kept on for some time. It was hard for them, too, for they had three children of their own and were keeping a brother and sister of mine. They would go in the barn and change their clothing before entering their home. It was a miracle; not one of their household was stricken. But—somehow, after things were adjusted to normal, this was all forgotten. They did not toll the church bell, as was the custom of the day, when beloved Maya was called home to glory. It was customary to toll the church bell at ten o'clock the morning after a person had died that belonged to the church. Johanes grieved because of this but was much too proud to ask them. I feel that this would have been the very least the church could have done for a couple who so earnestly labored during such a critical time, and who brought home the very bell that they would not toll. . . .

Lotta married and lived in the city a couple of years. Later they moved back to West Sweden, planning to settle there on a farm, but her husband decided to work in the mines one winter so as to help finance the farm. He was gone about six or seven months before she heard from him. He wrote saying he would be coming home in May. The month of May came and went but he never returned. Lotta could never find out what happened to him. Many people thought that he might have been robbed and killed as this often happened to the men returning from work with heavy payrolls. Lotta gave birth to a little girl, who died in infancy, and Lotta thereafter made her home with her father and two brothers. . . .

Chapter Eleven

. . . . Christmas of 1885 rolled around and two of my sisters, my aunt and I went home [from working in St. Croix Falls] on a vacation. One other sister was keeping house for Father. My aunt, uncle, and three cousins were there too. We were a family of thirteen over the holidays. Christmas morning four of us got up at three o'clock and walked seven miles to Jule Otte, the Christmas morning service. The closer we got to the church, the more people we saw, some of them carrying real torches made of pine roots.

Going home from the church, I met a nice young man that had recently come over from Sweden, though I did not know it at the time. I started to talk with him, and he did not answer. Thoughtlessly, I said, "Why don't you answer me? I hate a man that will not answer when I speak to him!" Then one of the boys told me that he did not speak English. "Why did you not say so, I can speak Swedish." He was tall, slender and handsome with dark curly hair. I thought his face would have been just perfect if his nose had been just a little smaller.

One of my sisters was keeping company with his brother. As we walked along we came to a new road. "Let's walk the new road," I suggested. We could not agree, though we would have all met on the same road again. My sister, the new Swede and I chose the new one. We passed an old bachelor's house on our way, so we agreed to go around and wish him a merry Christmas. He had an organ that he had made, and the young man could play a little so we played and sang a few Swedish songs. Finally the old fellow suggested breakfast. We helped him prepare a nice breakfast of pancakes, fried pork and coffee. He seemed so happy that to this day I feel good about it, for I know we brought Christmas Cheer to his heart.

There was another service at the church at ten o'clock so we left the old gentleman, arriving at church just in time for the service. My sister's friend and his brother lived with their sister in a house very close to the church, and we were invited to have lunch with them.

They boarded there as their parents were still in Sweden. After lunch all of us went to our home. We had a lake on our land and we spent the afternoon skating and sitting around the fire. My friend, Swede, stooped down and picked an evergreen from a vine (some call it Prince's pine) and pinned it on my coat. Sixty years have passed, but this little pine is still among my souvenirs. . . .

The following spring, in June, I packed all my belongings and went home to my father's house to keep house for him and one of my brothers, letting my sister go to the city for a while. There was a great deal of hard work to do, but plenty of fun, too. I was happy wherever I went, letting nothing worry me. My Swede was home for a few weeks, too.

Another year rolled by. Time passes so swiftly on a farm with a lot of work to do. One day, who should I see coming down the hill? It was my Swede. He had come home from the woods where he had been for six months. "Oh, my," I thought, "He looks just like a real American——Got his hat tipped just so and has learned to speak English, too. I guess I still stand in good with him, for I am the first girl he calls on after he has been gone all winter." We had supper and then he and my brother and I walked out to see his sister. . . .

We were married May 13, 1888. . . .

We settled on the farm. I learned to keep house much better than my mother-in-law had ever hoped that I would. At first she would scold me when I attempted to do some of the little fancy things, such as embroidering a child's garment or an apron saying that I ought to be doing something more useful. I thought there was time for both.

One fall I was embroidering some lilies on an apron that I had planned to give her as a Christmas gift. It was very fashionable for old ladies to wear big white aprons. She scolded me while I was making it. Her daughter once asked her if she would not like to have one like that some day, but in her odd way, she answered, "No, the sun will never rise on a day that I will wear an apron like that." Christmas came and she received it as a gift, placed under the Christmas tree at the church. She liked it and was very sincere when she thanked me, saying she was sorry she scolded me while I was making it. I told her everything was all right and that I understood. She always liked her apron and told her daughter to return it to me when she died, as was the custom of the day. Poor old dear, it had been hard for her to adjust herself to the American way of life. . . .

Sentenced to the Prairie
Mary Larrabee

William H. Larrabee would have been killed at Custer's Last Stand on Little Big Horn if he had not been in jail for desertion at the time. As his wife's first letter states, he traded a two-year prison sentence for ten years of life on the prairie. William and Mary Larrabee were the first white settlers in Foster County, Dakota Territory. They farmed and maintained a relay station. In her letters to an unidentified "Patty," sometimes called "Patience," Mary mentions the isolation of her life only in passing as she describes the beauty and plenty of her new surroundings. Her letters furnish a condensed history of progress in the Dakota Territory.

Source:
Elizabeth Hampsten, ed. To All Inquiring Friends: Letters, Diaries and Essays in North Dakota. *Grand Forks, ND: Department of English, U of North Dakota, 1979. 55-60.*

Dakota Territory, August, 1876

Dear Patty,

At last after travelling by rail, prairie schooner and ox team we arrived at Fort Totten to find that William's trial was on and he was found guilty and sentenced to two years in a Federal prison. I was simply crushed but after talking things over with our friends here and taking their advice, we got his sentence changed to ten years of life on the prairie; so my dear we will not see you for ten years, for we are going to live somewhere not very far from where we now are.

General L.C. Hunt is in command at Fort Totten and last winter several cavalry regiments were quartered here. We have just received word that Custer and the L Troops of the 7th Cavalry were all massacred June 20, 1876. This was one of the regiments quartered here last winter. We are all feeling frightened and dismayed about it. The Indians are restless and dissatisfied and are feeling very much elated over their victory.

Dakota Territory, Sept. 1876

Dear Patty,

A beautiful September day and at last we have left the post and are settled on the Fort Totten trail about thirty miles from Fort Totten. Mr. Larrabee bought out a man by the name of Joseph Hay who owned a log house near the James River Valley. The valley is sheltered by hills and is open to the east, where the waters of Lake

Belland come into the river through a little creek. It is a good place for raising stock and that is Mr. Larrabee's intention. We will also keep the relay station where the mail carriers and freighters can keep their relay horses.

Let me describe our surroundings. To the east lies Lake Belland, a nice little sheet of water with a few trees on the north and south shores. On the south and north the hills shut off the view. The river runs out of the valley to the west. Mr. Larrabee is very busy making hay and getting in supplies. The relay station will use up huge quantities of this for all the supplies freighted to Fort Totten and the Indian Agency go by our door along this trail. Herds of antelope pass near, grazing as they go, for in this valley is fine grass and running water, which is not often to be found, for you may travel miles upon the prairie without finding water. The geese and ducks and prairie chickens are here in immense numbers and sometimes they cover vast spaces. The sand hill cranes at a distance look like huge herds of cattle. About the lake is the breeding place of the ducks, and they will remain until the frosts send them southward.

You asked me about the buffalo. There are no buffalo here now as they left the region about Devils Lake about 1868. They used to be very numerous about here as the grass is good and there is plenty of water, but the Indians and Red River halfbreeds became so numerous and hunted them so persistently that they went west and south. They [made pemmican] of their flesh in immense quantities and sold it to the Hudson Bay and American Fur Companies.

May 24, 1877

Dear Patty,

We have no neighbors nearer than Fort Totten except the Indians, who visit us frequently, and so far as I know I am the only white woman in Foster County. We have a new baby at our house, a boy, which we have named Berkley Terry Larrabee, whose arrival on the 12th was very much dreaded by me because we had no doctors or nurses. This baby so far as we know is the first white child born in Foster County.

The little girls have come in with their hands full of some beautiful flowers and wanted to know what they were called. Hunting out my old Botany I found that they were the Pasque flowers with their quaint furry hoods which cover the buds. The hills are covered with them as they begin to bloom so early there is no grass and the leaves come after the flower. We welcomed them eagerly as they are the first but we will have an abundance of wild flowers all summer long.

The lake is full of fish and as they go up the Slummegullion Creek (so named by me because it is such a tiny creek beside our creeks at home). We get numbers which are a welcome change in our menu, though they are not so fine as the salt water fish at home.

Oh, how homesick I get for the sight of a white woman's face. I have seen none since I came here in September. The Indian women visit us frequently. Five came a few days ago. One is always the spokeswoman and introduces the others by pointing to them, "This Lizzie, this Fannie, this Mary." We always have to give them lunch when they come as they will remain until they are fed. We had five or six fat little puppies and Mr. Larrabee gave each of them one which was received with broad smiles and great pleasure. I was glad he had given them something that pleased them so much and mentioned it to William after they were gone, when he replied nonchalantly, "Oh yes, they will make them into a pot of soup." You can imagine my disgust as this was the first time I knew that they ate dogs.

September, 1877

Dear Patience,

Have just got settled after moving. We moved about a mile south of our last habitation. Mr. Larrabee has built a 6 room frame house, the first one in the county, where we will be much more comfortable than in the old log house. He will move all the buildings here, and there we will keep our relay station. It is in the bottom of the valley on the banks of the River James and is much more sheltered. The round topped hills are on the north and west and cut off from view, but to the south it is open with gently rolling prairie in the direction of the river. The trail travels along this rolling land towards the river which is called the James. Mr. Larrabee is busy getting in hay and getting in supplies. We will be very busy for we intend keeping a relay house here and he will need a great deal of provender to supply the animals. . . .

June, 1879

Dear Patty,

Your letter received and was glad to get all the news from home. There have been a few men who have come in here and stayed a few months but no one has brought their families or made any long stay, and to the best of my belief I am the only white woman in Foster County.

A new baby arrived at our house on May 12th. We have named him Charles Edward Larrabee and as his birthday is the same day as Berkley's they can both be able to celebrate their birthdays together. We are quite sure that these babies are the first white babies born in Foster County. As there are no other County organizations I have entered their births in the family Bible.

I forgot to tell you that we receive the mail three times a week. The name of our mail carrier is Edward Loomis. He stops at our house every night and keeps his relay horses there, then in the morning goes on to Fort Totten returning at night when he goes to Jamestown.

Lake Belland is named after an old Frenchman who lived there at the time the County was surveyed. He was what is known as a "Squaw man," having purchased a squaw from an Indian which it was easy to do, for a pony or something else.

There is a little lake north east of here which has had no name. An old blue cow of ours wandered up there and was lost for a few days; since then the Lake is known as Blue Cow Lake.

Have seen no white woman except the ones from the post in three years.

1881

Dear Patty,

Time passes quickly even on the prairie and we have been here five years. Two brothers named Smith, E. Dalefield and Herbert, have settled on the south side of the lake. They carry on a trade with the Indians, buying furs. This is the first settler near us, but neither of the brothers is married. This country looks beautiful—I wish you could see it. There is some talk of a R.R. coming through the county but it will not be within twenty miles of us. The R.R. is the North Pacific and there is talk of surveyers working in that part of the county brought in by the freighters and mail carriers. If such is the case we will not be here many years longer as we will not be so prosperous after the R.R. arrives. The travel then will leave the old trail and I scarcely know whether I will be glad or sorry.

1882

Dear Patty,

At last we have a real, bona-fide settler. He has taken a pre-emption on the south side of Lake Belland and is building a "wee brown soddy." He is working for Mr. Larrabee and will move his family here. His name is George Backen. My, it seems so comfy to have some woman here even if she is a couple of miles away. These people have some family and I am glad for the sake of our family, for our children will have some other children to play with.

It was a real fact about the R.R. and it has come as far as Jamestown. Another townsite is platted in this county and is called Carrington after Henry Carrington of Toledo, Ohio, of the Carrington Casey Land Company. This will bring in the settlers and soon we will see a shack on every quarter section. You may wonder what a quarter section is. It is 160 acres of land, 1/2 a mile long, and all the land here is surveyed in that way. The mail now instead of coming from Jamestown comes via Carrington, and a P.O. has been established here with Mr. Larrabee as postmaster.

April 1883

Dear Patty,

At last Foster County is coming into its own. The town of Carrington is booming. New settlers are coming in droves. Two passenger trains have reached Carrington and many who wished to come on the first train could not even find a foothold on the cars—men swarming over the tops of the cars and clinging to the railings on platforms.

Carrington has become the greatest boom town in the northwest. Still you can drive all day away from the railroads without seeing a sign of human habitation, bush nor tree, shack nor stack. There are no roads and we find our way across the prairie by reading the inscriptions showing range, township, and section placed on the surveyors' stakes.

As I have not written to you for so long I must give you a story of the blizzard that raged here this winter. It was one of the worst I have ever seen. The winter has been very cold and I scarcely see how the emigrants who landed in Carrington have existed, as there were no trains in there all winter. The snow was so great that the Northern Pacific abandoned everything until spring. A number of boarding cars were left there which the people used as homes and a quantity of R.R. ties which were taken possession of and used as fuel. Some provisions had been left in the cars when they were abandoned and these, and the jackrabbits they managed to kill, kept them alive through the winter. If it had not been for this I think that the few who stayed would have perished as no relief reached them until March '83 when the Northern Pacific train reached there.

1884

Dear Patty,

William and I just came home from Carrington where we went on business and I called on some of the wives of the new settlers. So many people have come in. There is a beautiful new hotel named the Kirkwood which is run in great style, Negro waiters and everything else accordingly. This is done to accommodate the class of people who are buying land, as many rich people from the east are coming in to buy land.

"A Farm Is Such a Hard Place for a Woman"
Laura Ingalls Wilder

Laura Ingalls Wilder is the one writer in this anthology that all readers will recognize. Little House on the Prairie *has been translated into dozens of languages. Many readers, however, have not read the story of the first four years of her marriage. This book was not published until 1971, after her death.*

The First Four Years *describes the frustrations and satisfactions of farming in South Dakota from 1885-1889. When Laura marries Manly Wilder, she tells him that she loves life on a farm and she loves the prairie, but "a farm is such a hard place for a woman." Nevertheless, Laura agrees to farm with Manly for three years because she loves the prairie grasses, the wild roses, and the spaciousness of the land. In December 1886 their first baby, Rose, is born. During the third year both Laura and Manly suffer from diptheria. Manly resumes heavy farm work before he is completely recovered and paralysis sets in; in fact, he never completely recovers. Nevertheless, at the end of the three-year period, Manly asks for one more year. This fourth—and last—year on the Dakota homestead is presented below.*

Source:
Laura Ingalls Wilder. The First Four Years. *Intro. Roger Lea MacBride. New York: Harper & Row, 1971. 98-134.*

Fall plowing was begun as soon as haying was finished, but the work was too hard for Skip and Barnum to do even with the help of the ponies. Trixy and Fly were small and could not pull with strength. They were intended only for riding. Fly objected strenuously at times, kicking savagely when her tugs were being hitched. Once when Laura was helping Manly hitch the horses to the plow and keeping watch of Rose at the same time, she lost sight of Rose. Immediately she stopped working with the harness, and looking quickly around the yard, said, "Manly, where is Rose?"

And a little hand pulled Fly's tail away from her body, on the opposite side of the four horses abreast, a little face showed between Fly and her tail, and Rose's little voice said, "Here I am!"

Now Manly's hands were not nearly so stiff and clumsy. Perhaps he could soon hitch the straps and buckle the buckles himself.

The team was tired at night. Laura could hardly bear to see them at the unhitching, Skip with his gay head hanging and Barnum's dancing feet standing so patiently still.

Manly said he would have to get another team, for he wanted to break sixty acres of sod and have the whole 160 acres ready to seed in the spring.

"But the three years are up. Do you call this farming a success?" Laura objected.

"Well, I don't know," Manly answered. "It is not so bad. Of course, the crops have been mostly failures, but

we have four cows now and some calves. We have the
four horses and the colts and machinery and there are the
sheep. . . If we could only get one crop. Just one good
crop, and we'll be all right. Let's try it one more year.
Next year may be a good crop year and we are all fixed
for farming now, with no money to start anything else."

It sounded reasonable as Manly put it. There didn't
seem to be anything else they could do, but as for being
all fixed—the five hundred dollars still due on the house
worried Laura. Nothing had been paid on it. The binder
was not yet paid for and interest payments were hard to
make. But Manly still might be right. This might be
when their luck turned, and one good year would even
things up.

Manly bought two Durham oxen that had been broken
to work. They were huge animals. King was red and
weighed two thousand pounds. Duke was red-and-white
spotted and weighed twenty-five hundred pounds. They
were as gentle as cows, and soon Laura helped hitch them
up without fear—but she fastened Rose in the house
when she did so. They were cheap: only twenty-five
dollars each and very strong. Now Skip and Barnum took
the ponies' place and did the light work, while the cattle
hitched beside them drew most of the load.

The plowing was finished easily and the breaking of
the sod was done before the ground froze. It was late in
doing so for it was a warm, pleasant fall.

The winter was unusually free of bad blizzards,
though the weather was very cold and there was some
snow.

The house was snug and comfortable with storm
windows and doors, and the hard-coal heater in the front
room between the front door and the east window. Manly
had made the storm shed, or summer kitchen, tight by
battening closely all the cracks between the board sheeting, and the cook-stove had been left there for the
winter. The table had been put in its place in the front
room between the pantry and bedroom doors, and Peter's
cot-bed stood against the west wall of the room where
the table used to stand. Geraniums blossomed in tin cans
on the window sills, growing luxuriantly in the winter
sunshine and the warmth from the hard-coal heater.

The days passed busily and pleasantly. Laura's time was fully occupied with her housework and Rose, while Rose was an earnest, busy little girl with her picture books and letter blocks and the cat, running around the house, intent on her small affairs.

Manly and Peter spent much of their time at the barn, caring for the stock. The barn was long, from the first stalls where the horses and colts stood, past the oxen, King and Duke, the cows and the young cattle, the snug corner where the chickens roosted, on into the sheep barn where the sheep all ran loose.

It was no small job to clean out the barn and fill all the mangers with hay. Then there was the grain to feed to the horses, and they had to be brushed regularly. And all the animals must be watered once a day.

On pleasant days Manly and Peter hauled hay in from the stacks in the fields and fed the animals from that, leaving some on the wagon in the sheep yard for the sheep to help themselves.

This was usually finished well before chore time, but one afternoon they were delayed in starting. Because the snowdrifts were deep, they were hauling hay with King and Duke. The oxen could go through deep snow more easily than horses, but they were slower, and darkness came while Manly and Peter were still a mile from home.

It had begun to snow: not a blizzard, but snow was falling thickly in a slow, straight wind. There was no danger, but it was uncomfortable and annoying to be driving cattle, wallowing through snow in the pitch dark and the storm.

Then they heard a wolf howl and another; then several together. Wolves had not been doing any damage recently and there were not so many left in the country, but they were still seen at times, and now and then they killed a stray yearling or tried to get into a flock of sheep.

"That sounds toward home and as though they were going in that direction," Manly said. "Do you suppose they will go into the sheep yard?"

"Not with Laura there," Peter answered. But Manly was not so sure and they tried to hurry faster on their way.

At home Laura was beginning to be anxious. Supper was nearly ready, but she knew Manly and Peter would do the night chores before they ate. They should have been home before now and she wondered what could have happened.

Rose had been given her supper and was sleeping soundly, but Nero, the big, black dog, was uneasy. Now and then he raised his head and growled.

Then Laura heard it—the howl of a wolf! Again the wolf howled, then several together, and after that, silence.

Laura's heart stood still. Were the wolves coming to the sheep yard? She waited, listening, but could hear nothing but the swish of the snow against the windows; or was that a sheep blatting?

Must she go into the sheep yard and see that they were all right? She hesitated and looked at Rose, but Rose was still asleep. She would be all right if left alone. Then Laura put on her coat and hood, lighted the lantern, and taking it and the dog with her, went out into the darkness and the storm.

Quickly she went to the stable door, opened it, and reaching inside secured the five-tined stable fork; then shutting fast the door again, she went the length of the barn, flashing her lantern light as far as she could in every direction.

Nero trotted ahead of her, sniffing the air. Around the sheep yard they went but everything was quiet except for the sheep moving around restlessly inside. There was no sight nor sound of the wolves until, as Laura stood by the yard gate listening for the last time before going back to the house, there came again the lone cry of a wolf. But it was much farther to the north than before. The wolves had gone by on the west and all was well, though Nero growled low in his throat. Laura hadn't known she was frightened until she was safely in the house; then she found her knees trembling and sat down quickly.

Rose was still asleep and it was not long before Manly and Peter were there.

"What would you have done if you had found the wolves?" Manly asked.

"Why, driven them away, of course. That's what I took the pitchfork for," Laura answered.

In December Laura felt again the familiar sickness. The house felt close and hot and she was miserable. But the others must be kept warm and fed. The work must go on, and she was the one who must do it.

On a day when she was particularly blue and unhappy, and the neighbor to the west, a bachelor living alone, stopped as he was driving by and brought a partly filled grain sack to the house. When Laura opened the door, Mr. Sheldon stepped inside, and taking the sack by the bottom, poured the contents out on the floor. It was a paper-backed set of Waverly novels.

"Thought they might amuse you," he said. "Don't be in a hurry! Take your time reading them!" And as Laura exclaimed in delight, Mr. Sheldon opened the door, closed it behind him quickly, and was gone. And now the four walls of the close, overheated house opened wide, and Laura wandered with brave knights and ladies fair beside the lakes and streams of Scotland or in castles and towers, in noble halls or lady's bower, all through the enchanting pages of Sir Walter Scott's novels.

She forgot to feel ill at the sight or smell of food, in her hurry to be done with the cooking and follow her thoughts back into the book. When the books were all read and Laura came back to reality, she found herself feeling much better.

It was a long way from the scenes of Scott's glamorous old tales to the little house on the bleak, wintry prairie, but Laura brought back from them some of their magic and music and the rest of the winter passed quite comfortably.

Spring came early and warm. By the first of April a good deal of seeding had been done and men were busy in all the fields. The morning of the second was sunny and warm and still. Peter took the sheep out to graze on the school section as usual, while Manly went to the field. It was still difficult for him to hitch up the team, and Laura helped him get started. Then she went about her morning's work.

Soon a wind started blowing from the northwest, gently at first but increasing in strength until at nine o'clock the dust was blowing in the field so thickly that Manly could not see to follow the seeder marks. So he came from the field and Laura helped him unhitch and get the team in the barn.

Once more in the house they could only listen to the rising wind and wonder why Peter didn't bring the sheep in. "He couldn't have taken them far in such a short time and he surely would bring them back," Manly said. Dust from the fields was blowing in clouds so dense that they could see only a little way from the windows, and in a few minutes Manly went to find Peter and the sheep and help if help were needed.

He met Peter with the sheep about four hundred yards or one-quarter of a mile from the barn. Peter was on foot, leading his pony and carrying three lambs in his arms. He and the dog were working the sheep toward their yard. The sheep could hardly go against the wind but they had to face it to get home. They had not been sheared and their fleeces were long and heavy. The poor sheep with their small bodies and little feet carrying such a load of fluffy wool caught too much wind. If a sheep turned ever so little sideways, the wind would catch under the wool lift the sheep from his feet and roll it over and over, sometimes five or six times before it could stop. Against the strength of the wind it was impossible for the sheep to get to its feet. Peter would lift it up and stand it on its feet headed right so it could walk into the wind. He was tired and the sheep dog and pony were powerless to help, so it was time for Manly to be there.

It took them both over an hour to get all the sheep the four hundred yards and into the yard.

After that they all sat in the house and let the wind blow. Their ears were filled with the roar of it. Their eyes and throats smarted from the dust that was settling over the room even though the doors and windows were tightly closed.

Just before noon there came a knock at the door, and when Manly opened it, a man stood on the step.

"Just stopped to tell you, your wheels are going round," he said, and with a wave of his hand toward the barn, he ran to his wagon, climbed in, and drove on down the road. His face was black with dust and he was gone before they recognized him as the man who had bought their homestead.

Laura laughed hysterically. "Your wheels are going round," she said. "What did he mean?" She and Manly went into the kitchen and looked from the window toward the barn and then they knew. Between the house and barn, the hay wagon with the big hayrack on it had been left standing. The wind had lifted it, turned it over and left it bottom side up. The wagon rested on the rack underneath, and every one of the four wheels was turning in the wind.

There was only a cold bite to eat at noon, for no one felt like eating and it was not safe to light a fire.

About one o'clock Laura insisted that she could smell fire and that there must be a prairie fire near, but no smoke could be seen through the clouds of dust.

The wind always rises with a fire, and on the prairie the wind many times blows strongly enough to carry flame from the fire to light grass ahead of the burning, so that the fire travels faster than the grass burns. Once Manly and Peter had raced toward a fire trying to save a large haystack that stood between it and them. They ran their horses' heads up to the stack and jumped off just as a blown flame lit the opposite end of the haystack. Each had a wet grazing sack to fight the fire. They scrambled up the stack and slid down the end, scraping the fire off and putting it out at the ground after it had burned back a little way from the end of the stack. They let it run down each side as a backfire and the main fire raced by and on, leaving the haystack with Manly and Peter and their horse untouched. The horses had stood with their heads against the stack where they could breathe.

The wind reached its peak about two o'clock, then slackened gradually, so slowly at first it was hardly noticeable, but it died away as the sun went down and was still.

Rose lay asleep with her tired, dusty little face streaked with perspiration. Laura felt prostrated with exhaustion, and Manly and Peter walked like old men as they went out to the barn to see that the stock was all right for the night.

Later they learned that there had been a prairie fire during the sixty-five mile an hour wind, a terrible raging fire that hardly hesitated at firebreaks, for the wind tore flames loose and carried them far ahead of the burning grass. In places the fire leaped, leaving unburned prairie, the flame going ahead and the wind blowing out the slower fire in the grass as a candle is blown out.

Houses and barns with good firebreaks around them were burned. Stock was caught and burned. At one place a new lumberwagon stood in a plowed field a hundred yards from the grass. It was loaded with seed wheat just as the owner had left it when he had gone from the field because of the wind. When he went back, there was nothing left of the wagon and its load except the wagon irons. Everything else had burned.

There was no stopping such a fire and no fighting it in such a wind.

It went across the country, leaving a blackened prairie behind until it reached the river, and then the wind went down with the sun. There it stopped, somewhere between fifty and one hundred miles from where it began.

There was nothing to do but re-seed the fields, for the seed was blown away or buried in the drifts of soil around the edges of plowed land.

So Manly bought more seed wheat and oats at the elevator in town, and at last the seeding was finished.

Then the sheep were sheared and the selling of the wool cheered them all, for wool was worth twenty-five cents a pound and the sheep averaged ten pounds of wool apiece. Each sheep had paid for itself and fifty cents more with its wool alone. By the last of May, the lambs had all arrived, and there were so many twins that the flocks had more than doubled. Lambing time was a busy time, both day and night, for the sheep must be watched and the lambs cared for. Among the hundred sheep there were only five ewes who could not or would not care for their lambs. These five lambs were brought into the house and warmed and fed milk from a bottle and raised by hand.

Rose spent her time playing in the yard now, and Laura tried to watch her as the little pink sunbonnet went busily bobbing here and there.

Once Laura was just in time to see Rose struggle upright in the tub of water that stood under the pump spout; and with water running down her face and from her spread fingers at each side, Rose said without a whimper, "I want to go to bed."

One afternoon, just after Rose had been washed and combed and dressed in fresh, clean clothes, Laura heard her shrieking with laughter, and going to the door, saw her running from the barn. "O-o-o," Rose called. "Barnum did just like this." And down she dropped in the dusty path, and with arms and legs waving, rolled over and over on the ground. She was such a comical sight that Laura could only laugh too, in spite of the wreck of the clean dress, the dirt on her face and hands and the dust in her hair.

Another time, Laura missed her from the yard and with fear in her heart ran to the barn door. Barnum was lying down in his stall and Rose sat on his side, kicking her heels against his stomach.

Carefully, so as not to disturb his body, the horse raised his head and looked at Laura and she was positive Barnum winked one eye. After that Laura tried to watch Rose closer, but she couldn't bear to keep her in the house with the spring so fresh and gay outside. The work must be done between moments of looking at Rose through the door and window.

Once again she was just in time to see Rose miss an accident by a narrow margin. She had evidently gone farther afield than usual and was just coming back around the corner of the barn. Then Kelpie, Trixy's latest colt, came running around the same corner with another colt chasing her. Kelpie saw Rose too late to turn, too late to stop, so she put an extra spring in her muscles and sailed over Rose's head, while Susan, the other colt, proving, as she always tried to do, that she could do anything Kelpie did, followed behind, going neatly over Rose's head.

Then Laura was there, and snatching Rose up, carried her in the house. Rose had not been frightened, but Laura was, and she felt rather sick. How could she ever keep up the daily work and still go through what was ahead. There was so much to be done and only herself to do it. She hated the farm and the stock and the smelly lambs, the cooking of food and the dirty dishes. Oh, she hated it all, and especially the debts that must be paid whether she could work or not.

But Rose hadn't been hurt and now she was wanting a bottle to feed one of the pet lambs. Laura would do the same: she'd be darned if she'd go down and stay down or howl about it. What was it someone had said in that story she read the other day? "The wheel goes round and round and the fly on top'll be the fly on the bottom after a while." Well, she didn't care what became of the top fly, but she did wish the bottom one could crawl up a little way. She was tired of waiting for the wheel to turn. And the farmers were the ones at the bottom, she didn't care what Manly said. If the weather wasn't right they had nothing, but whether they had anything or not they must find it somehow to pay interest and taxes and a profit to the businessmen in town on everything they bought, and they must buy to live. There was that note at the bank Manly had to give to get the money to buy grain for the re-seeding after the wind storm. He was paying three percent a month on that note. That was where the wool money would have to go. No one could pay such interest as that. But there was all the summer's living before another harvest. Her head spun when she tried to figure it out.

Would there be enough money to pay it? Their share of the wool money was only $125, and how much was that note? A bushel to the acre of seed wheat and $1 a bushel for the seed: $100. Sixty acres of oats and two bushels to the acre of seed: 120 bushels. At 42 cents a bushel, that would be $50.40. Added to the $100 for wheat the note must be for $150.40.

It seemed to make a great difference in the price whether they were selling wheat or buying it. To be sure, as Manly said, there were freight charges out and back and elevator charges. But it didn't seem fair even so.

Anyway, they should pay the note at the bank as soon as possible. If they had to do so they could buy a book of coupons at the grocery store and give a note for that at only two percent a month. It was rather nice that the merchants had got those books with coupons from 25 cents to $5 in twenty-five or fifty-dollar books. It was convenient and it was cheaper interest. They had not bought any yet, and she had hoped they would not have to. Somehow the thought of it hurt her pride worse than a note at the bank. But pride must not stand in the way of a saving of one percent. She wouldn't think about it any more. It was his business and he wasn't worrying.

As spring turned the corner into summer, the rains stopped and the grain began to suffer for lack of moisture. Every morning Manly looked anxiously for signs of rain, and seeing none, went on about his work.

And then the hot winds came. Every day the wind blew strongly from the south. It felt on Laura's cheek like hot air from the oven when she opened the oven door on baking day. For a week, the hot winds blew, and when they stopped, the young wheat and oats were dried, brown and dead.

The trees on the ten acres were nearly all killed too. Manly decided there was no hope of replanting to have the trees growing to fulfill the law for the claims.

It was time to prove up and he could not. There was only one way to save the land. He could file on it as a pre-emption. If he did that he must prove up in six months and pay the United States $1.25 an acre. The continuous residence would be no trouble, for they were already there. The two hundred dollars cash at the end of the six months would be hard to find, but there was no other way. If Manly did not file on the land someone else would, for the land would revert to the government and be open to settlement by anyone.

So Manly pre-empted the land. There was one advantage: Manly did not have to work among the trees any

more. Here and there one had survived and Manly
mulched with manure and straw from the barn. The
mulching would help keep the land moist underneath and
so help those trees to live. The cottonwood tree before
Laura's pantry window, being north of the house, had
been protected from the full force of the hot winds and
from the sun. It was growing in spite of the drought.
Laura loved all its green branches that waved just the
other side of the glass as she prepared food on the broad
shelf before the window and washed the dishes there.

No rain followed the windstorm, but often after that
cyclone clouds would form in the sky and then drift
away. It was cyclone weather.

One sultry afternoon, Manly was in town and Peter
was gone with the sheep. Laura finished her work and
she and Rose went out in the yard. Rose was playing
with her play dishes under the cottonwood tree on the
shady side of the house while Laura idly watched the
clouds more from force of habit than a real fear, for she
had become used to the danger of storms.

The wind had been from the south strongly in the
morning, but had died down, and now Laura noticed
clouds piling up in the north. There was a solid bank of
blackness and before it clouds rolled. Now the wind rose,
blowing hard from the south, and watching, Laura saw
the dreaded funnel-shape cloud drop its point toward the
ground from the wall of black. The light turned a
greenish color, and seizing Rose, Laura ran with her into
the house. She quickly shut all doors and windows before
she ran into the pantry to look again, from its window,
toward the storm.

The point of the funnel had touched the ground and
she could see the dust rise up. It passed over a field of
new breaking and the strips of sod were lifted up out of
sight. Then it struck an old haystack. There was a blur
and the stack disappeared. The funnel-shaped cloud was
moving toward the house. Laura lifted the trap door in
the pantry floor and taking Rose with her went quickly
through it into the cellar, dropping the door shut behind
her. Holding Rose tightly, she cowered close in a corner
in the darkness and listened to the wind shriek above

them, expecting every second that the house would be lifted and carried away. But nothing happened, and after what seemed hours but was really only a few minutes she heard Manly's voice calling.

Lifting the cellar door Laura carried Rose up the stairs. She found Manly standing by his team in the yard, watching the storm as it passed eastward less than a quarter of a mile north from where they stood. It went on blowing away buildings and haystacks, but only a sprinkle of rain fell on the parched earth. Manly, in town, had seen the storm cloud and hurried home so that Laura and Rose should not be alone.

There were no more cyclones, but the weather continued hot and dry, and August the fifth was especially warm. In the afternoon Manly sent Peter to bring Laura's Ma, and at four o'clock he sent Peter again to town, this time on his running pony for the doctor. But their son was born before the doctor could get there.

Laura was proud of the baby, but strangely she wanted Rose more than anything. Rose had been kept away from her mother for the sake of the quiet, and a hired girl was taking indifferent care of her. When Laura insisted, the girl brought Rose in, a shy little thing with a round baby face herself, to see the little brother.

After that Laura rested easily and soon could take an interest in the sounds from outside, knowing well, from them, what was going on.

One day Peter came to the bedroom door to bid her good morning. He had stuck a long feather in his hatband and as it nodded above his good-natured face he looked so comical that Laura had to laugh.

Then she heard him talking to his pony and calling his dog and she knew he was taking the sheep out. He was singing:

> Oh, my! but ain't she handsome!
> Dear me! she's the sweetest name.
> Ki! yi! to love her is my dooty,
> My pretty, little, posy-pink
> Jenny Jerusha Jane.

And Peter and the sheep were gone until night. Then she heard Rose playing with the pet lambs. They were so large now that three of them went out with the sheep, but the two smallest still hung around the back door and yard to be fed and played with. Often they pushed Rose over, but it was all in the game. Then she heard the hired girl refuse to give Rose a piece of bread and butter, speaking crossly to her, and that Laura could not bear. Calling from her bed, she settled the question in Rose's favor.

Laura felt she must hurry and get her strength back. Rose shouldn't be treated meanly by any hired girl, and besides, there were the wages of five dollars a week. They must be stopped as soon as possible for the time would come soon enough to pay a note.

Laura was doing her own work again one day three weeks later when the baby was taken with spasms, and he died so quickly that the doctor was too late.

To Laura, the days that followed were mercifully blurred. Her feelings were numbed and she only wanted to rest—to rest and not to think.

But the work must go on. Haying had begun and Manly, Peter, and the herd boy must be fed. Rose must be cared for and all the numberless little chores attended to.

The hay was going to be short of what was needed, for it had been so dry that even the wild prairie grass had not grown well. There were more sheep and cattle and horses to feed, so there must be more hay instead of less.

Manly and Peter were putting up hay on some land two miles away a week later. Laura started the fire for supper in the kitchen stove. The summer fuel was old, tough, long, slough hay, and Manly had brought an armful into the kitchen and put it down near the stove.

After lighting the fire and putting the tea kettle on, Laura went back into the other part of the house, shutting the kitchen door.

When she opened it again, a few minutes later, the whole inside of the kitchen was ablaze: the ceiling, the hay, and the floor underneath and wall behind.

As usual, a strong wind was blowing from the south, and by the time the neighbors arrived to help, the whole house was in flames.

Manly and Peter had seen the fire and come on the run with the team and the load of hay.

Laura had thrown one bucket of water on the fire in the hay, and then, knowing she was not strong enough to work the pump for more water, taking the little deed-box from the bedroom and Rose by the hand, she ran out and dropped on the ground in the little half-circle drive before the house. Burying her face on her knees she screamed and sobbed, saying over and over, "Oh, what will Manly say to me?" And there Manly found her and Rose, just as the house roof was falling in.

The neighbors had done what they could but the fire was so fierce that they were unable to go into the house.

Mr. Sheldon had gone in through the pantry window and thrown all the dishes out through it toward the trunk of the little cottonwood tree, so the silver wedding knives and forks and spoons rolled up in their wrappers had survived. Nothing else had been saved from the fire except the deed-box, a few work clothes, three sauce dishes from the first Christmas dishes, and the oval glass bread plate around the margin of which were the words, "Give us this day our daily bread."

And the young cottonwood stood by the open cellar hole, scorched and blackened and dead.

After the fire Laura and Rose stayed at her Pa's for a few days. The top of Laura's head had been blistered from the fire and something was wrong with her eyes. The doctor said the heat had injured the nerves and so she rested for a little at her old home, but at the end of the week Manly came for her.

Mr. Sheldon needed a housekeeper and gave Laura and Manly houseroom and use of his furniture in return for board for himself and his brother. Now Laura was so busy she had no time for worry, caring for her family of three men, Peter and Rose, through the rest of the haying and while Manly and Peter built a long shanty, three rooms in a row, near the ruins of their house. It was built only one thickness of boards and tar-papered on the outside, but it was built tightly, and being new, it was very snug and quite warm.

September nights were growing cool when the new house was ready and moved into. The twenty-fifth of August had passed unnoticed and the year of grace was ended.

Was farming a success?

"Well, it all depends on how you look at it," Manly said when Laura asked him the question.

They had had a lot of bad luck, but anyone was liable to have bad luck even if he weren't a farmer. There had been so many dry seasons now that surely next year would be a good crop year.

They had a lot of stock. The two oldest colts would be ready to sell in the spring. Some newcomer to the land would be sure to want them, and there were the younger colts coming on. There were a couple of steers ready to sell now. Oh, they'd likely bring twelve or thirteen dollars apiece.

And there were the sheep, twice as many as last year to keep, and some lambs and the six old sheep to sell.

By building the new house so cheaply, they had money left to help pay for proving up on the land.

Maybe sheep were the answer.

"Everything will be all right, for it all evens up in time. You'll see," Manly said, as he started for the barn.

As Laura watched him go, she thought, yes, everything is evened up in time. The rich have their ice in the summer, but the poor get theirs in the winter, and ours is coming soon.

Winter was coming on, and in sight of the ruins of their comfortable little house they were making a fresh start with nothing. Their possessions would no more than balance their debts, if that. If they could find the two hundred dollars to prove up, the land would be theirs, anyway, and Manly thought he could.

It would be a fight to win out in this business of farming, but strangely she felt her spirit rising for the struggle.

The incurable optimism of the farmer who throws his seed on the ground every spring, betting it and his time against the elements, seemed inextricably to blend with the creed of her pioneer forefathers that "it is better farther on"—only instead of farther in space, it was farther on in time, over the horizon of the years ahead instead of the far horizon of the west.

She was still the pioneer girl and she could understand Manly's love of the land through its appeal to herself.

"Oh, well," Laura sighed, summing up her idea of the situation in a saying of her Ma's, "We'll always be farmers, for what is bred in the bone will come out in the flesh."

And then Laura smiled, for Manly was coming from the barn and he was singing:

> You talk of the mines of Australia,
> They've wealth in red gold, without doubt;
> But, ah! there is gold in the farm, boys——
> If only you'll shovel it out.

Building Leslieville, Alberta
Mary C. Bailey

In 1927, Mary C. Bailey wrote her memories of the set-
tling and growth of Leslieville, Alberta. She begins with
the humor and difficulties in planning pioneer weddings,
including her own in 1904, and ends with the coming of
the railroad through Leslieville in 1911. Her descriptions
of the construction of the town's public buildings are
stories of determined people working together despite
differences in background. The first church building, for
instance, was shared by members of seven different
denominations. She concentrates as much on her observa-
tion of others as on her own feelings and mentions
several women who successfully coped with hardship and
cultural change.

While most of the selections in this anthology focus
on the lives of rural women, Mary Bailey's narrative gives
us a woman's view of a town whose growth and activities
are closely linked with the farming community.

Source:
Mary C. Bailey. "Reminiscences of a Pioneer." Alberta
Historical Review *15 (Autumn 1967). 17-25.*

On March 9th, 1904, George Bailey and I were married in the Methodist parsonage in Red Deer by Rev. John Toole, after we made a 40-mile drive with team and sleigh in 30 degree below zero weather. We had started out on the morning of March 8th, from my father's house near Leslieville, wearing all our warmest clothing: George with his own fur coat and I with my father's big fur coat. Our team was hired from a Norwegian named Pete Peterson, with whom George had worked in the camp, and the harness was decorated with bells which rang so musically that they helped us to endure the cold wind that threatened to reach us through all our thick clothes. I called them our wedding bells.

We stopped for the night at a homesteader's house a few miles out of Red Deer. It was quite dark and when George knocked at the door and asked if he could stay for the night—which was customary among settlers, as there were no regular stopping places—he met with: "I'm sorry sir, but my husband is away, and I don't keep gentlemen alone!" But when she found he had a lady with him, she made us very welcome and we did enjoy the warmth of the big one-room house after our long cold ride. George said afterwards that I saved his life that night; but for my presence, he might have had to sleep in a snowdrift.

Mrs. Pagh (that was her name) gave us supper, after which she showed me, with pardonable pride, how she spun sheep's wool into yarn on a spinning wheel, which was a complete mystery to me, much to her delight.

There were several children, one of which amused himself by giving the baby, Elmer, some pepper to eat, probably with the idea of entertaining us; if so, the stunt back-fired, producing a terrific hulla-ba-loo before Elmer was consoled. Sleeping arrangements were simple—a large bed in one corner that I shared with Mrs. Pagh, while George slept on the floor among the children. Next morning we found the weather much warmer. Our wedding was quite uneventful—no showers nor reception, but it was thrilling to step into that little log shack which was to be our future home.

My sister Fannie's wedding, however, was quite different. She had left her job in Red Deer and come home, as our father and brother George had joined a survey party under a Mr. Edwards and were away to the west somewhere. She and Merritt Case of Red Deer planned to get married in August of the same year. Fannie had chosen the 13th for her wedding day as that was our brother George's brithday, so both our father and brother were coming home for the great occasion which was to take place in the family home. Also, my husband George, who was working several miles away, expected to be there.

Accordingly, Fannie wrote her intended of her plans. He was working near Red Deer, and had plans of his own. He wrote to her, of course, but mails being what they were in those days, neither ever received the other's letter! The result was, that after several days of rain—which meant muddy roads and swollen streams, on the 10th day of August Mr. Case, driving a team and democrat, and Rev. Walter Daniels, a young Baptist minister who had recently begun his ministry in Red Deer, driving a team and light top buggy, arrived at the homestead for the ceremony. As they were not expected for at least 3 days, nothing was ready.

It is quite possible that Mr. Daniels had never before found himself in such a unique situation. After a 40-mile ride in the rain, over muddy trails, and across rivers that had to be forded, to perform a marriage ceremony, to find nothing prepared. However, hurried preparations were soon underway.

Meanwhile, Mr. Daniels discovered to his dismay that in his hurried departure from Red Deer, he had forgotten his book containing the marriage ritual. He felt confident, however, that he remembered the lines correctly; but to test his memory, tried to persuade our brother Charlie, aged 7, to stand beside me and repeat them. Charlie, however, firmly refused to do so, because, he said, "She's married already!" Finally, all difficulties were ironed out, necessary preparations completed, and the marriage ceremony performed, which made my sister Mrs. Merritt Case, and hers the first wedding performed in the district that was soon to be known as Leslieville. As we later learned, it was also the first marriage ceremony that Mr. Daniels had ever performed.

As Mr. Case fully expected to take his bride back with him to Red Deer, his feelings can be imagined when he found that it was not possible to leave her mother and Charlie alone, so, for a time at least, she must stay with them. Therefore, it was a very disappointed bridegroom who set out alone a few days later for the long trip back to Red Deer.

But Merritt Case was not the only one who felt aggrieved. When the absent members of the family arrived to "see Fannie married," and found it was all over, their reaction can be better imagined than described.

The year 1904 saw quite a number of new arrivals who settled mainly to the north and west of us. Land in Range 5, west of ours, was not open for homesteading until 1906, but many came and "squatted" on land of their choice before that date, after which they could file their claims.

Among these newcomers was the Reilly family who reached the district early in 1905. They came originally from Toronto in 1903, but had spent two years at the Indian Industrial School, a few miles from Red Deer, where Mr. Reilly was employed as instructor in carpentry. The family consisted of Mr. and Mrs. Reilly, four daughters and two sons. The house Mr. Reilly built for his family was of lumber, the first of its kind in our district, and was a scant mile south of the Thompson home, thus making the Reilly's the first near neighbors.

Up to this time our young brother Charlie had had no playmates except his dog, King, so it was not surprising that the two boys, the same age but for one day, became close friends. The Reillys were a talented family and proved to be a real asset to the community.

In the spring of 1905 Edmund Bureau brought his family from France to Red Deer where he left them, and continued west. He seemed to approve of our locality and squatted SE ¼, Sec. 26, Tp. 39, R. 5, West of 5th, and began to make place for a building on his property, which would serve as a hotel or store, and for living quarters for his family. He pitched a tent on the bank of Small Lobstick Creek, not far from where the Hudson's Bay trail forded it, and lived there while getting acquainted with the scattered settlers. His was an ambitious project in a country where log houses were standard housing; the fact that his building must be made of lumber brought about a few interesting happenings. To begin with, lumber was scarce and had to be hauled long distances on wagons in summer and on sleighs in winter. The nearest lumber mill was about eight or nine miles away, where a man named Joyce had set up a portable sawmill in a big spruce swamp. The lumber, though green, could be used for the framing of the building, but floors and finishing for other parts required dry lumber.

A middle-aged bachelor named Johnny Campbell was hired to haul the lumber. Johnny, as he was familiarly called, owned several horses of different temperaments, but they suited old Johnny, who was never known to get upset about anything. So one morning he rigged up three teams and three wagons, driving one outfit himself; a hired man handled the second outfit, and he hired my husband to drive the third team. There was no road, only trails, and in some places not even trails. Their way led to a ford across the Horseguard River, which they reached after safely descending a long, steep and crooked hill. The bank on the other side was very steep but not long and the remainder of the trip through brushy, open land was uneventful. They reached the mill site around noon, unhitched and fed the horses and ate their own lunches, which they carried with them; after that they loaded the three wagons with lumber and started back.

They had gone only a short distance on the soft, muddy road when Johnny's horses decided that they had had enough. Not being properly trained by their easy-going owner, they balked and did everything but pull; but with limitless patience and maneuvering on the part of two of their drivers, the wagons were finally moved to more solid ground. By then it was too late to get home that night, so the mill owner kindly allowed them to sleep in his camp and gave them supper and breakfast.

The homeward trip was quite trouble-free until they got the three outfits across the Horseguard River to the bottom of the long difficult hill. It was evident that no single team in the outfit could pull one of the loads up that hill, so they hitched the team from one of the wagons to the front of one of the others and started up the hill, with a man driving each team. All went well until they reached a steep place, when the lead team began to back down the hill. The others were of the same mind but they stumbled backward and fell down and slid until the load reached the bottom of the hill. Johnny, true to form, was not upset. He took out his pipe, leisurely filled it and lit it before he made any attempt to straighten out the mess; but all three loads were finally brought up the hill and reached their destination by mid-afternoon where the lumber was piled, ready for the carpenters.

Before leaving for home, my husband, who was young, ambitious, and badly in need of money, approached Mr. Bureau with a proposition to haul some of the lumber with his team of oxen. Mr. Bureau agreed to pay him $4.00 per 1,000 feet for hauling it. George had bought his oxen as three-year-old steers about 1½ years before. He broke them for hauling, using the yoke, and controlled them by a long rope tied around the near ox's horns. They were strong and dependable, and he lost no time in getting started on his job.

Leaving home at 6:20 every morning, with a gunny sack full of hay on board for his team's dinner and a hearty lunch for himself, he would reach Joyce's mill around noon, and unyoke the oxen and feed them. While they were eating he would load 500 feet of lumber on his wagon; as it was green and heavy, that was as much as his oxen could handle. When they had finished their hay, George would put the yoke on and hitch them up for the return trip. Then he would climb onto his load and eat his own lunch on the way. That was the pattern of all the trips he made during that fall and winter, whenever Mr. Joyce would have a load for him.

Every homeward trip, however, had extra work when they came to the bottom of the big hill. Here he would take off half of his load and haul the other half to the top where he would unload it. Then he drove back down and loaded up the 250 feet he left there, hauled it to the top, then reloaded the other half. To a man who was used to hard work, it was all easy at $2.00 a trip! The trail at that time ran close to the home of Mr. and Mrs. John Reilly, who had come to the district early in 1905; often that winter when it was quite cold, Mrs. Reilly would come out with a cup of hot tea which would taste especially good after his half frozen lunch.

Meanwhile, construction of Mr. Bureau's house began with Alex and George Thompson, Julius Armineau and one or two others of the settlers doing the carpentry work. As all of Joyce's lumber was green, he obtained dry seasoned lumber from some other source and being so much lighter enabled George to haul 1,000 feet at a load.

Each day when he got home the first thing he did was to unhitch the oxen, water them and put them in a good, warm stable, and fill their mangers with hay before he even went into our shack. I used to say that he thought more of his oxen than he did of me.

A year later Mr. Bureau's store was opened on the site which was to become "Leslieville." This store was a boon to the settlers in more ways than one. It not only sold them goods, it also bought produce from them; and as most of the stock came from Red Deer, it meant hauling jobs for those who had teams and wagons or sleighs.

Our closest post office was at Red Deer, and mail for the whole district was brought in by any settlers who had reason to make the long trip into town. For some time this mail was left at my father's homestead, which had gradually become sort of a gathering place for many of the young settlers to the west and north. My father's experience with Mr. Edwards' survey party had made him acquainted with the surveyors' markings on the corner stakes of each quarter section of the land, so he was able to help many settlers locate their claims. Many of these young men were quite unused to "roughing it," and they enjoyed the plain but comfortable home life of my parents' place.

Eventually, a post office was opened at a placed called Evarts, some twenty miles to the southeast; then, when another called Eckville was established on the east side of the Medicine River, only twelve or thirteen miles away, people in our district began to feel that they should have a post office of their own. Therefore, after petitioning the government at Ottawa, and having their application granted, a post office was opened in a corner of Mr. Bureau's store on January 1st, 1907, and was named Leslieville.

Our first mail carrier was a colorful character named Foster, who brought the mail from Red Deer to the new post office three times a week. He carried passengers, as well as mail, and entertained with songs, monlogues and outrageous stories. Mr. Foster became quite a celebrity; he was a kind man, and his tri-weekly trips into Leslieville were a welcome innovation to our uneventful lives, as he always had some news of the outside world to pass on to us.

Wherever people make their homes, they feel the need of some kind of religious services. Mr. and Mrs. Reilly, being staunch Methodists, early made their home available for services, and settlers began gathering there from near and far, regardless of denominational differences, to attend meetings which were conducted by any ministers in who came to our locality. The Reillys were musical people who possessed an organ, and their oldest daughter, Mattie, was also a fine singer. The first minister from the "outside" to hold a service was Mr. Patstone from Lacombe. He was followed by others whose names I do not recall, but they were generally students from the different denominational colleges, who spent their sum-

mers ministering to scattered congregations in the newly
settled west country.

About that time, a young man named Fred McNeil
came from London, Ontario, took up a homestead not far
from ours, and built a sod house, the only one of its
kind in the district. His parents, Mr. and Mrs. John
McNeil, were to follow him as soon as he had built a
house for them to live in. Mr. McNeil had for many
years worked as a motorman on the streetcars of London,
and his health had broken down. His doctors had ordered
him to "go west and live," so he went, but very unwill-
ingly. They brought all their furniture and all was well
until they reached Red Deer, when their troubles began.
They bought a team and wagon, got their stuff loaded
and started for the homestead; but not being accustomed
to such things as mud holes and crooked trails, fording
streams and balky horses (or horses of any kind), they
got discouraged, turned around and went back, thoroughly
disenchanted with the much vaunted "west." But Mrs.
McNeil was one of those who don't give up easily; her
husband's health demanded it, so later on they made
another attempt, and finally reached their son's homestead.

When Mrs. McNeil saw the sod house which was to
be her home, all her dreams of a cozy, comfortable little
cabin were shattered and she sat down and cried, but not
for long; she was a brave woman and optimistic, and so
she started making the best of setting up housekeeping in
her new domain. With the help of my husband and his
oxen, logs were hauled from a nearby ravine, and lumber
from a distant sawmill, a log house was finally built and
made warm and comfortable.

During the ensuing months this lady played an
important part in the lives and doings of the Leslieville
community. It was she who first saw the need of a
church building, and promptly started to do something
about it. The McNeils were Methodists, but the country
was fast filling up with people of different beliefs, and
little attention was paid to denomination. Mrs. McNeil
evolved a plan whereby a building could be built by the
settlers themselves all working together. Meetings were
called and plans were made to decide the size of the

building. The site was already settled as Mr. Bureau generously donated a square plot of land measuring half an acre. As most of the homesteaders were interested in the project, they went to work promptly and in a short time the required number of logs were hauled and piled at the building site. They were of spruce, cut from tall, straight timber which abounded in this western district, but had to be "dressed" or shaped for building by being hewed on opposite sides to a uniform thickness of about six inches.

To get this accomplished, Mrs. McNeil called on all settlers for a "hewing bee." Not every man who could chop wood was an expert at hewing, but all who were able turned out, and the hewing began. Some of the women of the district, led by Mrs. McNeil, brought lunch at noon for the workmen, and a good start was made. The first few bees were well attended, but gradually homestead duties and other important matters made it increasingly difficult for Mrs. McNeil to get a bee together. Once she sent penny postal cards around; another effort was an announcement in the post office reading:

WANTED——"1,000 men for a worthy cause!

Payment——Virtue is its own reward."

The hewing of the logs was finally completed, and everyone helped in the erection of the building. This job of chinking was undertaken by the women. The men fashioned paddles from poplar wood for putting on the mortar, and it was a gala day for all concerned. In those days any occasion that brought people together was a social affair, a time for fun and good-natured jollity, generally with something to eat, which was always a treat to those who happened to be bachelors. Afterwards a nephew of Mrs. McNeil cleaned the paddles and decorated them, finishing them with the date of the occasion; I still have my paddle.

The finishing of the interior of the building was done by John Reilly who was an experienced carpenter. He also made a pulpit and a large number of seats to accommodate future congregations. At one of the several meetings held concerning this project, the naming of the building was the subject of some controversy. As was often the case, Mrs. McNeil calmed the troubled waters with this suggestion: "Why not call it Bethel Union Church?" and the idea caught on, as it seemed a fitting name to a people of different faiths, Bethel meaning "God is in this place" and "Union" including all the different denominations.

The name settled, a Code of Rules was next drawn up regarding the use of the building. It was free to all recognized denominations, providing their hours of service did not conflict. There was to be a Board of Management composed of one representative from each of seven denominations, Methodist, Presbyterian, Congregational, Anglican, Baptist, Lutheran and Roman Catholic, and as long as these rules were adhered to, harmony prevailed. At times there were three services on Sundays, morning, afternoon and evening, usually Anglican Presbyterian and Methodist or Baptist.

The first service was held in the new church in late November, 1908, and as there was no visiting minister in the area at that time, a Sunday School was organized with Mr. Reilly as Superintendent.

Miss Mattie Reilly was an able organizer as well as musician, so she set to work to mould all the available musical talent the district provided, into a choir of many voices. This was the beginning of a pleasent era in the lives of the settlers. Most people enjoyed music, and many were the concerts and entertainments held in the church on week nights.

In time, young ministers were sent to the district by different denominational missions during the summer months. Some of these young men had little or no experience with the "wild west" and its inhabitants. One of the earliest of these was a Mr. Mabon, who, in all innocence, took as true all the tales that had been told him about savages and came to his mission field armed to the teeth. I never knew whether or not he carried a gun; but he came garbed like a Mountie, even to the spurs which, some declared, he wore even at night! However, Mr. Mabon soon discovered that we were a peaceable people and were kindly disposed toward all who came to minister to our spiritual needs.

Among these earlier ministers were Oscar Irwin, a Presbyterian, and Reg Edwards, a Baptist, both of whom boarded at Mrs. McNeil's at the same time in the summer of 1909. They were good friends, but often indulged in sly digs at each other in a good-natured way. Once, when Edwards came home from helping some settler in field work, he was showing Irwin his sore and blistered hands. Irwin, all sympathy, offered him some salve, adding "That is, if you think Presbyterian salve will do," then as an afterthought, "Maybe you had better *immerse* your hands first!"

The next newcomer was T.J. Warwick, from County Antrim, Ireland, a small man, very humorous and very Irish. He spent the winter among us. Another was Malcolm McKenzie McLean who was very, very Scottish. He was quite a singer, and "The March of the Cameron Men" was one of his favorites. A Mr. Scilly was sent in to our district by the Presbyterian Church in Red Deer. His introduction to us was, "I'm Scilly. Mr. Brown sent me!" But he was all right. It didn't take much to amuse us in those days. Mr. Heaven was the Anglican minister who served for a long time.

During this time, however, another pressing problem occupied the minds of the people who had children, and that was the need for a school. Accordingly, a school district was formed and named Prairie Rose. The lovely flower for which it was named bloomed in such abundance that it has since been chosen as the floral emblem of Alberta.

The first schoolhouse, located on the north bank of the Horseguard River, about two miles southeast of Leslieville, was built by Mr. Reilly. The secretary-treasurer was E.N. French, who, with his wife and family, lived south of the river, and started the village of Condor by building a store there.

Another school soon became necessary, and a second school building was built by Mr. Reilly, this time north of Leslieville on the Johnny Campbell quarter-section, at the foot of a very high, steep hill, known locally as "the Butte." This hill gave to the new school its name, the Butte School.

After completing a year at Prairie Rose, Anne Patterson became the first teacher at the new school, and put in a second year of service to our community. It must have been a grueling experience for a young lady of Miss Patterson's English background to work under the crude conditions that prevailed in this newly settled country, so altogether different from anything she had ever experienced; but, like many other newcomers, she had been able to adjust herself to the situations she had to cope with.

Another early teacher in the Butte School was Bessie Meston, member of a Scottish family who had settled on land to the west and north of Leslieville. Miss Metson later married Frank Patterson. Another was Jack McDonald, familiarly called "Pegleg" because he had lost a leg and always walked with a cane. Jack was very pleasant and well liked. He quit teaching, early, however, and went onto a farm near Eckville.

There was another teacher named Fullerton, I remember, chiefly because of the unique way he had of keeping order in his schoolroom. He kept a strap in his desk, and when his watchful eye caught some unsuspecting youngster in mischief, he would roll the strap into a ball and fire it at the hapless culprit. This treatment generally had better results than when the strap was applied in the customary manner.

Nearly all of the streams, both large and small, ran between high, steep banks. The old Hudson's Bay Trail, which was the main road into the West Country, ran along the north bank of the Horseguard River—not on the top, but on the slanting side. Many wagon wheels had worn deep ruts, the lower one being the deeper, giving the wagon a very uncomfortable slant, making riding anything but a pleasure. During those earlier years, the ruts grew deeper and deeper as more and more settlers braved the discomforts of the trip in, to start new homes for themselves.

When my father first settled in this district he had visions of another railroad running north and south, parallel to the Calgary and Edmonton line, but his dream was shattered by the discovery of the vast coal fields farther west. When the Brazeau Collieries started operations at Nordegg, a race began between the Canadian Northern and the Alberta Central Railways to be first to get a road built into Rocky Mountain House. It seemed that that company would be the one to get the job of hauling the coal out of Nordegg.

Both the C.N.R. and the A.C.R. were surveyed about 1909-1910, and grading operations began at once. This was a great boon to the settlers, as grades had to be made with plows, scrapers and shovels; settlers were hired to do this work, and almost everybody in the Leslieville district got a job, either by hand or with whatever teams and implements he had. The A.C.R., building west from Red Deer, was the first to reach our area, running a fairly straight line to Rocky Mountain House, and about 4 or 4½ miles south of Leslieville. Wages were good, $2.50 per day, less 75 cents for board, for a man single-handed; other wages depended on the number of horses he had on the job. This seemed almost a miracle to a man who had been working a 10-hour day for $1.00 and sometimes board himself!

The A.C.R. soon reached Rocky Mountain House, and began carrying passengers and mail as well. This ended the long "horse and buggy" mail route between Red Deer and Leslieville, and started a new one. Post offices had been established at Alhambra, Condor and Pitcox on the assumption that the A.C.R. would be serving them; Pitcox was the only one bypassed; its post office was moved to a location a little farther east, and the name changed to Hespero. Condor was nearest to Leslieville, so a carrier route was begun between the two places.

The C.N.R. grade reached our district in the summer of 1911, passing in a straight line through Leslieville on its way to Rocky Mountain House. We were now well provided with railroads, one half mile north of us, another 4½ miles south of us!

Gradually the little settlement began to take shape as a hamlet south of the railroad track. After McKinnon Bros.' first fire (the Bureau building), they started a new store on a different location, and other small business places sprang up here and there. At one time, two young men

came to Leslieville and started another store in a small
building they built on the other side of the Lobstick. The
business was known as King and Mitchell's, and for a
time they got considerable patronage, especially from the
west; but they did not stay very long.

The C.N.R. had finished their grade to Nordegg, and
had been hauling out coal for several years before they
began bringing mail into Leslieville. They made three
round trips a week—west to Nordegg on Mondays,
Wednesdays and Fridays, east on Tuesdays, Thursdays and
Saturdays. They also carried passengers which was a great
help to anyone who wanted to go to Red Deer. Up to
this time, we had to drive to Condor and catch the
A.C.R. on its eastern trip.

The coming of the railroad had brought many changes.
The Alberta Wheat Pool built an elevator, and the Nation-
al Company built another. Harry Him and his brother,
Louie, built a cafe. Another school was built, this time
within the hamlet; but before it was ready for use,
school was opened in the church with Kate Morrow as
teacher. After a time it was moved to the front of
Roddle's store, where it was kept until the new two-
roomed school was finished.

I have written this account of Leslieville's early days
mostly from memories; but I have received assistance
from a few friends to whom I offer sincere thanks,
especially to Charles H. Snell, Mrs. A. Holt, Mrs. Angus
Martin and Miss Margaret McKinnon.

Farming in Iowa
Ada Mae Brown Brinton

In 1977, Ada Mae Brown Brinton combined material from her many diaries and her unwritten, accurate memories to write a history for her family. The story begins in the 1860's when Ada's father and her mother's family moved to Iowa. Her mother had become engaged to her father while she was working in a textile mill in Massachusetts.

Ada traveled to Iowa and married Marion Brinton in 1914. The young man already owned a farm on which he built a new home in preparation for his marriage. Ada and Marion made a success of the farm and lived there until 1974, when Marion died. This edited portion of her manuscript gives us vivid accounts of home life, farming, dairying and social events in Iowa from the early 1900's until the Depression.

Source:
Glenda Riley, ed. "Eighty-Six Years in Iowa: The Memoir of Ada Mae Brown Brinton." Annals of Iowa 45 *(Winter 1981): 551-67.*

171

My father, Thatcher Brown, of Morrill, Maine, and his friend, Morrison Sanborn, of Grafton County, New Hampshire, came west by train in the spring of 1868. They stopped in Morrison, Illinois, to see the Horace Hinkson family, formerly from New Hampshire. After a brief visit my father, who was 23, and Mr. Sanborn continued by train on to Guthrie Switch, later known as Menlo, which was as far as the railroad extended west at that time.

My father purchased a farm south of Menlo, most of which was on well-laying ground. It did have a small creek and timber on the north end. Water and timber were considered very essential. . . . Papa bought a team and necessary farming equipment with which he "broke" the southern part of the farm and planted crops that same spring. He built protection for his horses and then started to build a house.

In 1869, my maternal grandparents of Grafton County, near Canaan, New Hampshire, Farnum and Sabra Ann Hinkson, journeyed to Illinois with their children: my Mother, Rhoannah, 21; teenage Adda; and younger brother Fred Oscar. They stayed with the before mentioned Horace Hinkson, brother of Farnum. There a team, wagon and supplies were purchased, and with them my grandfather and his son, Fred, proceeded on to Adair County, Iowa where my father was located. In due time my grandmother with the two girls traveled to Iowa, by train. Following are the excerpts from a letter Mamma wrote May 30, 1870, to Aunt Ada Brown in Massachusetts:

Having good weather, the prairie is green,
grass quite so tall so people are cutting it
for their horses. The flowers that grow here
are lovely bright colors that make a pretty
bouquet. "T" (Thatcher) is breaking sod,
hard work so we did not go to church. The
Methodist minister preached. (Apparently
denominations took turns.) The house is
generally filled. They go and carry their
babies. Sometimes there are over a dozen
little bits of things. They look as if they
should be at home. People are not at all
proud. They do not stop for looks. They
wear sunbonnets and big aprons to church.
The men ride on a board put across the
wagon if they are too poor to be able to
have a spring seat, and the women sit down
flat on the bottom of the wagon. That is
the West! The people around here do not
trouble to get acquainted with the Yankees,
as they call us. . . .

Earlier, during the time my father was in Lawrence,
Massachusetts, my mother was working in one of the
large textile mills there. My father and mother met in
Lawrence while attending the same Baptist church. After
coming to Iowa, they were married on Christmas day,
1869. My mother, Rhoannah Hinkson, was 21, Thatcher
Brown was 24. . . . My father was a hard working
man—was said to remark that he could outwork any team.
However, he broke his health doing so and had to give
up farming. He then bought the dairy farm just east of
Stuart where I was born and he began doing carpenter
work. He had learned the carpenter trade from his Uncle
Elisha Merriam in Lawrence, Massachusetts, under whom
he served his apprenticeship. . . . The dairy Papa operat-
ed was a type conforming to that date. Milk was carried
in 5 and 10 gallon cans in a covered four-wheel wagon
drawn by one horse. There were regular customers. When
a hand bell was rung in front of a house, the customer
would bring out containers and the milk was poured

either into a pint or quart tin measure according to the amount desired. Milk tickets were sold in advance in $1.00 amounts—red printed tickets for quarts and green for pints.

The dairy farm was sold in 1893 or 1894. In '94 my parents, sister Luella and I went "back east" to visit relatives and attend a Brown family reunion. . . .

After selling the dairy farm and the trip back east in 1894, my father built a nice cottage of 1½ stories, plus a full basement. This was located out "on the hill" on Nassau Street, west of the business part of town. . . .Those of us who lived out on the hill, as it was called, were sort of set apart from the rest of the townspeople, for there were no houses connecting that area for many years. . . .Upon moving out on the hill my father continued with a small dairy—he usually had three to four cows. It was my job to deliver the milk. We had a faithful driving horse by the name of "Fannie." She was hitched to an open buggy. Fanny knew the route as well as I did. When in a block where there were three or four houses to which I was to deliver—I carried the bottles in a heavy wire container which held eight bottles of milk in exchange for empty ones with tickets—and as I proceeded down the block Fannie walked along the street without any instruction, ready to pick me up at the last house. While this milk business continued it meant work for my mother to keep the bottles clean and filled. Due to the fact that my father always kept only Jersey or Guernsey cows, our customers were among the people who could afford and preferred the quality of milk. I came to know these families personally (many remained good friends the rest of their lives), as new people were seldom added to the list and the route was confined to a small area—three or four blocks in the central part of town—as the quantity of milk was limited.

My parents attended church regularly and I was brought up to do so. In my teenage years this required five services a day on Sunday: Sunday School, Morning Service, Junior League in the afternoon as a teacher, Epworth League in the early evening followed by the Evening Church Service. Each year Evangelistic services were usually conducted for a week to ten days in the church by an outside evangelist and a "music leader." I accepted Christ during one of these meetings, was baptized and joined the Methodist Church on August 6, 1906.

As a young child I was "entertained" in various ways during church services. I remember lying in the pew with my head on my mother's knees so as to watch the glitter of many spangles on the beautiful chandelier which was hung from the center of the high ceiling of our church. I also would listen to the ticking of my mother's watch when she would say, "Listen to the little boy chopping wood." In the summer she carried a fan which folded completely out of sight into the handle case. Upon pushing a slide button the fan would open out into a fluted circle with a handle—that fascinated me. Another form of entertainment was provided by my mother's allowing me to try on her mitts—they were a form of gloves used in summer, made of knitted silk without fingers, open beyond the knuckles. . . .

My parents were loyal church workers. My mother was President of the Ladies Aid Society for ten years. The Ladies Aid met every two weeks in homes and indeed they did work! They raised money by piecing quilt blocks and then quilting them, by tying comforters, tearing and sewing carpet rags, making aprons and sunbonnets and other wearing apparel. Mamma and Lue made all of the fancy sunbonnets which became very popular. They took special orders as to color, for the sunbonnets were white on the outside with a solid color underneath. The crown was machine stitched with rows of stitching about one-fourth inch apart. . . .The Ladies Aid Society at one time sold vanilla and lemon extract which came from a company in gallon jugs. The jugs were kept in our basement and Mamma transferred the extract into glass bottles and labeled them with proper stickers. I also remember about a large Scripture Cake being made one time in a new dish pan. The recipe was typed and given with the purchase of a piece of the cake. All of the ingredients in the cake had been mentioned in the Bible.

In our church there were two special programs each year in which youngsters took part and for which much preparation was made—Children's Day, the second Sunday of June, and the Christmas Program, always given on Christmas Eve. I served on committees for these programs in my teen years and know what a lot of patience and time is required as there were always some children who were hard to restrain. The programs were made of Sunday School individuals and classes singing, speaking pieces, and performing drills. . . .

For Christmas there was always a large evergreen tree decorated by tinsel and lights. At the close of the program Santas Claus would appear from the entrance to the auditorium causing great excitement by his costume and chatter. At the time of my earliest recollection presents were hung on the tree. The packages were labeled for the smaller children (presumably from their parents). The names were called out by Santa and specified helpers delivered the packages. I well remember a large beautifully dressed doll hanging rather high on a branch. Naturally each little girl hoped the doll might be hers. This caused envy and disappointment to such a degree that these gifts were discontinued. Instead, cute little paper boxes filled with candy and nuts were given to each child from the teacher of each class. These classes of younger children were called forward, one at a time, and the boxes were handed out. Then the classes of older children were called and each child received an orange or a polished apple.

There were always evening church services in all of the churches in my day. A large tree grew on the outer edge of the sidewalk almost directly in front of the Methodist Church. Some of the young fellows congregated under the tree to wait for girls to come from the evening service. It must have been too handy as it was cut down eventually!

At four I started my school experiences as a first grader at Whittier School House (West School). The first and second grades were in the basement in a room which was halfway underground with tall windows of eight panes. We entered the basement through a one-story wooden-type building at the center of the brick school.

This covered the stairway leading down. Then to the east of this wooden structure was a cement outside stairway with bannisters which led up to the double doors opening into a hallway. In good weather scholars lined up in two rows and at a signal given by the teacher in charge who was standing in the doorway we marched up the stairs. . . .There was a large playground to the south of the building and wooden walks led to two outhouses, one for girls and one for boys, and each divided into two separate compartments. There was a well with a pump in the northwest area of the front yard. Walks were across the north and west sides of the grounds with tall soft maple trees on these sides.

I went to High School at twelve years of age, which was too young. At that time there was an Assembly Room where Freshman, Sophomore, Junior and Senior year students did their studying and from which the students marched out to appointed classrooms as the piano was played. School began at nine o'clock with "chapel." At this time Scripture was read by faculty members, the Lord's Prayer was recited by faculty and students and then there was a singing session. These songs (not popular music) were openly requested by the students. On one occasion the Principal, a man greatly disliked, in the process of correcting one of the big boys in the assembly room got into an awful scrap. The boy was knocked on the floor on his back and the Principal was choking him until he was getting blue in the face. Some girls cried and ran from the room, others screamed, whereupon some of the other boys pulled the Principal off.

I did not go to school beyond the middle of my junior year. My big handicap was algebra. I had gotten a poor start in the subject my Freshman year and was having to repeat second year algebra in my Junior year plus the regular Junior year studies. I was discouraged and at Christmas time I got a clerking job in the J.B. Grove store and quit school. . . . Later I regretted that I was allowed to quit, but it was not an uncommon thing to do at that time.

I did continue to clerk on Saturdays and on call until eventually I became a fulltime clerk. I always liked it, learned a great deal and knew women from far and near. The store drew trade from other towns, many coming on passenger trains which were then available.

For a number of years "Bates Hall" was the location of all entertainment features [in Stuart]. That was in the second story of the building occupied by the George Ryan Dry Goods Store. The Reverend Billy Sunday conducted some meetings in Bates Hall. There were musicals and public gatherings of all kinds there. In observance of Lincoln's birthday a program was given in Bates Hall and I spoke the poem which was said to have been Lincoln's favorite, "Why should the Spirit of Mortal Be Proud?" In addition I sang an operetta there, sang a solo for a high school graduation, and our Stuart Quartette (of which I was a member) participated in a musical there and I was in a play. The Country Club put on a dandy play at Bates Hall—the play was repeated because it was so well accepted. A traveling stock company appeared at Bates Hall, producing a different play every two weeks. A Lecture Course, consisting of varied high-class entertainment over a period of three or four weeks in the wintertime, was held at either Bates Hall or the High School Assembly Room.

There were some very cold winters. . . .Everyone wore warm knit long-sleeved and long-legged underwear either plain cotton, fleece lined or wool. Feminine attire included long stockings, summer and winter, usually two petticoats which were starched and worn under light-weight dresses in the summer. (My mother knit fancy stitched underskirts for us for winter wear.) Remember, we rode in open conveyances and in summer there was no air conditioning. In the winter soapstones, hot water in jugs, heavy horse blankets and buffalo robes were used extensively when riding. "Buffalo robes" were originally made from the hides of buffalo, later from the hides of cattle or horses.

In my years at home with my parents we had feather beds on our beds in the winter months. These were ticking filled with soft feathers from duck or goose breasts. It was the most wonderful feeling to sink into them and keep warm. They were somewhat lumpy. When making the bed, my mother used a wooden yardstick to even the top so that it would be perfectly smooth.

The arrival and departure of passenger trains at depots was always a major event, not only of interested persons gathered to greet those arriving or to bid "adieu" to those leaving, but there was usually a news reporter on hand and there were idle bystanders on the platform. The interior of small town depots was much the same. In the center of the room was a tall pot-bellied stove. Wooden benches with curved backs and smooth seats were around the perimeter of the room. I can still hear the chatter of the telegraph keys as they ticked endlessly in the office. At Division Centers the trains took on water and coal. Stuart was a Division Center. It was interesting to see the heavy hand trucks on the depot platforms. The trucks were wheeled out for baggage, express and mail sacks. In later years mail bags were suspended at a certain spot and as the train passed a long heavy, hook reached out and pulled the bag into the mail car. There was also a train, the Guthrie Center Branch, which made the round trip to Guthrie Center each day. There were also plenty of freight trains. We lived a block from the track but we were so used to them that the noise did not bother. . . .

In the early 1900's Stuart's streets were either dusty or muddy. There was no solid ground of any kind. Hitching rails were along Main Street. Flies in the stores were a pest, drawn largely from the sweat and manure of the horses.

I was young when I learned to ride horseback, having a nice sized riding horse, larger than a shetland pony, which I greatly enjoyed. . . . At one time in my career I had a tailored tan-colored riding outfit made with a full-length divided skirt. . . . All of my youth I had horseback rides before breakfast as my father always got up at 4 A.M. to do chores and would bridle and saddle my horse in readiness for me. He continued to do this as long as I was home.

In the winter, with sufficient snow, sleighs and bobsleds were used extensively. Nothing can ever replace the pleasure of slipping smoothly over the snow. Another pleasure was to hear bells and chimes attached to the har-

ness. My father had a long string of bells about the size
of golf balls which were fastened around the body of the
horse. Marion [her fiance] had chimes the size of base-
balls which were fastened on a leather piece. At times, of
course, there were "spills" from the sleighs and bobsleds,
either purposely or otherwise, but the falls were cush-
ioned by snowdrifts.

In our church two special services were often the
same Sunday: The School Baccalaureate in the evening and
the Memorial in the morning. At the Memorial service
the members of the G.A.R. followed by Veterans of the
Spanish American War and their auxiliaries marched down
the front aisle carrying flags and were seated in the
center seats. It was an impressive sight as I recall to see
the white-haired Civil War soldiers. Their auxiliary was
called "Woman's Relief Corps." There was a window in
the Methodist Church carrying symbols of two Civil War
organizations.

On the 31st of May, Memorial Day, there used to be
celebrations held at the North Oak Grove Cemetery. The
G.A.R. soldiers rode out from town while the people
walked. A band led the march. There was a small band-
stand in the cemetery situated with rolling ground to the
west where people sat on the ground for the program.
Usually the band played and a speaker gave a suitable
address. One year the "Stuart Quartette" (I was one of the
singers) sang a couple of songs as part of the program.

The Fourth of July used to be really celebrated. I
always had some firecrackers which were fun to set off.
My father showed me how to place one under an empty
tin can to make a big noise. Also, he put a couple of
long nails in the end of a lightweight pole of some kind
in which a firecracker was placed as soon as it was
lighted and the pole rose in the air. It seemed a safe way
to shoot off the larger firecrackers. . . .

Our house was thoroughly cleaned each spring and
fall. Carpets were taken outside and either thrown over
the clothesline or put on the grass where a carpet beater
was used to remove the dust. The dining room in my
parents' house was covered by rag carpet. . . . It was
made from clothing discarded in our family. The clothing

was washed and torn into strips which were sewed end to
end, rolled into balls and sent to someone who had a
loom on which to weave any length desired. It was fun
to try to discover some former dress. The width of the
woven strips was 36 inches, so the strips were sewed
together for the width required by the room.

Marion and I were engaged in 1913. In the fall of
1914 preparations were made for the building of a house
on the farm owned by Marion two miles west of Stuart
up on a high spot from which the view of the countryside was wonderful in all directions. Marion bought books
of house plans and we discussed plans in them. Papa was
consulted as well as Marion's father. Rock for the
foundation was laid by Roy Morrison, a reliable mason.
The floor of cement covered the entire basement under all
of the house with a garage under the large front porch.
Papa and a contractor in Stuart built the house. Somewhere Father Brinton had seen finishing casings used in
framing doors and windows which were different from
any used in our vicinity. They had a smooth curved
exterior. He ordered the lumber from a Minnesota lumber
company. I was most grateful in all future years when
cleaning for this extra effort on his part, for other
casements usually had ridges which were dirt catchers.
White pine was used in the house. . . .

Our wedding was in my parents' home on December
9, 1914. We invited only our immediate families. . . .
The wedding was at "high noon" followed by a very nice
luncheon. The second course of the luncheon was a slice
of brick ice cream with a lavender bell in the center. . . . and angel food cake plus fruit cake which had
been made from a recipe used at weddings in Mama's
family. My wedding dress was silk crepe—dainty flowers
on a deep purple background. I had a cream-colored
chiffon shoulder cape trimmed by deep cream lace on the
sleeves. Marion wore a vested dark blue suit. The weather
was good but later snowflakes fell on us as Bert Chittick
[Ada's brother-in-law] drove us in an open buggy to the
railroad depot to take the train, which came shortly after

two o'clock, to Des Moines. We stayed at the Savery Hotel. The great evangelist, Billy Sunday, was holding meetings not far from the hotel. We attended, and for the first time we heard the song "Brighten the Corner Where You Are" and never forgot the tune and the words. . . .

In Omaha we looked for furniture and purchased a brown leather covered large chair. . . .Among other gifts, Father Brinton had slipped me a $100 bill. This was spent for the chair. We received very useful gifts, many of which were used all our lives. . . .

Our years were busy happy ones. For years after moving to the country I still took part in various activities in town. I often drove to Lue's and to my parents' home. In fact I was away in the afternoon almost daily. Marion always inquired at noon if I had plans to go. If so, he harnessed a horse and left it hitched to the buggy all ready for me. After we had a car he made sure all was in readiness for me.

Marion had been a charter member of the Stuart Country Club. I was initiated. The club was a most worthwhile organization and the leading one of the vicinity. Most of the time the members were farm couples within the neighborhood. We were active for 55 years. Our topics and discussions were based on those of leading issues concerning the betterment of our homes, of our county and naturally concerning farm improvement. We had many good times together, meeting once a month in our homes. At no time did we play cards. We often had prominent outside speakers. At one time Henry A. Wallace, who later became Secretary of Agriculture and then Vice President of the United States, was our speaker. . . .

Corn picking was done by hand, throwing the husked ears into a wagon as a reliable team kept slowly walking ahead without interruption except to be turned at the end of the row. Marion picked 100 bushels a day, much above the average. At noon and at night the corn was shoveled by scoop into the corn crib. Marion was in the field by daybreak. That meant husking mittens getting soaked by the frost on the corn husks. Our kitchen range would have mittens laid on the oven door to dry out during that season of the year. As time went on Marion's third finger on his right hand became somewhat curved which he always said was caused by his grabbing the ear of corn off the stalk with a brass husking peg worn on his finger.

Sowing oats was accomplished by loading the seed into the wagon box with a mechanism on the end which could be adjusted as to the amount of seed allowed to go through and be evenly spread over a certain area. This was the only farming operation in which I helped. Marion drove the team (later, the tractor) while I rode in the wagon box to see that enough grain was being pushed into the spreader—not a hard job!

During the years when our family was growing up and we had hired men I did a great deal of canning of fruit, vegetables and meat—chicken, beef and pork which we raised. Thus we did not have a problem of going to the butcher shop in town except when large roasts were required to feed the twenty or more threshers, plus the women who helped prepare the food. Bread, pies and cakes were baked at home, of course. In reading my diary of 1935, I came upon the following menu for threshers at our home that year: mashed potatoes, beef roast, gravy, ham loaf, baked kidney beans, creamed corn, home made cottage cheese, dill pickles, apples cooked with lemons, plum jelly, fresh rolls and butter (both home made), two kinds of cake, home made ice cream, iced tea, coffee and cream.

During my early days on the farm and during World War I, everyone was making their own soap for laundry work. Of course on the farm where home butchering was done it was an easy thing to have the required grease. Tallow was melted along with hog fat—in fact the tallow presumably made better soap, but it was not used alone. I am going to record a recipe which should produce good results: 5 lbs. grease, 5 qt. of cold *soft* water, 1 cup lye, $\frac{1}{2}$ cup ammonia, $\frac{1}{2}$ cup Perfex can also be dissolved and added. Dissolve lye in a little soft water. Mix with all ingredients. Stir until creamy and it thickens. Pour mixture to set into enamel, stoneware, or a wooden box lined with white cloth. (We used the latter.) Don't get mixture on hands until the hard soap stage.

The job of washing clothes was quite different from nowadays! In town my mother used a copper boiler in which to boil white clothes and to heat the wash water. At least she had good facilities for those days. The pump was outside the door of the cement floored room in the basement which opened up onto the ground level. We had a stove down there, so water didn't have to be carried far. If the water was hard, some lye was put into the boiler of water which brought a thick foam up on the top. The foam was dipped off. Often some bluing was added. The washing machine was hand propelled. On the farm my machine was run by a small gasoline motor until we had electricity—I also had a double tub machine. Time was saved with that as one tub could be used for rinsing. Later I had an enamel lined electric machine and finally we had a modern washer and dryer installed on our back porch. We always had soft water in our entire water system on the farm. Our large cistern filled from gutters around the roof of the house. Water was heated by pipes running through the cook stove and stored in a tank back of the stove.

For refrigeration, butter and sweet cream were placed in a bucket which was lowered on a rope down to the top of the water in the well. When our house was built, Marion had a hole, perhaps ten feet deep, made in the basement floor. The hole was cemented like a cistern. A dumb waiter with shelves was lowered and raised by a small chain on a pulley. This kept food reasonably cool.

The principal fuel for our cook stove during the summer was cobs, as they made a quick hot fire, though frequent refueling was necessary. It was a chore to keep enough cobs available. Many were picked up from hog feed lots. These had a distinctive odor not appreciated! The cattle feed bunks and the horse feed boxes in the barn provided the other cob sources. Wood, if available around the place, and coal were also used in the cook stove. In our early days there were two or three small spots north of town where coal was mined, but it was a poor grade (too much slate or too soft) and choked up the stove and pipes.

Stuart had Chautauqua for a number of years. This was held in a large tent on the grounds of the West School for a week in August and provided entertainment for both afternoon and evening shows. This was well attended and people came from Menlo and Dexter, as well as the Stuart community, to enjoy the programs. The advent of radio spoiled the Chautauquas.

Saturday night was the time when farmers particularly "went to town." Chores and supper were hurried up as it was important to park one's car in a favorable spot so that after grocery buying the car could be used from which to watch others going by. Among other errands the men would drop in at the barber shop to wait for a haircut and shave (in many cases decidedly changing their appearance for the better). The younger members of a family located their friends and spent a little money on confections to their liking and walked up and down the street. If fortunate enough to have arrived in town for the early picture show, the young people often went there and afterwards knew where to find their parents "passing the time of day" with a friend or two. I am sorry to say that we often saw those who had taken a "drink" or two too many at one of the Beer Parlors or the Pool Hall. Some unfortunate hired men had little left in their pockets after a Saturday night in town.

We had some exceedingly rough years in the 1930's during the Depression and Drought. We had to count our pennies, for prices for farm products touched bottom. Many supposedly well-to-do people lost all they possessed. In most cases home farms were mortgaged in order to buy more land. Then, when prices for farm products dropped, the income wouldn't cover the indebtedness and *all* was lost. One of our good neighbor friends had a few days left before foreclosure. We were told of his determination not to lose. He took an unprecedented chance and called President Franklin D. Roosevelt personally, stating his dilemma. Our friend was told that help would come, and the bank was ordered not to proceed with its intended foreclosure. . . . We found help from an old friend who was one of the few people who had money. He loaned us what was needed and insisted that if we could not pay the interest when it came due that we were not to worry, just pay when possible.

Of course we went through some hard times—the Depression and Drought. We tried to spend our money wisely and therefore we enjoyed many extras that came within our lifetime. We did not use tobacco or liquor. We suffered the loss of two children. But we were blessed by two very precious girls whom we tried to guide in the right ways of life, and they did not disappoint us.

We lost Marion on April 28, 1974, at the Dexter, Iowa, Hospital. I had no thought of leaving the home Marion and I had enjoyed for close to sixty years but this was suddenly changed by events on October 9, 1974.[1] Following this experience, my family insisted that I could no longer live in my home on the farm. By great luck there was a comfortable one-bedroom apartment vacant in Stuart's Retirement Apartments and I have lived here since October, 1974. . . .

---

[1] On this date her home was burglarized; her children decided it was no longer safe for her to live there.

"I Have Planted Flowers Everywhere"
Elinore Pruitt Stewart

If you have seen the film Heartland *then you already know part of Elinore Pruitt Stewart's story. She wanted a homestead for herself and her daughter, so she answered a newspaper ad and went to work for Clyde Stewart on his homestead near Burnt Fork, Wyoming. In addition to working for Stewart, she filed on an adjacent claim. During the next four years she married Stewart, bore four children and "proved up" on her homestead. In* Letters of a Woman Homesteader, *Elinore describes her daily chores, her horseback rides through the country, and the people she meets.*

In a letter written on 2 December 1912, Elinore tells her friend about her marriage to Stewart. She also lists the satisfactions she has experienced in Wyoming. She says, among other things, that she has "loads and loads of flowers which I tend myself." Although it is not apparent in this passage, her flowers are essential to her psychological well-being. In another collection of letters, Letters on an Elk Hunt, *Elinore eloquently describes the role that flowers play in her life:*

> *The cattle died in piles and the horses died in other piles and I didn't want to write to anyone. But I can tell you, my dear, that it is a relief when things get to their worst. You know what the worst is*

then and can begin to plan better things.
That's what I have done. I have planted
flowers everywhere.

Source:
Elinore Pruitt Stewart. Letters of a Woman Homesteader.
1914. Foreword by Gretel Ehrlich. Boston: Houghton
Mifflin, 1988. 15-21, 137-42, 184-92, 213-16.

Dear Mrs. Coney,

This has been for me the busiest, happiest summer I can remember. I have worked very hard, but it has been work that I really enjoy. Help of any kind is very hard to get here, and Mr. Stewart had been too confident of getting men, so that haying caught him with too few men to put up the hay. He had no man to run the mower and he couldn't run both the mower and the stacker, so you can fancy what a place he was in. I don't know that I ever told you, but my parents died within a year of each other and left six of us to shift for ourselves. Our people offered to take one here and there among them until we should all have a place, but we refused to be raised on the halves and so arranged to stay at Grandmother's and keep together. Well, we had no money to hire men to do our work, so had to learn to do it ourselves. Consequently I learned to do many things which girls more fortunately situated don't even know have to be done. Among the things I learned to do was run a mowing-machine. It cost me many bitter tears because I got sunburned, and my hands were hard, rough and stained with machine oil, and I used to wonder how any Prince Charming could overlook all that in a girl he came to. For all I had ever read of the Prince had to do with his "reverently kissing her lily-white hand," or doing some other fool trick with a hand as white as a snow-flake. Well, when my Prince showed up he didn't lose

191

much time in letting me know that "Barkis [1] was willing," and I wrapped my hands in my old checked apron and took him up before he could catch his breath. Then there was no more mowing, and I almost forgot that I knew how until Mr. Stewart got into such a panic. If he put a man to mow, it kept them idle at the stacker, and he just couldn't get enough men. I was afraid to tell him I could mow for fear he would forbid me to do so. But one morning, when he was chasing a last hope of help, I went down to the barn, took out the horses, and went to mowing. I had enough cut before he got back to show him I knew how, and as he came back manless he was delighted as well as surprised. I was glad because I really like to mow, and besides that, I am adding feathers to my cap in a surprising way. When you see me again you will think I am wearing a feather duster, but it is only that I have been said to have almost as much sense as a "mon," and that is an honor I never aspired to, even in my wildest dreams.

I have done most of my cooking at night, have milked seven cows every day, and have done all the hay-cutting, so you see I have been working. But I have found time to put up thirty pints of jelly and the same amount of jam for myself. I used wild fruits, gooseberries, currants, raspberries and cherries. I have almost two gallons of cherry butter, and I think it is delicious. I wish I could get some of it to you, I am sure you would like it.

We began haying July 5 and finished September 8. After working so hard and so steadily I decided on a day off, so yesterday I saddled the pony, took a few things I needed, and Jerrine and I fared forth. Baby can ride quite well. We got away by sunup and a glorious day we had. We followed a stream higher up into the mountains and the air was so keen and clear at first we had on our coats. There was a tang of sage and of pine in the air, and our horse was midside deep in rabbit-brush, a shrub just covered with flowers that look and smell like golden-

---

[1] Reference to Dickens' *David Copperfield*.

rod. The blue distance promised many alluring adventures, so we went along singing and simply gulping in summer. Occasionally a bunch of sage chickens would fly up out of the sagebrush, or a jack rabbit would leap out. Once we saw a bunch of antelope gallop over a hill, but we were out just to be out, and game didn't tempt us. I started out, though, to have just as good a time as possible, so I had a fish-hook in my knapsack.

Presently, about noon, we came to a little dell where the grass was as soft and as green as a lawn. The creek kept right up against the hills on one side and there were groves of quaking asp and cottonwoods that made shade, and service-bushes and birches that shut off the ugly hills on the other side. We dismounted and prepared to noon. We caught a few grasshoppers and I cut a birch pole for a rod. The trout are so beautiful now, their sides are so silvery, with dashes of old rose and orange, their speckles are so black, while their backs look as if they had been sprinkled with gold-dust. They bite so well that it doesn't require any special skill or tackle to catch plenty for a meal in a few minutes.

In a little while I went back to where I had left my pony browsing, with eight beauties. We made a fire first, then I dressed my trout while it was burning down to a nice bed of coals. I had brought a frying-pan and a bottle of lard, salt, and buttered bread. We gathered a few service-berries, our trout were soon browned, and with water, clear, and as cold as ice, we had a feast. The quaking aspens are beginning to turn yellow, but no leaves have fallen. Their shadows dimpled and twinkled over the grass like happy children. The sound of the dashing, roaring water kept inviting me to cast for trout, but I didn't want to carry them so far, so we rested until the sun was getting low and then started for home, with the song of the locusts in our ears warning us that the melancholy days are almost here. We would come up over the top of a hill into the glory of a beautiful sunset with its gorgeous colors, then down into the little valley already purpling with mysterious twilight. So on, until, just at dark, we rode into our corral and a mighty tired, sleepy little girl was powerfully glad to get home.

After I mailed my other letter I was afraid that you would think me plumb bold about the little Bo-Peep, and was a heap sorrier than you can think. If you only knew the hardships these poor men endure. They go two together and sometimes it is months before they see another soul, and rarely ever a woman. I wouldn't act so free in town, but these men see people so seldom that they are awkward and embarrassed. I like to put them at ease, and it is to be done only by being kind of hail-fellow-well-met with them. So far not one has ever misunderstood me and I have been treated with every courtesy and kindness, so I am powerfully glad you understand. They really enjoy doing these little things like fixing our dinner, and if my poor company can add to any one's pleasure I am too glad.

Sincerely yours,
Elinore Rupert

The New House

December 1, 1911

Dear Mrs. Coney,

I feel just like visiting to-night, so I am going to "play like" you have come. It is so good to have you to chat with. Please be seated in this low rocker; it is a present to me from the Pattersons and I am very proud of it. I am just back from the Patterson ranch, and they have a dear little boy who came the 20th of November and they call him Robert Lane.

I am sure this room must look familiar to you, for there is so much in it that was once yours. I have two rooms, each fifteen by fifteen, but this one on the south is my "really" room and in it are my treasures. My house faces east and is built up against a side-hill, or should I say hillside? Anyway, they had to excavate quite a lot. I had them dump the dirt right before the house and terrace it smoothly. I have sown my terrace to California poppies, and around my porch, which is six feet wide and thirty long, I have planted wild cucumbers.

Every log in my house is as straight as a pine can grow. Each room has a window and a door on the east side, and the south room has two windows on the south with space between for my heater, which is one of those with a grate front so I can see the fire burn. It is almost as good as a fireplace. The logs are unhewed outside because I like the rough finish, but inside the walls are perfectly square and smooth. The cracks in the walls are snugly filled with "daubing" and then the walls are covered with heavy gray building-paper, which makes the room very warm, and I really like the appearance. I had two rolls of wall-paper with a bold rose pattern. By being very careful I was able to cut out enough of the roses, which are divided in their choice of color as to whether they should be red, yellow, or pink, to make a border about eighteen inches from the ceiling. They brighten up the wall and the gay paper is fine to hang pictures upon. Those you have sent us make our room very attractive. The woodwork is stained a walnut brown, oil finish, and the floor is stained and oiled just like it. In the corners by the stove and before the windows we take our comfort.

From some broken bamboo fishing-rods I made frames for two screens. These I painted black with some paint that was left from the buggy, and Gavotte fixed the screens so they will stay balanced, and put in casters for me. I had a piece of blue curtain calico and with brass-headed tacks I put it on the frame of Jerrine's screen, then I mixed some paste and let her decorate it to suit herself on the side that should be next her corner. She used the cards you sent her. Some of the people have a suspiciously tottering appearance, perhaps not so very artistic, but they all mean something to a little girl whose small fingers worked patiently to attain satisfactory results. She has a set of shelves on which her treasures of china are arranged. On the floor is a rug made of two goatskins dyed black, a present from Gavotte, who heard her admiring Zebbie's bearskin. She has a tiny red rocking-chair which she has outgrown, but her rather dilapidated family of dolls use it for an automobile. For a seat for herself she has a small hassock that you gave me, and behind the blue screen is a world apart.

My screen is made just like Jerrine's except that the cover is cream material with sprays of wild roses over it. In my corner I have a cot made like a couch. One of my pillows is covered with some checked gingham that "Dawsie" cross-stitched for me. I have a cabinet bookcase made from an old walnut bedstead that was a relic of the Mountain Meadow Massacre. Gavotte made it for me. In it I have my few books, some odds and ends of china, all gifts, and a few fossil curios. For a floor-covering I have a braided rug of blue and white, made from old sheets and Jerrine's old dresses. In the center of my room is a square table made of pine and stained brown. Over it is a table-cover that you gave me. Against the wall near my bed is my "dresser." It is a box with shelves and is covered with the same material as my screen. Above it I have a mirror, but it makes ugly faces at me every time I look into it. Upon the wall nearby is a match-holder that you gave me. It is the heads of two fisher-folk. The man has lost his nose, but the old lady still thrusts out her tongue. The material on my screen and "dresser" I bought for curtains, then decided to use some white crossbar I had. But I wish I had not, for every time I look at them I think of poor little Mary Ann Parker.

I am going to make you a cup of tea and wonder if you will see anything familiar about the teapot. You should, I think, for it is another of your many gifts to me. Now I feel that you have a fairly good idea of what my house looks like, on the inside anyway. The magazines and Jerrine's cards and Mother Goose book came long ago, and Jerrine and I were both made happy. I wish I could do nice things for you, but all I can do is to love you.

Your sincere friend,
Elinore Rupert

The Homesteader's Marriage and a Little Funeral

December 2, 1912

Dear Mrs. Coney,

Every time I get a new letter from you I get a new inspiration, and I am always glad to hear from you.

I have often wished I might tell you all about my Clyde, but have not because of two things. One is I could not even begin without telling you what a good man he is, and I didn't want you to think I could do nothing but brag. The other reason is the haste I married in. I am ashamed of that. I am afraid you will think me a Becky Sharp[2] of a person. But although I married in haste, I have no cause to repent. That is very fortunate because I have never had one bit of leisure to repent in. So I am lucky all around. The engagement was powerfully short because both agreed that the trend of events and ranch work seemed to require that we be married first and do our "sparking" afterward. You see, we had to chink in the wedding between times, that is, between planting the oats and other work that must be done early or not at all. In Wyoming ranchers can scarcely take time even to be married in the springtime. That having been settled, the license was sent for by mail by Mr. Pearson, the justice of the peace and a friend of long standing. I had never met any of the family and naturally rather dreaded to have them come, but Mr. Stewart was firm in wanting to be married at home, so he told Mr. Pearson he wanted him and his family to come up the following Wednesday and serve papers on the "woman i' the hoose." They were astonished, of course, but being such good friends they promised him all the assistance they could render. They are quite the dearest, most interesting family! I have since learned to love them as my own.

Well, there was no time to make wedding clothes, so I had to "do up" what I did have. Isn't it queer how sometimes, do what you can, work will keep getting in the way until you can't get anything done? That is how

---

[2] Reference to Thackeray's *Vanity Fair*.

it was with me those few days before the wedding; so
much so that when Wednesday dawned everything was
topsy-turvy and I had a very strong desire to run away.
But I always did hate a "piker," so I stood pat. Well, I
had most of the dinner cooked, but it kept me hustling
to get the house into anything like decent order before
the old dog barked, and I knew my moments of liberty
were limited. It was blowing a perfect hurricane and
snowing like midwinter. I had bought a beautiful pair of
shoes to wear on that day, but my vanity had squeezed
my feet a little, so while I was busy at work I had kept
on a worn old pair, intending to put on the new one
later; but when the Pearsons drove up all I thought about
was getting them into the house where there was a fire,
so I forgot all about the old shoes and the apron I wore.

I had only been here six weeks then, and was a
stranger. That is why I had no one to help me and was
so confused and hurried. As soon as the newcomers were
warm, Mr. Stewart told me I had better come over by
him and stand up. It was a large room I had to cross,
and how I did it before all those strange eyes I never
knew. All I can remember very distinctly is hearing Mr.
Stewart saying, "I will" and myself chiming in that I
would, too. Happening to glance down, I saw that I had
forgotten to take off my apron or my old shoes, but just
then Mr. Pearson pronounced us man and wife, and as I
had dinner to serve right away I had no time to worry
over my odd toilet. Anyway the shoes were comfortable
and the apron white, so I suppose it could have been
worse; and I don't think it has ever made any difference
with the Pearsons, for I number them all among my most
esteemed friends.

It is customary here for newlyweds to give a dance
and supper at the hall, but as I was a stranger I preferred not to, and so it was a long time before I became
acquainted with all my neighbors. I had not thought I
should ever marry again. Jerrine was always such a dear
little pal, and I wanted to just knock about foot-loose
and free to see life as a gypsy sees it. I had planned to
see the Cliff-Dwellers' Home; to live right there until I
caught the spirit of the surroundings enough to live over

their lives in imagination anyway. I had planned to see the old missions and to go to Alaska; to hunt in Canada. I even dreamed of Honolulu. Life stretched out before me one long, happy jaunt. I aimed to see all the world I could, but to travel unknown bypaths to do it. But first I wanted to try homesteading.

But for my having the grippe, I would never have come to Wyoming. Mrs. Seroise, who was a nurse at the institution for nurses in Denver while I was a housekeeper there, had worked one summer at Saratoga, Wyoming. It was she who told me of the pine forests. I had never seen a pine until I came to Colorado; so the idea of a home among the pines fascinated me. At that time I was hoping to pass the Civil-Service examination, with no very definite idea as to what I would do, but just to be improving my time and opportunity. I never went to public school a day in my life. In my childhood days there was no such thing in the Indian Territory part of Oklahoma where we lived, so I have had to try hard to keep learning. Before the time came for the examination I was so discouraged because of the grippe that nothing but the mountains, the pines, and the clean, fresh air seemed worth while; so it all came about just as I have written you.

So you see I was very deceitful. Do you remember I wrote you of a little baby boy dying? That was my own little Jamie, our first little son. For a long time my heart was crushed. He was such a sweet, beautiful boy. I wanted him so much. He died of erysipelas. I held him in my arms till the last agony was over. Then I dressed the beautiful little body for the grave. Clyde is a carpenter; so I wanted him to make the little coffin. He did it every bit, and I lined and padded it, trimmed and covered it. Not that we couldn't afford to buy one or that our neighbors were not that kind and willing; but because it was a sad pleasure to do everything for our little first-born ourselves.

As there had been no physician to help, so there was no minister to comfort, and I could not bear to let our baby leave the world without leaving any message to a community that sadly needed it. His little message to us had been love, so I selected a chapter from John and we had a funeral service, at which all our neighbors for thirty miles around were present. So you see, our union is sealed by love and welded by a great sorrow.

Little Jamie was the first little Stewart. God has given me two more precious little sons. The old sorrow is not so keen now. I can bear to tell you about it, but I never could before. When you think of me, you must think of me as one who is truly happy. It is true, I want a great many things I haven't got, but I don't want them enough to be discontented and not enjoy the many blessings that are mine. I have my home among the blue mountains, my healthy, well-formed children, my clean, honest husband, my kind, gentle milk cows, my garden which I make myself. I have loads and loads of flowers which I tend myself. There are lots of chickens, turkeys, and pigs which are my own special care. I have some slow old gentle horses and an old wagon. I can load up the kiddies and go where I please any time. I have the best, kindest neighbors and I have my dear absent friends. Do you wonder I am so happy? When I think of it all, I wonder how I can crowd all my joy into one short life. I don't want you to think for one moment that you are bothering me when I write you. It is a real pleasure to do so. You're always so good to let me tell you everything. I am only afraid of trying your patience too far. Even in this long letter I can't tell you all I want to; so I shall write you again soon. Jerrine will write too. Just now she has very sore fingers. She has been picking gooseberries, and they have been pretty severe on her brown little paws.

With much love to you, I am
"Honest and truly" yours,
Elinore Rupert Stewart

The Joys of Homesteading

January 23, 1913.

Dear Mrs. Coney,—

I am afraid all my friends think I am very forgetful and that you think I am ungrateful as well, but I am going to plead not guilty. Right after Christmas Mr. Stewart came down with *la grippe* and was so miserable that it kept me busy trying to relieve him. Out here where we can get no physician we have to dope our-selves, so that I had to be housekeeper, nurse, doctor, and general overseer. That explains my long silence.

And now I want to thank you for your kind thought in prolonging our Christmas. The magazines were much appreciated. They relieved some weary night-watches, and the box did Jerrine more good than the medicine I was having to give her for *la grippe*. She was content to stay in bed and enjoy the contents of her box.

When I read of the hard times among the Denver poor, I feel like urging them every one to get out and file on land. I am very enthusiastic about women home-steading. It really requires less strength and labor to raise plenty to satisfy a large family than it does to go out to wash, with the added satisfaction of knowing that their job will not be lost to them if they care to keep it. Even if improving the place does go slowly, it is that much done to stay done. Whatever is raised is the homesteader's own, and there is no house-rent to pay. This year Jerrine cut and dropped enough potatoes to raise a ton of fine potatoes. She wanted to try, so we let her, and you will remember that she is but six years old. We had a man to break the ground and cover the pota-toes for her and the man irrigated them once. That was all that was done until digging time, when they were ploughed out and Jerrine picked them up. Any woman strong enough to go out by the day could have done every bit of the work and put in two or three times that much, and it would have been so much more pleasant than to work so hard in the city and then be on starva-tion rations in the winter.

To me, homesteading is the solution of all poverty's problems, but I realize that temperament has much to do with success in any undertaking, and persons afraid of coyotes and work and loneliness had better let ranching alone. At the same time, any woman who can stand her own company, can see the beauty of the sunset, loves growing things, and is willing to put in as much time and careful labor as she does over the wash tub, will certainly succeed; will have independence, plenty to eat all the time, and a home of her own in the end.

Experimenting need cost the homesteader no more than the work, because by applying to the Department of Agriculture at Washington he can get enough of any seed and any kinds as he wants to make a thorough trial, and it doesn't even cost postage. Also one can always get bulletins from there and from the Experiment Station of one's own State concerning any problem or as many problems as may come up. I would not, for anything, allow Mr. Stewart to do anything toward improving my place, for I want the fun and experience myself. And I want to be able to speak from experience when I tell others what they can do. Theories are very beautiful, but facts are what must be had, and what I intend to give some time.

Here I am boring you to death with things that cannot interest you! You'd think I wanted you to homestead, wouldn't you? But I am only thinking of the troops of tired, worried women, sometimes even cold and hungry, scared to death of losing their places to work, who could have plenty to eat, who could have good fires by gathering the wood, and comfortable homes of their own, if they but had the courage and determination to get them.

I must stop right now before you get so tired you will not answer. With much love to you from Jerrine and myself, I am

Yours affectionately,
Elinore Rupert Stewart

Two Young Women Homesteaders
Edith Eudora Kohl

When Edith Kohl published her book Land of the Burnt
Thigh *in 1938, a* New York Times *book reviewer announced that it was "one of the most interesting books of
Western settlement" to have appeared in a long time. Two
factors contributed to the popularity of the book. First, it
demonstrated that there were still pioneers struggling in
the wilderness in the first decade of the 20th century.
Second, it brought to the reader's attention that some of
those pioneers were single women. In 1907 Edith and her
sister, Ida Mary Ammons, attempted to establish a
homestead near Pierre, South Dakota. While they lacked
the usual resources for "proving up," they had other kinds
of talents that enabled them to establish their claim: they
taught school, published a newspaper* (The Wand), *ran a
printing shop, a store and a post office.*

*In the following passage Kohl shows the suffering
endured by a whole community. In desperation, Kohl goes
to the Indian chief to beg for help. The Indians provide
assistance, but the chapter ends with another disaster—a
prairie fire.*

Source:
Edith Eudora Kohl. Land of the Burnt Thigh. *New York:
Funk, 1938.*

The Thirsty Land

"You'd better do a little exhortin'," Ma told me on my return to the claim. "And if you get any collections, turn some of them in for the good of the store."

"Isn't business good?"

"Business is pouring in. It's money I'm talking about; there won't be any money until the crops are threshed—which will be about Christmas time out here. Now in Blue Springs——"

I didn't hear the rest of it. In the city I had been struck by the lavish spending of money, money which was at such a premium out here. There was something shockingly disproportionate in the capacity to spend by city people and those on farms.

"At least, the crops look good."

"But," Ida Mary pointed out, "they need rain, and the dams are beginning to get low."

"What about the wells the settlers are digging for water supply?"

"They get nothing but dry holes," she told me. "Some of the settlers brought in well-drills, but they didn't find water. They don't know what to do."

All other issues faded into the background before the urgency of the water problem. I packed my city clothes deep down in the trunk, never to be worn again, and went to work!

A casual glance revealed no sign of the emergency we were facing. The Lower Brulé was a broad expanse of

green grass and grain, rippling gently in the breeze like
water on a quiet sea. Sufficient moisture from the snow
and early rain had been retained in the subsoil for
vegetation. But we needed water. With the hot weather
the dams were going dry. There had been increased
demands for water this summer, and there had not been
the late torrential rains to fill the dams as there had been
the year before.

"What are we going to do?" I asked the other settlers.

"Haul water until we can get wells. We'll have to dig
deeper. Perhaps we have just not struck the water veins.
After this we will follow the draws."

Water-hauling again! But haul it from where? There
was no supply in the country sufficient for the needs of
the region. Drills would cost money, and few settlers had
any money left. There was no sign of rain, and an
oppression weighed upon everyone as of impending
evil—the fear of a water famine.

First we had come to understand the primitive
worship of fire. Now we began to know that water is as
vital to life as air itself. It takes experience to bring
home the meaning of familiar words.

In the meantime the tall waving crops brought land
agents with their buyers. At the first sign of water
shortage more claims were offered for sale, and by that
time there were a few deeded tracts put on the market.
Loan agents camped at the settlement, following up
settlers ready to prove up. One could borrow more than a
thousand dollars on a homestead now.

The money coming through our hands on relinquish-
ments, options, government payments, etc., was mainly in
bulk and growing beyond the coffee cans and old shoes
where we secreted money awaiting deposit at the bank.
We did need a bank on the Brulé.

During the long hot summer weeks, when it did not
grow dark on the open plain until far into the night, a
great deal of traveling was done at night. It was easier
for man and horse. On moonlight nights that white light
shining through the thin atmosphere made the prairie as
light as day, but ghostly; moonlight softened the contours
of the plains and robbed them of their color; sounds

traveled great distances, seeming to come from space; the howling of coyotes down the draw, the shrill, busy sound of insects in the long grass, the stamping of the horses in the barn, accentuated the stillness; they did not break it. Even the prairie wind came softly, sweet with the scent of hay, not lifting its voice on those hushed nights.

With the stillness invading one's flesh and bones, and the prairie, washed by moonlight, stretching out beyond one's imagination, I wondered that I had ever feared space and quiet.

But out of the silence would come the rhythmic thud of a horse's feet and a loud hail. The Ammons settlement was a day-and-night institution. With a loud knock on the door would come the identification. "It's Alberts!" Or Kimball, or Pinchot—real estate agents. "I've got a man here who wants to pay a deposit on N.W. quarter of section 18. We're on our way to the Land Office. Want to be there when it opens."

One of us would light the print-shop lamp, make out the papers, take the money, and stumble back to bed. A sign, "CLOSED," or "NEVER CLOSED," would have been equally ineffective in stopping the night movement on the Strip. Homesteaders living miles away came after the long day's work to put in their proving-up notices. They must be in the paper the following day to go through the five weeks' publication before the date set at the Land Office. During those scorching weeks their days were taken up by hauling water and caring for things at home.

With those urgent night calls we did not stick a gun out as had the Presho banker. We were not greatly perturbed about the possibility of anyone robbing us. A burglar who could find the money would accomplish more than we could do half the time, so outlandish had the hiding places become. Imbert insisted that we keep a loaded gun or two on the place, but we knew nothing about handling guns and were more afraid of them than of being molested.

Ada put up her folding cot at night in the lean-to kitchen, and one day she brought a rawhide whip from home and laid it on the 2 x 4 scantling that girded the walls—"the two-be-four" she called it. "You don't need a gun," she said in her slow, calm voice. "Just give me a rawhide." With that sure strong arm of hers and the keen whip, one would never enter without shooting first.

There were a few nights when we woke to find Ada standing still as a statue in her long white cotton nightgown, straw-colored braids hanging down her back, rawhide in her right hand, only to find whoever had prowled around had driven on, or that it was Tim Carter, the lawyer, coming home from town intoxicated, talking and singing at the top of his voice.

During that clock-round period the days were usually quiet and we worked in shifts as much as our many duties permitted. "Come on, girls," Ma would call, "this ice tea is goin' to be hot if you don't come and drink it. Now this isn't made from dam water. Fred hauled it over from the crick. (Fred Farraday did things like that without mentioning them.) It's set in the cave all day. Now the Ladies' Aid back in Blue Springs sticks a piece of lemon on the glass to squeeze in—just to get your fingers all stuck up with. I never was one for mixing drinks."

Ma poured an extra glass for Van Leshout, who had just come in with letters to mail. "Tomorrow we'll have the lemonade separate. Come on, Heine, don't you want a glass of tea?"

"Naw." Offering Heine tea was the one thing that shook his calmness.

"You don't expect he-men like Heine to drink tea," protested Van Leshout. A sly grin on Heine's face which the artist quickly caught on paper.

"Pa drinks it," from Ma, with the snapping of the jaw which in Ma expressed emphasis. Poor old Pa was the shining example of masculinity in her eyes.

Like a sudden breath the hot winds came. The dams were getting dangerously low. The water was dirty and green-scummed and thick. And Ada's folks lost a horse and a cow—alkalied.

The drier it became the whiter the ground on the alkali spots. We had no alkali on the great, grassy Brulé, but there were strips outside the reservation thick with it, and the water in those sections contained enough of it to turn one's stomach into stone.

Carrying the mail from the stage, I saw along the trail horses and cattle leaning against the fences, or lying down, fairly eaten up with it, mere skin and bones; mane and tail all fallen out, hoove dropped off.

A number of settlers had not a horse left that could put his foot to the ground to travel. Every day there were a few more horses and cows lying dead over the pastures. Gradually, however, most of the afflicted stock picked up, got new hooves, new manes and tails.

The livestock, even the dogs and the wild animals on the plains, drank from little holes of reservoirs at the foot of the slopes until the water became so hot and ill-smelling that they turned away from it.

But the settlers skimmed back the thick green scum, dipped up the water, let it settle, and used it. The dam water must be boiled, we warned each other, yet we did not always wait for a drink of water until it had been boiled and cooled. Late that summer, when the drying winds parched the country, the dams became the only green spots left on the yellow plains. But the dry for rain was no longer for the fields, it was for the people themselves.

A few narrow, crooked creeks cut their way through the great tableland of prairie. But they were as problematic as the Arkansas Traveler's roof in that they overflowed in the rainy season when we did not need water, and were dry as a bone when we did need it. The creeks were dry now—except the water holes in the creek beds and a few seep wells which homesteaders living near the creeks had dug and into which water from the creeks had seeped.

Proving-up time came for a few, and the ones who had not come to farm left as soon as they proved up—at least until the following year. And the situation was so serious we were glad to have them go—the fewer there were of us the less water we would need.

To add to the troubles of the homesteaders, there were increased activities by claim jumpers. Almost equal to the old cattle-rustling gangs were the land rustlers who "covered up" land as the cattle thieves did brands, making mavericks out of branded stock. Technicalities, false

filings, or open crookedness were used to hold rich
valleys and creeks and water holes open—or to block the
settler's proof title.

Because the problem was a federal one, the courts and
men like Judge Bartine were powerless to act in the
matter. The West needed fearless representation in Washington. If John Bartine were elected, westerners said, he
would fight the land graft. "But there must be a strong
campaign against it on the ground," he emphasized. "The
frontier newspapers can become the most powerful agency
in abolishing this evil."

"Could *The Wand* help?" I asked.

"Its influence not only would be effective," he assured
me, "but it would set a precedent and give courage to
other little proof sheets."

So *The Wand* took up the issue, using what influence
it had to bring a halt to the activities of the claim
jumpers. And the homesteaders continued their battle for
the thirsty land. Whisky barrels and milk cans were the
artillery most essential to keep this valiant army from
going down in defeat. They were as scarce as hen's teeth
and soared sky high in price, so great was the demand
on the frontier. Barrel and can manufacturers must have
made fortunes during the years of water-hauling in the
homestead country.

The size of a man's herd, and thus his rank as a
farmer, was judged by the number of barrels and cans
surrounding his shack or barn.

Ida Mary bought a barrel and several new milk cans.
"You cannot use the barrel for water," Joe Two-Hawk
said. "It is yet wet with fire-water." He drained a pint or
more of whisky from it. It would have to be burned
out. No one wanted fire-water these days.

Across the hot stretches, from every direction, there
moved processions of livestock being driven to water;
stoneboats (boards nailed across two runners), with barrels
bobbing up and down on them, buggies, wagons, all
loaded with cans and barrels.

Ida Mary and I led our livestock to a water hole three
miles away, filling water cans for ourselves. The Ammons
caravan moving across the hot, dry plain was a sorry

spectacle, with Ida in the vanguard astride old Pinto, her hair twisted up under a big straw hat. Lakota insisted upon jumping the creek bed, and we were not trained to riding to hounds. In the flank, the brown team and Lakota, the menagerie following behind. Coming up from the rear, I sat in the One-Hoss Shay behind Crazy Weed, the blind and locoed mare, with the water cans rattling in the back end of the buggy. I too wore an old straw hat, big as a ten-gallon sombrero, pushed back on my head to protect my sunburnt neck, and an old rag of a dress hanging loose on my small body, which was becoming thinner.

The sun blazed down on the shadeless prairie, and the very air smelled of heat. The grain was shriveled and burnt. And for shelter from the vast furnace, a tar-paper shack with a low roof.

As we reached the creek, Crazy Weed, smelling water, leaped to the creek bed, breaking the tugs as she went, leaving the horseless buggy, the empty cans and me high and dry on the bank.

We patched up the tugs, fastened them to the single tree with hairpins, hitched up Pinto, drove down to the water hole and filled our cans.

When we got back to the settlement we saw Lone Star on Black Indian, waiting for us. He dismounted, threw the reins to the ground and carried the water cans into the cool cave.

"Don't know what we're goin' to do with the range stock," he said anxiously, "with the grass dried up and the creeks and water holes on the range goin' dry."

"Lone Star," I said, "don't you think it's going to rain soon?"

Yesterday I had asked Porcupine Bear, and he had shaken his head and held up one finger after another, counting off the moons before rain would come.

"What will become of the settlers?" asked Ida Mary.

"The quicker these homesteadin' herds vacate," Lone Star answered in that slow drawl of his, "the better for everybody. The hot winds have come too early. Goin' to burn the pastures, looks like; hard to find water now for the cattle."

He handed us two flasks of cold water. "Brought 'em from the river; filled 'em while the water was cold early this morning."

Cold, clear water! We drank great long draughts of it, washed ourselves clean and fresh in a basin half-full of water.

One day Tim Carter came by sober. "The damn homestead is too dry for a man to drink water, say nothing of whisky," he stormed. "I'm going to have water if it takes my last dollar."

He brought in a drill. For several days neighbors helped with the drilling; others flocked around with strained anxiety, waiting, waiting for that drill to strike water.

The one scorching afternoon the drillers gave a whoop as they brought up the drill. "Oil! Oil! There's oil on this drill. Damned if we ain't struck oil!"

Tim Carter's straight, portly figure drooped. He put his hands in his pockets, staring aghast at the evidence before him. "Oil!" he shouted. "Who in hell wants oil? Nobody but Rockefeller. It's water we want!"

"Pack up your rig, boys," he said in a tone of defeat, as though he'd made a final plea in court and lost the case. A discouraged, disheartened group, they turned away.

Thirst became an obsession with us all, men and animals alike. Cattle, breaking out of pastures, went bawling over the plains; horses went running wildly in search of water. People were famished for a cold drink.

"I don't believe we ought to drink that water," I heard Ida Mary tell Ma Wagor, as she stood, dipper in hand, looking dubiously into the bucket.

"Oh, never mind about the germs," Ma said. "Just pick out them you see and them you can't see oughtn't hurt anybody. You can't be persnickety these days." With all that we could see in the water, it did seem as though the invisible ones couldn't do much harm.

With the perverseness of nature, the less water one has the thirstier one becomes. When it is on tap one doesn't think of it. But down to the last half-gallon, our thirst was unquenchable.

The store's supply of salmon and dried beef went begging, while it kept a team busy hauling canned tomatoes, sauerkraut, vinegar. People could not afford lemons, so vinegar and soda were used to make a refreshing, thirst-quenching drink.

Homesteaders reached the point where the whole family washed in the same quart of water. A little more soap and elbow grease, the women said, was the secret. Most of the water used for household purposes did double or triple duty. The water drained from potatoes was next used to wash one's face or hands or dishes; then it went into the scrub bucket. Potato water kept one's hands and face soft, we boasted; it was as effective as face cream.

But I was not a tea-cup saver by nature. Could the time and scheming of those pioneer women to save water have been utilized in some water project, it would have watered the whole frontier. But gradually we were becoming listless, shiftless. We were in a stage of endurance in which there was no point in forging ahead. We merely sat and waited—for rain or wells or whatever might come.

And always when we were down to the last drop, someone would bring us water. I never knew it to fail. One such time we looked up to see Huey Dunn coming. He had made the long trip just to bring us water—two whole barrels of it, although we had not seen him since he moved us to the reservation.

It was so hot he waited until evening to go back. He was in no hurry to return: it was too hot to work. But when had Huey ever been in a hurry? We sat in the shade of the shack, talking. He had dug a well, and his method of fall plowing—fallowing he called it—had proved successful.

Starting home toward evening, he called back, "If you girls take a notion to leave, you needn't send for me to move you—not until you get your deed, anyhow." I only saw him once after that—Ida Mary never again.

Ida Mary was seeing a lot of a young easterner that summer, an attractive, cultured boy who had taken a claim because he had won it in a lottery and it was an adventure. Imbert Miller had gone into the land business. He was well fitted for the work, with his honest, open manner, which inspired confidence in landseekers, and his deep-rooted knowledge of the West.

One day I looked up from my work with a belated thought.

"Imbert hasn't been here for some time. What's the matter?"

"He is to stay away until I send him word. I've got to be sure."

When there was any time for day-dreaming those days I conjured up pictures of snow banks and fountains and blessed, cooling rain, and long, icy drinks of water. The water had alkali in it and tasted soapy in cooking. But it was water. And we drank it gratefully.

The old man from the Oklahoma Run came over. Stooped and stiff, he leaned on his cane in the midst of a group of settlers who had met to discuss the drought and the water problem.

"Now, down in Oklahomy," he began, "it was hotter than brimstone and the Sooners didn't draw ice water from faucets when they settled there." Sooners, we took it, were those who got on the land sooner than the others. "Water was imported in barrels. Buying water was like buying champagne and worse to drink than cawn liquor."

"What did they do?"

"Well, suh," he went on, the long mustache twitching, "one of the fellahs down there was a water witch. He pointed out where the water could be got. Divining rods. That's the solution for the Strip."

But finding expert water witches was almost as difficult as finding water. They had to be imported from some remote section of the West. The witches, as we called them, went over various parts of the reservation, probing, poking with their forked sticks.

The divining rod was a simple means of locating water, and it had been in common use through the ages, especially in arid regions. It was used in some instances to locate other underground deposits. These rods were pronged branches, sometimes of willow, but preferably of witchhazel or wild cherry.

If there were water close to the surface, the divining rod would bend and turn with such force that it was hard to keep the prongs in hand. It was said to work by a process of natural attraction, and was formerly regarded as witchcraft or black magic.

Our divining rods refused to twist or bend. If there were water on the Strip, the witches missed it; either that, or it was too deep for the rods to detect. One of the experts said there was indication of some kind of liquid deposit far underground.

The settlers shook their heads and said there must be something wrong with the witches or the divining rod, and Ma Wagor declared, "I never did have any faith in them little sticks."

The hot winds swept the plains like blasts from a furnace. There was not a shelter as far as the eye could see except those little hot-boxes in which we lived. As the sun, like a great ball of fire, lowered to the horizon, a caravan topped the ridge from the north and moved slowly south across the Strip. A wagon and a wobble-wheeled buggy, its dry spokes rattling like castanets, went by. Following behind were the few head of stock-horses whinnying, cows bawling, for water. A panting dog, tongue hanging out, trotted beside the wagon. They were shipping out. The railroads were taking emigrants back to the state line free.

Leaving a land of plenty—plenty of everything but water.

A number of homesteaders who had come to stay were getting out. Settlers were proving up as fast as they could. They wanted to prove up while they could get loans on the land. Loan agencies that had vied with one another for the business were closing down on some areas. Despite the water famine, the Brulé had built such prestige, had made such a record of progress, that it was still holding the business. Western bankers kept their faith in it, but the lids of the eastern money-pots, which were the source of borrowing power, might be clamped down any day.

The railroads were taking people back to the state line free, if they wished to go. It seemed to me, exhausted as

I was, that I could not go on under these conditions, that the settlers themselves could not go on without some respite.

I walked into the Land Office at Pierre and threw a sheaf of proof notices on the Register's desk. He looked at them with practiced eyes. "These haven't been published yet," he said.

"I don't want them. I'm leaving the country. I came to get nine months' leave of absence for myself and all those whose time is not up. That would give us until next spring to come back and get our deeds."

He leaned over his desk. "Don't pull up and leave at this critical time, Edith," he said earnestly. "There are the legal notices, the loans, the post office—we have depended on you so much, it would be putting a wrench in the machinery out there."

He looked at me for a moment. "Don't start an emigration movement like that," he warned me.

I was dumfounded at his solemnity, at the responsibility he was putting upon me. It was my first realization of the fact that *The Wand* had indeed become the voice of the Brulé; that where it led, people would follow. If my going would start a general exodus, I had to stay.

I walked wearily out of the Land Office, leaving the proofs on his desk. It seemed to me that I had endured all I could, and here was this new sense of community responsibility weighing on me!

A young settler drove me home, and I sat bleakly beside him. It was late when we got near my claim, and the settlement looked dark and deserted. Suddenly I screamed, startling the horses, and leaped from the wagon as there was a loud crash. The heavy timbers of the cave back of the store had fallen in.

I shouted for Ida Mary, and there was no answer from the shack or the store. If she were under that wreckage. . . . Frantically we clawed at the timbers, clearing a space, looking for a slip of a girl with long auburn braids of hair. It was too dark to see clearly, and in my terror I was ripping the boards in any fashion while Jack strove to quiet me.

"What's the matter?" said a drowsy voice from the door of the shack. It was Ida Mary, who had slept so heavily she had not heard our arrival or our shouts or the crash of the cave-in.

I ran to her, sobbing with relief. "The cave's fallen in. I thought maybe you were in it."

She blinked sleepily and tried to comfort me. "I'm all right, sis," she said reassuringly. "It must have gone down after I went to bed. Too much sod piled on top, I guess. Now we'll have to have that fixed."

As I lay in bed, shaking with fatigue and nerve tension, Ida mumbled drowsily, "Oh, the fresh butter Ma brought me is down in that cave." And she fell asleep. A few moments later I too was sleeping quietly.

The nights were the life-savers. The evening, in which the air cooled first in the draws, then lifted softly to the tableland, cooling the body, quenching the thirst as one breathed it deeply. The fresh peaceful night. The early dawn which like a rejuvenating tonic gave one new hope. Thus we got our second wind for each day's bout.

The next day the proof notices I had turned in to the Land Office came back to me without comment. I explained to Ida Mary what I had done. "I told him we were going back, and he said I must not start an emigration movement. I applied for leaves of absence while the railroads are taking people to the state line free."

"And what," inquired Ida Mary dryly, "will they do at the state line? Go back to the wife's kinfolk, I suppose."

She was right, of course. I began to see what this trek back en masse would mean. What if the land horde went marching back? Tens of thousands of them milling about, homeless, penniless, jobless. Many of them had been in that position when they had stampeded the frontier, looking to the land for security. With these broad areas deserted, what would become of the trade and business; of the new railroads and other developments just beginning their expansion?

We were harder hit than most districts by the lack of water, but if that obstacle could be solved the Brulé had other things in its favor. The words of the Register came back to me: "Don't start an emigration movement."

The Wand came out with an editorial called, "Beyond the State Line, What?" It was based on Ida Mary's terse comment, "Back to the wife's kinfolk," and concluded with my own views of the economic disaster which such a general exodus would cause.

It took hold. Settlers who were ready to close their shacks behind them paused to look ahead—beyond the state line. And they discovered that their best chance was to fight it out where they were—if only they could be shown how to get water.

No trees. No shade. Hot winds sweeping as though from a furnace. And what water one had so hot and stale that it could not quench thirst.

We could ask our neighbors to share their last loaf of bread, but it was a bold, selfish act to ask for water. I have seen a gallon bucket of drinking water going down; have seen it get to the last pint; have held the hot liquid in my mouth as long as possible before swallowing it.

The distances to water were so long that many times we found it impossible, with all the work we had on hand, to make the trip; so we would save every drop we could, not daring to cook anything which required water.

One of the girl homesteaders came over with an incredible tale to tell. She had visited one of the settlers outside the reservation gate who had a real well. And his wife had rinsed the dishes when she washed them.

Ma prophesied that she would suffer for that.

Heine said one day, "My pa don't wanta leave. We ain't got no moneys to take us, Pa says."

There were many families in the same position. Get out? Where? How? . . . .

Of one thing there was no doubt. The grass on the Indian lands *was* greener than the grass on the settlers' lands. Through their land ran the Missouri River, and they had water to spare. While the homesteaders were famishing and their stock dying for water, it was going to waste in Indian territory. That areas was as peaceful as though the whole frontier were filled with clear, cool streams.

So Ida Mary and I went to the Indians for help. I presume we should have gone to the Agency, but we had never seen the government officials in charge, and we did know the Indians. . . .

We went before the chief and his council with form and ceremony. The old chief, dressed in dignified splendor, sat on a stool in front of his wigwam, a rich Navajo rug under his feet. He had been a great leader, wise and shrewd in making negotiations for his tribe. He looked at me and grunted.

I explained at length that I had come to him from the Brulé white men for help. But I got no farther. He threw out his hand in a negative gesture. The old warriors of the council were resentful, obstinate. They muttered and shook their heads angrily. No favors to the whites who had robbed them of their lands!

I sat down beside the chief while I talked to him, and then to other members of the council—to Porcupine Bear, Little Thunder, Night Pipe. The Indian demands pomp and ceremony in the transaction of affairs. These wanted to hold a powwow. But I had no time for ceremony.

The Indians had *minne-cha-lu-za* (swift-running water). We had none. If some of the settlers could run stock on their hunting ground where they could get to water, and if we could have water hauled from their lands, we would pay.

The old chief sat as immobile and dignified as a king in court. We soon learned that the Indian horse-and-bead traders are a different species from the high powers of the tribe sitting in council, making treaties. It was like appearing before a high tribunal.

"Take Indian lands. All time more," grunted one of them.

"The settlers' land is no good to the Indian," I argued; "no water, no berries, no wood, no more value. The government is making the whites pay money, not giving them allotments as they do the red men."

If they would not give us *minne-cha-lu-za,* I went on, we could not print the paper any more, or keep *she-la,* or trade for posts.

They went into ceremonious council, and delivered their concession officially by an interpreter, Little Thunder I think it was, attired in all his regalia of headdress with eagle feathers, beaded coat, and fringed breeches.

It appealed to their sense of power to grant the favor. At last the whites had to come to them for help. Whether the deal was official or unofficial, no one cared. In those crucial days Washington seemed to the homesteaders as remote as the gold gates.

We took a short-cut back. There was not a single building anywhere in sight, and the only moving thing was a herd of range cattle going slowly toward water. . . .

Some of the settlers turned stock over on the Indian lands after our negotiations, and the Indians hauled loads of life-giving water to the print shop now and then. Our collection of antique animals we turned loose to go back and live off the Indians.

"Might be it will rain," Heine said one day. "Did you see that cloud come by in front of the moon last night?"

But it wasn't a cloud. It was smoke.

"Wild with Heat and Thirst"
Anna Langhorne Waltz

Anna married a Baptist missionary pastor in 1911 and left her family's home in Pennsylvania. Two years later she and her husband filed on a claim near White River in Mellette County, South Dakota. Anna, with her five-month old daughter Dorothy, moved onto the claim. They lived there for 14 months, the time required to establish residency and "prove up." Her brother-in-law George and his wife Ruth lived on the adjoining homestead.

The following excerpts from Anna's memoirs focus on her last months on the homestead in the summer of 1914. She describes the unbearable heat as well as the prairie fire that swept across the land. After putting the fire out, however, the settlers put together an enormous chicken dinner to celebrate their victory over the fire. In the last episode, "Wild with Heat and Thirst," Anna reveals her most horrifying ordeal when, through a series of mishaps, she spills the drinking water and has no water for the baby.

Source:
Anna Langhorne Waltz. "West River Pioneer: A Woman's Story, 1911-1915. Parts Three and Four." South Dakota History *17 (1987): 242-48, 285-95.*

Summer

Another hot day! The summers in this prairie country are something to be avoided if possible. There are no trees, and the heat of the sun beats down on everything with relentless fury. Every living thing seems to wilt, ourselves included. Even the prairie dogs and coyotes stay down in their caves, and the snakes are loathe to crawl. There is no refrigeration, no ice, and not even a cold drink of water. Everything is hot—HOT!

We had not had a cool drink all summer, except for the few times we had driven into the village. By the time we arrived home over the hot, dusty trails, we were ready for more, but there was only warm water from the can down the cave. For days the heat had been intense, with the thermometer going up and up, day by day, until it reached 120 degrees.

We would hope for the blessed cooling of a shower, but each day the sun would set in a brassy sky that gave no promise of relief. Some days, a few light clouds would appear, and we would hope so much that they would gather into storm clouds. Instead, they would float silently away or vanish into the blue of the sky.

The sun's rays beating directly down on the roof of the soddie made it most unbearable, so I fixed up a cot down the cave, where I would carry baby for her morning nap and stay until the sun went down. We actually lived in the cave all during the extreme heat. So I was a cave woman, was I? Well, I did feel rather "cavey" but was very thankful for its being there, regardless of its not being the most beautiful place in which to find relief from the heat.

Dot was ten months old now and would amuse herself for hours by playing on the cot with her toys and chatting to them. She was making a few sounds like words, but it was mostly gibberish. It was fun to talk to her and have her chatter in answer. Her little naked body would feel as if it were on fire, so I would take a wet cloth, dampen her all over, and fan her. She seemed to realize I was doing something to make her comfortable. I took her food down with us to try to keep it from spoiling, so I did not have to leave her alone for very long at a time.

The thermometer outside would register between 115 and 120 degrees, but I knew inside the soddie during the heat of the day it was much higher. I would go inside to get something we needed and then rush down in the cave again, panting from the heat as if I would lose my breath. It was like opening an oven door and walking in. Everything I touched was hot—not warm, but hot—as if it would burst into flames. The very air seemed to scorch one's body clear through to the bones.

I had an uncomfortable feeling about staying down the cave at night, even though it took the soddie most of the night to cool off just a little. I was always on the alert for snakes, and when the coyotes started to growl and howl, I was ready to go inside. The heat would be so suffocating when we entered the soddie that I would spread a large rubber sheet on the floor, put baby on it, get a basin of water, and keep sprinkling her with it, telling her it was little raindrops from heaven. We would play it was raining until she was overcome with sleep, and then I'd put her in her little bed for the remainder of the night. I did this for so long that even after it had cooled off, Dot wanted to play "ain" every night before she went to bed.

I thought it would never cool off. After ten or more days of this dreadful heat, my garden was a wreck, with everything burned to the ground. This cut off our supply of fresh vegetables for the remainder of the summer, which was a real hardship out here so far from the trading post at White River. The few creeks were dry long since, and the river was so low it was almost impossible to scoop water into our barrels.

I would walk around the garden, where I had worked so hard and where everything had looked so promising and could hardly realize that it was gone—all gone. There was nothing left but dried-up vines and withered vegetables. It was hard to take, but I tried to think how much worse it could be—*that* I was soon to discover.

Prairie Fire

From the abundant rains early in the spring, the prairie grass was thick and high, although it was very brown now from the lack of moisture and from the intense heat. In places, the old tumbleweed had grown as high as a man, especially in the ravines where they were sheltered from the strong winds. These, also, were brown and dried out.

Early one afternoon, I saw smoke far to the west. Then I thought about how fast a prairie fire could travel over the dried-out prairie grasses and tumbleweed. The tumbleweed tears loose from the soil and goes rolling across the prairie at a terrific speed when the wind blows strong, as it usually does. If there should be a fire, this tumbleweed would spread it rapidly.

We had plowed a fireguard around the soddie, but it had become overgrown with weeds, and they were dry and chippy and would catch fire in a twinkling. If the weeds started to burn, I knew the soddie would, too, because dry brown grass was sticking out all over, making it look like a bristly porcupine. The wind was not in the right direction to bring the fire our way, and it was miles away from us. But to see even a tiny volume of smoke out on the prairie is cause for apprehension.

I went inside to get a lunch for baby. When I stepped outside a couple of hours later, I could smell the smoke and discovered the wind had changed and was blowing a strong gale from the west. I went to the west side of the soddie and, looking off in the distance, realized the fire was surely coming our way. It was still a long distance off, but I knew how quickly it could reach us with such a strong wind blowing. I ran to the pole and sent up the distress signal to attract the attention of my neighbors.

It was not long before George came over on one of the horses, leading the other one. He and Ruth had seen the smoke and prepared to come over for us even before they saw the signal. He told me to gather together whatever I could and get ready to leave quickly. Ruth, he said, was hitching the ponies to the wagon and would drive us all to the river, where we would be safe from the flames.

I was so confused I hardly knew what to grab first. This was one situation I had not anticipated. George helped me put some things—food and furniture—down the cave, where we thought they might escape the fire. I hurriedly grabbed all that I could of baby's clothing and some of my own. Piling baby's basket bed full, we jumped on the horses and crossed the canyon to their place as fast as we could. George held baby's bed, with her in it, in front of him on the saddle. I had several bundles hooked on my saddle and in my arms. The smoke was getting closer and thicker now, and we knew every minute counted.

When we reached their place, George gave instructions to put all our things in the wagon immediately and drive like lightning, regardless of trails, to the river. We took a can of water along so we could wet towels to put over our faces to keep from breathing too much smoke. George and the men from the creek bottom were staying to fight the fire.

Ruth and a son of a neighbor to the south drove the ponies, and the children and I huddled down in the bottom of the wagon. I kept the towels in circulation, taking the dry ones and handing back wet ones to the drivers and children while keeping one tied over my own face. I had fixed a tent-like affair over baby's bed by covering it with a heavy wet blanket, so she was fairly well protected as long as she stayed covered. But it was quite a task in itself to watch that she did not kick the blanket down on herself.

Ruth kept urging the broncos on to a swifter pace. They became quite excited from the constant urging and the strong smell of smoke. They kept snorting, tossing their heads, and shaking their manes and tails in a frenzied fashion. The drivers took turns and kept us going in a direct line toward the river. We did not follow the regular trail, so this made very rough going. The smoke was so dense now that we could not see the sky. It seemed like night was closing in on us. The surrounding territory looked as if it was shrouded in a heavy black veil.

We kept rushing madly on toward our goal and were cutting the space between us and the river by angling across the prairie as much as possible. We were going at quite a speed when, just before we reached the river, the left rear wheel of the wagon struck a buffalo wallow with such force that off came the wheel. Ruth pulled the broncos to a stop as quickly as possible. The children and I were all tossed to the corner of the wagon, but we were not hurt, just a little shaken up. Our water was almost gone anyway, so there was not much to spill.

The ponies were hurriedly unhitched, and for the remainder of the distance we rode horseback, all piled on the best we could, with Rover trotting along beside. We had to leave the wagon where it was, not knowing whether the fire would reach it or not.

We made it to the river, where we met a number of other women and children. All the men had stayed behind to fight the fire. The smoke had obscured the sky, so we did not see the clouds that were bringing us release and relief in a sudden downpour of rain. The rain reached the section out by the soddie long before it reached us, so the men had providential help in time to save the soddie and the other homes to the east. There were no homesteads to the west. Castaway lived out there, and we learned later that the fire had burned over a great deal of his land, but the dugout where he lived had been passed by since it was down over the ridge in the side of a canyon.

The men came galloping to the river to see how we had fared and to tell us that the fire had been brought under control without damage to our homes. We were, indeed, very fortunate. The men looked frightful. Their faces were blackened with smoke, soot, and the dust from the dirt bags they had wielded against the fire. Their eyes were bloodshot, and there were streaks where the rain had run down their faces and arms.

We let the ponies walk all the way home. Poor things, they had been so loyal and faithful in their race to the river and safety. The fire was out, but that awful smoky, burnt smell lingered for many days, and the atmosphere was like a fog. After the shower, the sun came out, but it did not look real through the smoke. It had a weird appearance, as if it were trying to penetrate some black curtain and struggling to give us its light. The whole range looked unreal.

Baby and I stayed with George and Ruth that night. They were concerned lest another fire start from some stray sparks being whipped into flames by the wind, as sometimes happens.

The next morning when we reached the soddie, all the prairie toward the west was black and dreary looking. The fire had come within about a half mile of the soddie. I tried to keep from looking in that direction because it was very depressing, but with it all there was so much to be thankful for. No one had lost his life, and our homes had been spared.

To offset the tension everyone felt from the effects of the fire, we planned to have a prairie-chicken dinner and get-together. Actually, it was to be a Thanksgiving dinner. There was, indeed, great thanksgiving in our hearts for God's intervening to prevent a greater destruction of life and belongings. The rain had come at the most opportune time. The fire had driven the prairie chickens our way as they tried to escape the flames, so for a week or more this section was just about overrun with them. The few men in this territory declared a holiday to go hunting together to get all the prairie chickens we would need for a big feast.

This time we were to meet at Noble and Maud Wickland's on the creek bottom. They had a real palatial frame dwelling of three rooms and an attic. The attic was reached by climbing a ladder on the outside of the house and entering through a small opening, but it was a grand place to store things and was the envy of all the women in the vicinity.

Early in the morning, the men took the women in a wagon over to Wickland's, where we were to prepare vegetables and other things while the men went after the chickens. We had a real happy time together, bustling around getting things ready.

It was not long before the men came back with enough chickens to feed a regiment. They said that in one place the birds were so numerous they could almost pick them up off the ground with their hands without having to shoot them. After the chickens were plucked, it looked like there were enough feathers to make a feather bed. All this was done outside, and feathers were flying in every direction. It looked almost like a snowstorm. I never saw so many chickens in my life. There were dozens of them.

With everyone sharing the task, it did not take long before the chickens were in the pan, frying and popping in the hot grease and being turned over and over until each piece was a rich golden brown and ready to eat. We carried it out to the table in the yard in huge kettles, and it was truly a feast. There was plenty of fluffy mashed potatoes and gravy, homemade pickles, heaps of homemade bread and rolls, butter, buffalo berry jelly, and chokecherry and wild plum jam. I think all the women brought as many kinds of homemade pickles and wild fruit jellies and jams as they could to show off their skills in culinary art—much to the satisfaction of everyone present. And the chicken! There was so much of it that after everyone had eaten all they could manage, every woman took enough home to last for several days.

Wild with Heat and Thirst

Ruth brought the ponies and buggy over because Dot and I were driving to White River to meet Daddy. Ruth had told me that they had to go to the village on business, so they would drive in along with us. (I am sure they did not want us to go alone.) I said how glad I was to have them go at the same time and that she should ride in the buggy with us. I dressed baby in all her pretty things, put on my best "bib and tucker," and off we went, full of joy and expectation.

The stage from the railroad would arrive in the late afternoon, but we could not get there too soon to suit me, so we started in the morning. We took our lunch and ate it down by the river, making a gala day of it. When we saw the dust from the stage a long way off, my heart started to pump a little faster. It was bringing our loved one to us, and this time baby and I would go back with him.

As the stage drew nearer, I kept getting more excited inside until I was afraid I would have to shout to keep from "busting." How proud I was to have Dot look so sweet and be able to walk to her daddy and talk to him. Just as the stage drove up to the trading post, I put baby down in front of me so she could walk to her daddy instead of being carried. My heart almost turned a flip-flop waiting for it to come to a complete stop. As last it stopped, and out stepped three men—and not one was Daddy.

What was wrong? Surely he was in the back seat and playing a joke on us. I went closer and peeped in the car but saw no one. I asked the stage driver if he had seen my husband get off the train, and he said he had not. My world was toppling around me! Where was my husband? He had never before disappointed me when he had made definite arrangements. Something unusual must have happened, or else he was sick.

We waited in the post office until the mail was sorted, but there was no letter from him. Ruth was so sympathetic and felt so badly about my disappointment. We waited until almost sundown, thinking perhaps he might come to White River in a private car, but he had written that he would come on the stage. We could not wait any longer, so we drove back home depressed, not knowing why he had failed to come.

Ruth drove with us over to the soddie, where I had fixed everything so pretty in anticipation of his arrival. We discussed many reasons why, perhaps, he could not get here, but I thought surely there would have been a letter or some message explaining the situation.

Ruth came in to stay awhile with me. During our conversation I said, "I even marked the day of his coming on the calendar, and here it is," handing the calendar to her.

She studied it a little, then looked up at me and said, "Anna, here is the reason he didn't come today—look, you marked the date in May instead of in June. You didn't tear May off, so you are four days ahead of time."

I looked at the calendar and, sure enough, there it was—May. I had been so eager to mark the date that I had marked the wrong month. I felt so silly and stupid, but it was a relief to know that it had been a mistake and that nothing was wrong. A heavy load was lifted from my heart.

The next day, Art Mountain went in to White River, and when he came back he stopped by George and Ruth's with a telegram for me, which Ruth immediately brought over. It was from my husband, and it was very disappointing. Instead of coming in four days, he would be delayed because of a funeral and a wedding and would not get here until the following week.

"Another disappointment," I said, "but I guess I can take it."

"I'm so sorry," Ruth said. "And we've already made arrangements to be gone for three days or more because we thought Pierce would be here with you."

I told Ruth that I wouldn't mind being alone for such a few days and they should go right ahead with their trip. They had been so wonderful to us all along the way that I just couldn't interfere with their plans.

"I'll be so busy getting things together that I want to take with me, I won't even notice being alone," I said. "So you folks go right ahead."

"We just wouldn't go now," Ruth said, "not with you being alone and the heat as bad as it is, but it seems this will be the only time we'll be able to get away for the rest of the summer." They decided to leave two days later and would be back before my husband arrived.

The next evening the whole family drove over to bring some extra milk, to see if I had enough water, and to say goodbye. They were leaving the next morning. George looked in the water barrel, which was almost full, and then asked about our drinking water. I told him we had plenty in the can in the cave. He said they had some extra, but seeing I had enough, they would pour what they had in a few pans and buckets for the chickens and the dog. They had left adequate food for all the animals for the time they would be gone, and Noble Wickland was to ride over each evening to see that all was well with the stock. Because they were to leave before daylight, we said our goodbyes, and they left our place early.

When I woke up the next morning, I knew they were gone—gone for three or more days—and I did feel terribly alone. The days had been getting hotter and hotter. Every day we were expecting it to cool off, but it was doing just the opposite. As the sun rose higher, I could feel the heat coming through the roof. When I went out where the sun could shine on me, I felt it burn. This would be a scorcher of a day!

It was time for baby's bath, so I went out to the barrel to dip some water for the bath and for washing. When I lifted the lid, I found the barrel entirely empty! The barrel rested on some planks to keep it off the ground, and after investigating, I saw a large hole in the bottom. A small animal of some kind had gnawed through the wood during the night, and my precious water had run out. What was I to do with my neighbors gone!

There was still some drinking water down the cave, so I thought I would get a little of that to bathe baby and wash a few things for her. I took a small bucket, went down the cave, and poured out as little water from the can as I thought I could possibly manage with. As I came up the steps, I stumbled and fell, spilling every drop out of the bucket. I knew I could use no more now for bathing or washing until the folks got home. We would need what was left for drinking.

I gave baby a dry rub with a soft turkish towel and changed her clothes. Other things could wait until some other time. I could use a little of the drinking water for cooking, if I were very saving, so I felt all would be well for a few days. It would be pretty hard to have our water limited when the days were so hot.

I went down the cave and brought up a little drinking water—just a very little—because I discovered there was less in the can than I had thought. I wanted to be very saving with it, but before noon it was gone, and baby was coaxing for more. Finally I decided to go down and get a little more just for her.

I took a small pitcher and started down the cave. I had gone down only two steps when on the third step I saw a huge snake. I was so frightened I could not tell whether it was a rattlesnake or a bullsnake. I quickly turned, took the two steps in one, and ran to the soddie for the broom. I was hoping the snake would crawl out while I was after the broom because I had never killed a snake and didn't relish the thought of doing it. When I got back, it had gone down three more steps. I was afraid to fight it down inside the cave so came up and left the door open, hoping it would see the sun and crawl out to the light, as they so often do.

Baby was crying now for a drink, and I was dreadfully thirsty, too. But between me and our precious water was this big snake, which I was afraid to encounter in close quarters. Baby was still crying "wawa" and "dink," so I went back in the soddie and stayed for some time to give the snake time to crawl out. It was scorching hot inside the soddie. I kept trying to comfort baby, but water was what she wanted, so she refused to be comforted. I knew how she felt. I thought I would make another try.

When I went back to the cave again, there was no snake on the steps or anywhere in sight. I ventured very cautiously down the steps, broom in hand, stopping on each one and peering around, but there was no snake. I felt sure now that it had crawled out of the cave. I got to the last step, and before stepping down on the ground, I looked all around again. Seeing no snake, I went over to the water can and reached down for the handle, when what did I see coiled behind the can but the snake! I was filled with fear, but I was desperate for water. I grabbed the can and made a dash for the steps.

I was partway up when the handle of the can came loose, and the can slipped from my grasp, tumbling down the cave and hitting each step as it went. I looked down and saw that the fall had knocked the spout off the can, and there was the last of the water running out on the dirt floor, making it muddy and sloppy. I was so wild with thirst that I was tempted to run down and scoop the water up with my hands and drink it. But I thought of baby and knew I did not dare risk going down in the cave with that frightful snake. Every drop of our water was gone! Gone, and what could I do? Baby was still calling for a drink.

I dragged myself up the remainder of the steps, closed the door of the cave, looked all around the parched prairie with the sun beating down relentlessly, and for the first time felt defeated. Had my neighbors been at home, it would have been a simple matter to run up the "out of water" signal, and soon we would have gotten some. What should I do? I couldn't leave baby. She could not walk any distance over the prairie, and I could not carry her in this terrific heat. The Mountains, who lived on the creek bottom, were our nearest neighbors, and that was too far to attempt to walk at any time, much less under this blistering sun. If I waited until night—well, that was not to be considered, with the coyotes and wolves prowling around. Then, too, it was the dark of the moon, and I knew in the darkness I would get lost even if I tried to go. I felt panicky!

It was late in the afternoon. Baby had gone to sleep fretting and crying for water. I knew Noble Wickland would be over at George and Ruth's place sometime to care for the stock so thought I would put up a distress signal on the pole. Perhaps, if he came before dark, he

would see it. I got out the signals I had and ran them all
up the pole.

When baby awoke, the first thing she wanted was
water. I tried to divert her, but it did not work. How
could it, when she was so thirsty? I took her outside to
see the cloth moving in the wind on top of the pole, but
the diversion was of short duration. That everlasting
begging for water, I thought, would unnerve me. Such a
little thing as a drink of water, and Yet I was not able
to give her any.

The night came on with no relief. Noble had not seen
the signal, I was sure, or he would have been here. All
night long, baby cried out in her sleep for water. How
could I stand it! To be alone in the daytime, when one
can see in all directions and things on the outside are
visible, is quite different from being alone when night
drops its curtain of darkness and all is blotted out except
the inside of the soddie and the eternal wailing of the
coyotes outside. Now, adding to that was baby crying for
water. I got into bed hoping and praying that the morning would bring relief. I hardly slept at all. All night
baby was hot and restless.

In the morning, the sun came up as hot as ever—even
hotter, it seemed. I hoped baby would sleep late, but she
was awake early crying for water. I gave her some milk,
but it was warm. That was not what she wanted. I let
the signals stay on the pole, but no one came. Baby
became very fretful, and that was not like her. I felt her
little soft, naked body. It was so hot, and I didn't even
have a damp cloth to sponge her off. I could not take
her down the cave because of the snake. I tried to think
what to do, but there was no solution. Baby kept following me around, begging for water.

Early in the afternoon, she fell asleep. I went outside
and started walking around the soddie. I would stop on
each side and look off in the distance, hoping and
praying again that someone would come from some
direction. I circled the soddie many times and kept
looking in all directions. There was nothing but the
sunblistered prairie and the hot-looking sky—heat and
more heat—and thirst! My own lips were parched. I

dreaded to have baby wake and start that fretful cry for
water. Poor dear little thing, how little she knew what
agony I was enduring in my sympathy for her. The
situation seemed utterly hopeless. I was nearly wild with
thirst and heat.

Not the faintest breath of a breeze was stirring—a
most unusual thing for this country. It was so silent and
still, one could almost hear the great silence. It made my
head swim. Solitude impenetrable! The silence was closing
in around me like some great monster ready to spring
and devour me. And the heat! Always the heat! I became
dazed, bewildered. A vague heaviness of spirit weighed
me down. A coyote began to howl down in the canyon,
and I started in with it, screaming as loud as I could.
Something inside of me seemed to snap. The last thing I
remembered, I was pulling at my hair and running.
Running from what? Solitude, disappointment, heat,
thirst—oh, the terrible thirst. My lips were cracking. I
suppose there are limits of endurance in all of us.

They picked me up out on the west range—two
homesteaders, a man and his wife, from out beyond Cut
Meat. They were on horseback, hunting their stray cattle.
They found me exhausted and in a daze. How long I was
gone I do not know. They recognized me from the color
and abundance of my hair. All my hairpins were gone,
and it was streaming down my back to my ankles. When
they spoke to me, all I could say was "water," "baby,"
"snake," and then I lapsed into unconsciousness.

The man put me on his horse and held me there until
they got me back to the soddie. There they looked for
water but could find none. Guessing the situation, the
husband jumped on his horse and galloped down to the
Mountains' on the creek bottom. How wonderful people
are! There seems always to be the divine spark of love
and sympathy for others in distress.

When I came to myself, I was in my own bed in the
soddie, with a damp cloth on my head. Hilma Mountain
was wetting my lips with water. Water! Precious water!
Since then, I have often wondered how much any of us
really appreciates the wonderful blessing of water.

The first thing I asked about was my baby. Hilma had taken care of her, sponging her and giving her drinks at intervals. They told me that she was standing at the door, crying and trying to get out, when they brought me home, but Rover was standing guard and wouldn't let her push the screen door open. She was crying for water, and her little lips were cracked and bleeding. The screen door opened out, and she could easily have gotten out on the hot prairie but could not have gotten back in. Often, when I had gone outside to hang clothes on the line or down the cave to get food, I would say to Rover, "Don't let baby out. Keep her inside while I'm gone." He would look at me and blink and seemed to understand because when she would push the screen open, he would bark and push it shut with his paw. It was amusing to see him take care of her, and this time it proved a true blessing.

He was such an understanding dog. He always went with me when I took a walk while baby was sleeping. Perhaps he did go with me for a short distance this time. I do not know, but I am sure he realized that something was wrong and felt it was his responsibility to look after baby, for he had stood guard where he was needed most.

My rescuers said they had looked for water even down the cave. When they saw the upset can and the empty barrel, they realized something unusual had happened. Around the barrel, it was still a little damp, and the floor of the cave was still quite wet. The man said he did not see the snake in the cave but had not looked around. After finding the upset can, he came right out and rushed down to Mountains'.

He went down the cave again after I spoke about the snake and saw that it was still there. I think it enjoyed having a cool place to stay. The man killed it but had quite a battle doing it. It was a very large rattlesnake and put up a strong fight for its life. The man asked me if I wanted the fifteen rattles connected to its tail, but I did not care for any souvenir that would remind me of that snake. Nor did I need anything to recall the experiences.

Hilma and the others asked me why I had started to run west, where no one lived. This I could not answer. I

did not know where I was going. I just went. I am sure
it was an answer to prayer because, had I gone another
direction, there would have been no one to pick me up.

Then everything turned out so well—we got water, the
snake was killed, and these wonderful neighbors were
taking care of us. So, my prayers had been answered.
The homesteader and his wife lived so far away that they
had to start for home. It was impossible for me to
express my gratitude to them. They had saved baby's life
and mine. They felt so happy and yet were so humble
about being of real service.

Hilma Mountain stayed with us until George, Ruth,
and the children came back two days later. Hilma was a
grand person, many times putting her own duties aside to
help others. Art, her husband, was just as fine in
wanting to help everyone in any way he could. Even
with all the work he had to do on his own place, and
with Hilma staying with me, he took time to haul me a
barrel of water. He said he didn't want anything like this
to happen again if he could prevent it.

It had been quite an ordeal, but through it I had
learned many precious lessons that would linger with me
all my life.

Farewell

The fourteen months of my homesteading were over,
and I would soon be leaving the Rosebud Indian Reservation of South Dakota. When the day came for my
husband to arrive, Ruth brought the ponies and buggy
over to take us to White River.

"Daddy is coming today," I said to Dot. "Let me
pretty you up."

She ran to me clapping her little hands. Yes, once
again we were getting "prettied up" for my husband's
arrival. This time I was sure he would get here because
the stage driver had gotten word that if the train were a
little late he was to postpone starting out, if possible,
until it arrived. George, Ruth, and the children were
going to the village, too, as they were expecting a mail-
order package.

Ruth and baby and I rode in the buggy, and George took the children in the wagon. It was the same old creek trail, but somehow this morning it looked so different. Everything was different—Daddy was coming!

As we rode along, Ruth and I talked of many things—my stay on the homestead, the things that had occurred, and the good times we'd had together.

"Ruth," I said, "all these experiences have been a blessing to me. I have learned so much more about many things."

I truly felt that I now knew more about the real values of life, our responsibilities to others, and the beauty that can be found in everyone's soul if we will only take the time to search for it. I had had such marvelous and spectacular answers to prayer that it had taught me the lesson of a stronger faith and trust in the Lord. I would always remember that it was out here on the lonely creek trail that God had spoken to me. That alone was worth more to me than anything material ever could be.

We reached the village and went directly to the post office. There was just one card for me, but that one card meant everything because written on it was one word, "Coming!" the stage was a little late, but at last we saw it coming over the ridge. When it stopped, the first to get out was my husband. There was a great reunion! He could hardly believe that Dot was such a big girl, big enough now to walk to him.

Back at the homestead, it did not take us long to assemble our personal belongings and distribute the others among the neighbors. Billy, Babe, the buggy, and Rover were to stay with George and Ruth. As we packed all the personal things that we were taking, it began to look a little bare in the soddie.

On the evening before our departure, the neighbors from far and near came to say goodbye and give us a farewell party. How sincere everyone was! I was experiencing conflicting emotions—one of great joy that our family would be united and the other a deep feeling of regret at leaving my splendid neighbors and friends.

The ponies and buggy had been left with us for the night so we could get an early start in the morning. Our luggage was packed and we were all ready to go shortly after dawn. George, Ruth, and the children were to follow in the wagon as far as White River, where we would take the stage to the railroad. It had turned cooler, and the morning was lovely and clear.

When we reached the trail at Coyote Butte, I asked my husband to stop the ponies so I could look back once more at the soddie. These thoughts kept running through my mind: Goodbye, dear old soddie, you were our protection in many ways. You and I alone are the only ones who know the happy moments that were spent beneath your roof, as well as the long, lonely hours of days and nights with no one near. The tears came in my eyes as we started on.

"Sorry to leave?" my husband asked.

"Oh no," I replied, "but there will always be memories."

I took another look back. The little old soddie looked so lonely and forsaken, perched there on the rim of the canyon and silhouetted against the western sky. Many times, when life has been hard and complex in places along the way, there have been moments when I have longed for the quietness and solitude of my little old soddie.

The wind still blows, making its weird moaning sound through the prairie grass; the coyotes still howl in the night; the tumbleweed still grows, breaks loose, and tumbles across the prairie like a coyote on the run; the wild horses still roam the range, snorting and neighing and kicking the dust; the snakes still crawl and rattle. But I am not there to hear them.

There Was Something Sweet and Clean about the Harvest
Era Bell Thompson

Era Bell Thompson's story is the only one we know about growing up black and female on a prairie farm. We've chosen a chapter from her book, American Daughter, *that describes the first year on a farm in south-central North Dakota in 1914. Her father, whom she calls "Pop," works the farm with his son, Tom. In fact, her account shows that Tom was the better farmer. While the mother sticks pretty much to the "inside" work, Era Bell participates in all the outside activities.*

Era Bell demonstrates an intense awareness of the prairie landscape as well as the tasks associated with plowing, planting, and harvesting. Although still a young girl, she found the work challenging, exhilarating, and sometimes overwhelming. Haying is her favorite time in the farm cycle. After a day's work driving the stacker horse, she concludes that there is "a sacredness about it that filled us with the inner happiness that comes of a day's work well done."

In the most moving section of her narration she describes the family's discouragement after a day's work harvesting their meager crop. The supper table is bare except for the usual potatoes. Pop and Tom begin arguing. Just then one of their neighbors drives up, discovers the barrenness of the table, and returns a few hours later with bags of flour and sugar and cans of staples.

Source:
Era Bell Thompson. American Daughter. *St Paul: Minnesota Historical Society P, 1986. 31-57.*

By the end of March we were firmly ensconced on the Hansmeyer place, but without my brother Dick. His faith in Father's agricultural instincts was still a bit shaken, so he hired out to Charley Koch, nearer town and convenient to the pool hall. And we were short one hand.

High winds and the tepid spring sun sent the snow scurrying down hillsides in tiny rivulets, honeycombing the scattered drifts that clung to the shady sides of the knolls until they slowly crumbled and disappeared into the ever thirsty soil, revealing the Hansmeyer farm, rough, rocky, and recalcitrant.

Everywhere there were rocks, millions of rocks pimpling the drab prairie, large blue-gray boulders, free and bold in their shallow pockets; long, narrow slits of rocks surfacing the soil like huge cetacean monsters; sharp stone peaks jutting from the horny earth. Pale-gray sage and dull buffalo grass flecked the fields, and here and there were red-brown patches of stiff buckbrush sheltering a coyote's den. In the slough at the north end of the pasture was long, dry marsh grass, flat from the recent weight of the snow. Purple crocuses blossomed reluctantly on thick, furry stems among the rocks and boulders.

We watched the transformation with heavy hearts. "Well," Pop said sadly, "we ain't never gonna want for no tombstones!"

Major, still lank and scrawny but surprisingly swift, munched hungrily around the big yard, our only bit of animal life and our sole means of transportation. Uncle

John agreed to take Harry and me to school, providing we met him on the road a mile to the south. Tom delivered us, Harry behind him, hanging onto his middle, and me in front of him, astride Major's thin neck, arms flying helplessly as he galloped the horse over snow and ice, through puddles of mud and water, unmindful of my tearful pleas and the scrambled food inside the dinner buckets. John never waited for us; most of the time we overtook him like cowboys in a western thriller, only there were no Indians....six months and still no Indians!

Father and Tom spent the early spring days mending fences, repairing the windmill, and trying to prop up the sagging barn, while Mother scrubbed the little house until it was clean and bright. Every day Tom rode out over the range in search of the Hansmeyer horses, but it was April before he sighted them and ten days later when he brought them charging into the corral. All but two got away.

Mother watched Tom lure the horses into the barn and follow and carefully close the door, while Pop took a safe position outside the barn window, club in hand. "Tony!" she screamed. "Don't let the boy go in there alone; he'll be killed!"

"He ain't alone, Mary; I'm takin' care of him. You better go in the house." Pop was breathing hard, his knees were rigid, and he was having trouble with his bloods. The Dutch said, "Go inside"; the Indian said, "Stand still." The other bloods raced up and down his veins and said, "Lord! Lord! There's no hidin' place down here!"

From within came a high, shrill whinny, the sound of thudding bodies, splintering stalls. The old barn moved ominously. "Tom! Tom!" called Mother weakly.

Pop took a quick peek inside and covered his face. All he could see was flying hoofs. There was another commotion, the door flew open, and a small sorrel mare, eyes glazed, ears back, nostrils distended, charged out into the corral, stood on her hind legs, and pawed freedom's air. Pop dropped his club and disappeared around the side of the barn—the far side. Instinct was more reliable than blood.

Tom went for Old Gus, the drunken bachelor who lived below the hill. Together they got the mare back into the barn, harnessed both horses, and hitched them to a dilapidated buggy, Tom holding the bridles while Gus climbed in and gathered up the reins.

"Let 'er go!" called Gus, through his whiskey.

Tom released the broncos and jumped to one side. "Yippee!" he cried, and swung on as the buggy lurched by. The horses made a new gate through the yard fence and tore down the muddy road on a dead gallop as Gus sat waving his bottle and yelling in Norwegian. Tom took the reins and guided the horses up a big hill. For two hours they raced up and down the hills, in and out of rutty roads, the buggy groaning and creaking as it bounced off rocks, out of holes. Tired and panting, bodies steaming and covered with lather, Tom brought the erring horses home. The buggy was a shambles, Gus was stone-sober, but we had a team.

The reputation of Hansmeyer's broncos and the fame of Tom's horsemanship (thanks to Gus) brought people from near and far. Every Sunday the yard was filled with the wagons and buggies of those who came to watch and help us break our horses. In the house jolly farm women opened baskets of food, while Mother made pot after pot of strong coffee for the inevitable lunch that followed the show.

Pop's equestrianism was manifested in various safe ways, such as naming the horses after race horses he had known. His favorite team was Buck, a handsome buckskin devil with a dark-brown seam running down the center of his back, and Dixie, a fat, little dapple ball of hell. Pop made his maiden trip into town without mishap. An hour later the horses returned on a dead run, heads up, heels flying, a picture of rhythmic beauty. Turning in the gate on two wheels, they stopped only when the buggy lodged in the barn door. Pop and one seat was missing. By being careful, he had gotten them into town and tied to the iron railing at the bank. While he was negotiating a loan for more feed and equipment, Buck worked his way free and rammed his head under Dixie's chin, breaking her halter rope. Pop and the banker ran out in time to see them racing down Main Street.

"And you'll need another buggy," the banker said, without emotion.

"Yes," Father sighed, "another buggy. But, man, did you see them rascals run!" There were few people, thereafter, who didn't see them, for Thompson runaways became legendary.

Mother couldn't keep me from the horses after Harry learned to ride. I fell off or was thrown off with disconcerting regularity, but backed the jittery broncos against wagon wheels and fences and climbed back on until I was able to race with my brothers and no favors asked.

The farm people were kind and friendly to us, encouraging and advising, offering the use of their tools and machinery, even bringing a pig or a chicken to help us get started. Old Gus offered fresh milk. The first time Harry and I went after it, we found him lying on a pile of dirty quilts, his bottle and pipe beside him. A huge stack of cold pancakes lay on the back of the cook-stove, more pancakes than we had ever seen, even in the heyday of Pop's cookery, and certainly never such large, sturdy ones.

Gus laughed. "You want some pannie cakes?" We shook our heads and edged toward the door.

"You never see so many, yah? Aye, make pannie cakes for whole veek. Aye no like to cook!" Gus spat out but not quite clear of the bed. He looked at our tight brown faces and roared. "You take tandy, maybe? Come, aye give you tandy." He reached for a dirty tin box near the bed. "Come, little Tovey Gustus." He held the sticky peppermint toward me. I fled out the door and up the hill, but the name followed, and I became "Tovey Guts" to my brothers the rest of my life.

Nell and August Nordland felt close to us, for they, too, had come from Iowa. The Nordland farm, some five miles away, was a prosperous place, with a roomy house and one of the largest and most modern barns in the township. Towheaded Skippy became Harry's pal, and the friendship between Jewel and me blossomed with that of our parents. When I visited their farm, I rode their ponies and played in the mammoth loft of the big barn, rolling down mounds of hay, sliding through floor chutes into the managers of startled horses, admiring—at a safe distance—the beautiful tan stallion who chafed and fretted in a private box stall. There was always homemade ice cream and cake with thick frosting for dinner, and, when I spent the night with Jewel, I wore her pretty night-gowns and slept in a soft bed between real linen sheets. I could never ask Jewel to stay at our house. There wasn't room.

Father heard it first. "Mary, Mary!" he cried. "Did you hear that?" Mother ran out the door into the early-morning sun. Pop shaded his eyes with his hand as he peered around the yard. From a fence post across the road came the clear, unmistakable notes of a meadow lark. "Shush, you all, don't scare that bird!" We stood at the door, scarcely breathing. The bird sang out again, then flew away. "Reminds me of Virginia. Never knew I'd be glad to hear a little bird sing." Pop looked toward the dying grove. "Wonder what he do for trees?"

There were more meadow larks and later there were robins. Droves of raucous crows sometimes blackened the air, and white-winged sea gulls swooped gracefully overhead. Pop wondered what they did for sea, but he didn't ask. It was, indeed, a strange country. We gazed with awe upon the prairie rose, a delicate pink flower growing close to the ground, whose thorny stem belied its tender beauty. As the wild rose was the official state flower, so was the gopher, commonly called the flicker-tail, its namesake. Since these little squirrel-like animals destroyed grain, a bounty was placed upon them. Tom and Harry got a couple of rusty traps from Gus and hunted with fairly profitable results, considering the bounty was only three cents a tail. Sometimes Skippy brought his .22 over, and the boys picked them off as fast as they stuck their heads out of their holes. Tom was intrigued. He worried Pop for a shotgun, but he didn't get far until we saw the timber wolf while we were eating breakfast one morning. He came from behind the barn, trotted close under the window, and went calmly down the road. Pop froze in his chair.

My first pet was a puppy Dick brought home on one of his casual visits and asked me to keep for him. Sport was beautiful, with long, tawny hair that turned blonde with the snow and deepened to bronze in the summer sun. His snowy white chest and white-trimmed face were the markings of a collie, but Sport was part shepherd, part coyote. He was a companion dog, not one for herding cattle or flushing game, but a dog I could love and trust, that would follow me to the ends of the earth.

The frost was barely out of the ground when Pop took the boys out to the field to show them how to handle a plow. He made the first row in something like record time, the plowshares occasionally digging into the ground, but more often scooting over the top, miraculously dodging the rocks. My father was too involved with reins and the business of remaining upright to manipulate the lever. The speed of the horses increased with the commotion from behind, and Tom and Harry rolled over on the ground howling with laughter as our father disappeared over the hill. Tom finished plowing.

Home from school at night, Harry and I changed our clothes and hurried out into the field to watch the shining shares slide along beneath the stubborn sod, turning over long rows of damp, blackish earth like unending dusky curls. We walked behind the plow in the shallow, trenchlike furrows, watching for earthworms, or sat on the velvety upturned soil and let its warm earthiness seep up into our bodies.

Sometimes Harry took the plow. He was thirteen now, growing straight and tall, growing away from me and my child's world, seeking the companionship of Father and Tom, and I found it increasingly difficult to tag along.

Mother, too, began to make demands upon my time. She found tasks inside the house, little-girl tasks like setting the table, doing dishes, sewing my clothes, or endless pounding on the clabber in the stone churn until fine flakes of gold appeared around the cover and gathered inside, forming a floating isle of butter. My dislike for housework often brought me into violent conflict with Mother. As I grew, the oak table, with its four sturdy legs, began to fail me as a place of refuge, and Mother reached some part of my anatomy no matter how much I squirmed.

I emerged one day from one of those skirmishes, burning and humiliated. With Sport at my heels, I went to my hideaway on the sunny side of the haystack, behind the barn. "Damn," I whispered. Nothing happened; lightning did not strike me dead. "Damn it!" I said aloud. Sport looked at me curiously, then looked away with that quiet indifference dogs possess. For a long time I stared off into the distant hills; I'd go there some day. I'd run away from these colored folks and go live with the Indians. There must be Indians somewhere. I watched a white fluff of cloud drift slowly across the sky, then another and another, forming the head of an angel, a horse with horns, an ethereal castle edged in gold floating silently by. On and on they came, swifter now, darker and closer together, crossing between me and the sun, casting dark shadows on the prairies. Suddenly there was a flash of lightning and a clap of thunder that brought Sport and me to our feet. The rain caught us before we reached the house. I buried my head in my mother's apron, while Sport lay quivering beneath the bed. It was the first storm of spring, the one that awoke the snakes. The rain ceased as quickly as it had begun, the sun came out, and, when I opened my eyes, Mother pointed to a giant rainbow. All the way across the sky, from horizon to horizon, stretched the shining ribbon of colors, both ends resting firmly on the ground. There was no pot of gold. "Damn!" I said, softly, under my breath, and another, illusion was destroyed.

Suddenly, it was warm, alive spring. The sting was gone from the morning air, and the thin layers of ice disappeared from the water trough; the two chickens were cackling and laying unfertile eggs, the prairie grass took on a greenish hue, and my heavy winter coat felt like suit of armor.

Father borrowed more money. Now he borrowed money on the things he had borrowed money for, on the things that did not yet exist—the crop yet unplanted. This time the money was for seed and a new seeder. Tom had done all he could, handicapped as he was by inexperience, poor machinery, poorer land, and horses that ran away every morning and collapsed every night. And Pop—he wasn't much help either.

Somehow we buried the funny little seeds in the rebellious earth, and great was our joy when the first scared shoots escaped from the stubborn soil and fought for a place among the rocks and weeds. The garden lagged. Sweet-potato and canteloupe [sic] seeds that Pop so hopefully planted—against the neighbor's protests—lay still in their strange, cold beds and died. Only the potatoes prospered.

Under the two hens, Mother placed the eggs our friends had given us, and in due time strange things came from the nests. Besides the downy yellow chicks came noisy little ducks and scrawny, speckled baby turkeys. The mortality rate was high, more than one dying from my handling, but some lived and grew into ugly, half-naked things that ran chirping and peeping in shrill monotones about the yard, and I no longer loved them.

On Sundays, Mother and Father walked arm in arm through the pasture to the grain fields to sit on the sunny slopes and dream and plan for the farm that some day would be ours. We did not go to church, for there was none except the little Lutheran church in Driscoll. It must have been hard for them, my parents, to give up their worship. We still sang the old hymns and said the long prayers over the food, but the boys scoffed at the family Bible-reading and grew cynical of Pop's religion, critical of his leadership on the farm. Father felt himself slowly losing his position as head of the house. Tom's strength, Tom's ideas, Tom's plan of work was sturdy, sound; always in the end his way was best. In major issues Pop stormed and commanded, then withdrew. Tom said nothing, went on with his plan. Succeeded. Mother stood as a buffer between them; it was she and Tom who signed the last mortgage while Father sulked.

At the program that marked the close of the school year, I was to give all eight stanzas of "The Village

Blacksmith," dressed in white. Mother mended and starched my white eyelet dress and took the ribbon from her wedding gown to make a sash and bows for the ends of my short braids, but my lingerie consisted solely of black sateen bloomers. Mother ripped open a flour sack and made a remarkable pair of straight-legged drawers. Somehow Harry got them before I did, and for a while it looked as though the blacksmith and the chestnut tree were going to be stood up.

"Tovey flour britches," said Harry. "Old Lady Pillsbury's gonna say, 'Who dat in my sack!'"

Clouds gathered in my eyes.

"Umm umph!" Tom joined in. "You gonna look just like a fly in a glass of buttermilk!"

"Mamma!" I wailed. There was no response. I turned to Father for help, but he looked at me in all of my whiteness, his face worked oddly, and suddenly he bolted for the barn.

The smithy got two and a half stanzas that night. "You can hear him swing his heavy sledge," I swung my dark arms to the right. "With measured beat and slow." I pivoted far to the left. Too far. The "bury" began to separate from "Pills," and I retired before the audience became fully aware of a sudden disunity in the garment industry.

Anxiously we scanned the sky for clouds, watched them slowly gather, disappear, gather, come closer, then skirt our dry fields, drop their white curtains of rain on some distant prairie. And when the precious drops did come to us, we waited for the cold that brought the hail that beat down the growing grain, mercilessly pounding out the half-ripe kernels. Usually hail came in regular paths, hail belts, and farmers living in these areas protected themselves with hail insurance—if they could afford it—or waited and watched and cursed God when it came. We waited and watched and praised God, for to us it did not come.

Spring faded into hot summer. A rain now, followed by the burning sun, meant black rust, those little dark specks of blight that rotted the stocks of the grain. It rained and the sun came out, and our spring wheat was beautifully blighted.

Then there were days and weeks when no rain fell, no clouds appeared. A dry, hot wind seared the crops, scorched the earth, and dried up the little slough until stiff alkaline rings formed a chalky mosaic in its hard, cracked bed. The heat increased. There were still days, silent, hot, motionless days when not a blade of grass stirred, not a stalk of grain moved. You didn't talk much then; you hated to break the prairie silence, the magic of its stillness, for you had that understanding with nature, that treaty with God. There was no need for words. The silence wore hard on those who did not belong.

The twenty-acre strip of flax clung stubbornly to its greenness as the short, tough stems swayed in the hot July wind; then overnight the whole field burst into delicate blue flowers, miniature stars against the yellow mustard blooms that clutched at their throat and strangled their growth. The blue flowers disappeared as quickly as they had come, and tiny bulbs of seed began to form in their place, to brown and ripen too quickly in the searing wind.

Only the potato vines remained green, and, but for watering, they too would have withered, for when the wind did blow and the windmill turned, we caught the tepid water in barrels and hauled it to the field. In the quick coolness that came with the dusk, the thirsty plants drank the water and, like the potato bugs, survived. Passing farmers shook their heads. Nobody but a green-horn would water potatoes.

Haying time, to me, was the happiest time of the year. As soon as Tom got in a few days with the mower, our whole family took to the field. We arose early, while the air was still fresh and cool, before the sun was up and drove to the hayland we had rent-ed—through the courtesy of the bank. Harry drove the rake, making long windrows, while Tom followed with the wooden-toothed buckrake, gathering up the hay into little doodles. As stacker man, Pop was in his glory, again head of his family. The first few loads he rounded and packed to form the bed of the stack, then began the building, the piling-on, the spreading-out, the tramping-down. It was a creative thing, this building a stack, rising higher and higher in the sky, above earthly things. He was master of all he surveyed up there, in his grassy chariot, rising nearer to the Glory Road, closer to the Golden Stairs. He took Mother with him sometimes, and together they would stand in silence and look away over the prairie. Away over Jordan.

My first job was driving the stacker horse, one so slow he would have stopped at the stake if I hadn't pulled on the reins. When I had mastered this task, I was taught to drive the hayrake. I couldn't manage the buckrake because it took weight and strength to bear down on the teeth and accuracy to deposit the hay on the stacker carrier. Hidden rocks were an ever present danger to the buckrake as well as to the blade of the mower. They didn't let me drive that either.

At noon we unhitched the horses, fed them, and sat down under the shade of the rack to eat. It wasn't much of a meal: hard slices of summer sausage, potato salad, soupy with vinegar, hard-boiled eggs, bread, and butter-milk. Sometimes cookies. We brushed aside the flies that suddenly came out of nowhere and ate steadily, silently, leaving nothing.

Afternoons were hardest, for then we fought the heat and hay needles and the horseflies and the mosquitoes and the droves of flying ants, those schools of black devils that descended upon us and crawled through our clothing and down our necks, biting and stinging. When they were very bad, the mosquitoes and the ants, we made smudges of oily rags or dampened hay. From old gunny sacks, the boys rigged up bizarre fly nets for the horses and put straw hats on them, tying fringed rags around their noses to keep the botflies from depositing their wormy eggs. They made sport of our poverty, with bandannas hanging under their battered straw hats, raggedy shirttails flying, sleeves shredded to the armpits, looking like something right from the Fijis, and it was little wonder the horses ran away.

The coming-home on a load of hay in the warm silence of twilight—the slow rhythm of tired horses, the

muffled rattle of the harness on those tied behind, the
hayrack creaking under its burden as we moved slowly
across the prairie in the shallow road of our making—had
a sacredness about it that filled us with the inner happiness that comes of a day's work well done.

Having no produce to sell, we were without the small
cash income which tides the dirt farmer over the lean
summer months, and our borrowed funds again gave out,
our food and credit with it. The gay pastoral picture
changed. There wasn't much fun haying when you were
hungry. The boys became irritable, and high haystacks
made Pop's head swim. Secretly each one of us wished
for a rain that would send us in from the field for a
few days' respite, but no rain came, so Harry broke the
mower wheel, which was just as effective.

The second day we were home Mother set the dinner
table out in the yard to escape the heat of the cookstove
and scraped the bottom of the flour bin to make the thin
milk gravy for the boiled potatoes, for we had no more
bread, had no meat. We gathered around the table, not
eager, but curious to see what she could find to put into
the dishes. At breakfast we had tried the porridge made
from flax seed, but it was a sorry mess, far worse than
the hand-ground oats and fruits of earlier experimenta-
tion.

"What'd I wash my hands for?" demanded Harry. "We
ain't got nothing to eat!"

Tom studied his brother's hands carefully. "Look at
those bear claws, son. What makes you think you
washed?"

"They're cleaner'n yours. You can't talk."

"Why, son," Tom spread his short fingers out against
the patched tablecloth, blew at an imaginary speck of
dust on his grimy, broken nails, "Look at my lily-white
hands; there's simply no comparison!"

"What you call that black stuff—pigment?"

"Them's veins, blue veins where flows the blood of
potentates."

"You all stop that crazy talk an' eat." Pop started the
potatoes down the table.

"I pass," said Tom.

"Me too," said Harry.

I pushed my plate away. "I want bread and jelly; I'm tired of potatoes."

"Where'd you see any jelly, in the catalogue?" Harry was sarcastic.

"Listen, children, eat your dinner. It's all we have. It's the last of the flour and lard, sugar's gone too. Maybe we can have some mustard greens tonight, maybe I can find some not too strong," said Mother hopefully.

Tom looked accusingly at Father. "Why don't you go to town and get some food? We've got to eat. We can't sit here an' starve!"

"What am I goin' to git food with, tell me that? I've borrowed, I've mortgaged everything we got—things we ain't got. Banker won't let me have no more money. Store won't give me no more credit, not with everything burnin' up."

"What about Uncle John?" asked Harry. There was silence.

"I'd rather starve than ask him. I've done the best I can; somehow the Lord will provide."

"And in the meantime we go hungry!" Tom was bitter now.

Pop stood up, his plate untouched. Defeat was written deep in the lines of his face.

"Sit down, Tony, someone's going by." Mother pulled him down as two spirited horses, hitched to a fine black buggy, came dashing up the road, slowed down at our gate and turned in.

"Hello there!" A voice boomed out. "I'm Carl Brendel, your neighbor—don't git up, I yust stop by to see how you git along."

Pop went over to the buggy and shook his hand. He recognized him now; it was Big Carl, the German widower who lived in the tiny speck of a farm far to the northeast. "This is a surprise, neighbor, won't you have some dinner?" Father was embarrassed.

"Yes," said Mother, "won't you get out and join us?"

Carl Brendel tried not to look at the bare table. "Nein," he said, "I yust et. On my vay to town; thought maybe I bring you somet'ings."

"Thanks, much obliged, but we ain't needin' nothin' jest now." Pop shifted his feet and looked out over the prairie.

"Yah, yah," said Carl quickly. "I go now." He picked up the reins, the horses whirled, and he was gone.

That evening Brendel returned. He was lifting sacks out of his buggy when Pop came up from the barn. "I bring you some little t'ings I t'ink maybe you need," he explained, resting a hundred-pound sack of flour against the house, beside the big sack of sugar.

"God bless you!" said Pop, tears running down his face. "God bless you, man! Mary, Mary!" he cried: "Come here an' see what the good Lord has brought us, jest come an' looka here!"

Mother clutched my father's arm; she could not speak. I came in from the yard, Sport close to my heels, and stood beside the pretty horses, watching the big man with the red hairs on his hands as he set more food on the ground. There were canned goods and staples, meat and lard. Carl Brendel smiled as he worked, not looking at Father and Mother. When he had finished, he pulled a little sack from his pocket and held it out to me.

"Here, little girl, here iss candy for you. I bring dis all for you." I looked at Mother. She nodded her head, and I took the sack, mumbling my thanks. The big man smiled and climbed into his buggy.

Pop moved then; he grabbed Brendel's arm. "Mister, I've got no money; I can't pay you now. God knows we need this food..."

"Nein, nein! I no vant money. Ven you git it you pay me if you vant. I got money, I your neighbor, I help you. Dot iss all." He whipped up the horses and drove away.

Far down the road, he looked back. The man and woman were still there in the yard where he had left them, but they were kneeling now, praying and thanking their God.

That night was Christmas—Christmas in the middle of August. Harry washed both of his hands, and I brought my jelly beans to the table and lined them up in a colorful circle in front of my plate. There wasn't a potato in sight. Once more the plates were hopefully stacked in front of Father, who beamed as he passed them out, laden with good food.

"Oh, I tell you, children, the good Lord will provide!"

"Yes, man!" grinned Tom. "Him and Mister Brendel!"

We were still waiting for the new mower wheel when Harry ran into the house shouting, "Fire, prairie fire!" Three miles away was a vast cloud of smoke, now and then the blaze showing through, red and angry. Swiftly it moved northward, toward the square black house on the top of the hill, toward the Widow Weiss—and our hay-field! Starting at the railroad tracks, where section men were burning off the right-of-way, it had spread rapidly over the dry grass, gathering momentum as it went, leaving behind it a smoldering path of blackened prairie.

We stood in the yard, stunned, sick with dread. Old Gus came thundering up through the pasture, his horses on a dead run. "Fire!" he screamed. "It's headed for da Widow Weiss! Hurry, man, hurry! Git in my wagon, aye take you!" Pop started for the barn, turned, started for Gus's wagon, went to the house for his hat. "Git sack, blanket, git somet'ing to fight wit," yelled Gus, pulling hard on the nervous horses.

Tom disappeared into the granary, came out with an armful of sacks. Harry ran to help him. I clung to my mother's dress. The wind increased as we stood there, fanning the fire; closer to the house. Another wagon dashed by, headed for the fire; across the field more wagons joined in the procession.

Pop ran out of the house with his hat, handed it to Mother, then jumped into the wagon beside Gus. "Don't git excited!" he shouted. "Don't nobody git excited!" Mother reached for Harry as he ran toward the wagon, but he eluded her and jumped in on top of the sacks and blankets, tumbling down among the barrels and buckets of water as the team started off. "Tom!" called Pop. "Where's Tom?"

Tom came charging out of the barn astride Major. They took the corral fence in one leap, cut down through our pasture and hurtled the gate, Major's thin yellow legs stretching out into long, even strides. They disappeared beneath the hill, the clatter of the wagon behind them, shot up over the next hill and the next like greased lightning, growing smaller and smaller, farther and farther ahead of Pop and Gus and Harry, catching up, passing others.

Mother and I could make out the moving forms now, see them running about like tiny figurines, now silhouetted against the blaze, now enveloped by the smoke. The Weiss house vanished from view. Mother covered her face with her hands. Big, black columns of smoke arose as the men frantically beat the flames with wet sacks.

"Look!" I cried. "The house is still there. There it is, Mom!"

She opened her eyes. "Thank God!" she breathed. But our precious hayland and our menfolk were still in danger.

Jumping the firebreak, the headfire went within half a mile of our hayfield, then burned itself out at an old slough bed. They fought the side fires until late in the evening. They had saved the widow's house and most of her stock, but the other buildings, the grain, a few chickens, an old sow—all were destroyed.

Slowly the wagons began to trickle back toward home. Tom came first, smudged and scorched from head to foot. Major's tail was much shorter; he held it high and carefully now. Gus let Harry off at the gate, and right behind came Uncle John and Pop. Side by side they had fought, and, somewhere in the smoke and flame, they had also fought their differences and buried the hatchet. Uncle John stayed for dinner.

"You'd better git that firebreak plowed, Tony, an' right away," he said, smearing a piece of hot cornbread with yellow butter.

"Yes," said Father, "first thing in the mornin'. You hear that, Tom?"

"Now in the old days," John continued, "we'd catch a big steer, split 'im in two, an' tie the bloody halves beteen two horses an' drag it through the flames to put out a fire!"

Mother winced. I pushed my Jello aside and left the table.

"Musta been big fires them days," ventured Pop, trying to get away from the blood-and-guts trend.

"Yes siree!" John held his cup for more coffee. "All this country's been burnt up sometime or 'nother. That's what makes the land good. After a big fire, a fire say twenty miles wide, hundred miles long, the prairie was full of dead buffalo, stampeded and burned to a crisp. Bones make good fertilizer." He grinned at Pop's scowling face.

As fall drew near, the intense heat subsided. There were quiet, silent days when the grain fields were hills of whispering gold, undulating ever so softly in the bated breeze. So warm, so tranquil was the spell that one stretched out on the brown, dry earth, whose dead, tufted prairie grasses made the lying hard, but put even the breeze above you. The sun alone stood between you and the blue sky of your God.

Time stood still.

By harvest time the heat had done it's damage, the rust taken its toll—it was a bad year for farmers. Our crop was no better, no worse, than that of thousands of others far more experienced than we. Borrowing Gus's binder, Tom and Harry harvested our meager crop, then Gus hired the whole family to do his shocking—that is, all except Father, who suddenly developed rheumatism.

There is an art in shocking grain, just as there is an art in cooking or catching rivets or shooting a basketball through the net. Tom and Gus walked along tossing the bundles together, setting them up like tenpins, with quick, precise strokes, while we staggered awkwardly under our burdens, unable to make the shocks stand still. But for all the sweat and strain, we loved it. There was something clean and sweet about the harvest, something biblical about the reaper and the golden sheaves of grain.

A couple of days in the hot sun, and mother willingly retired to the house to cook for the menfolk. I wasn't much good either, but I tagged along behind the others and made two dollars a day. It was my first job.

Gus liked having us there. "Aye no drink a t'ing, now," he assured Mother. "Aye only drink ven aye lonesome, but now have party like in ole country. Yah, yah, you cook lots of t'ings; I pay for dem, have like party, yah?" Later in the day Mother heard his cracked voice ringing out over the fields as he sang the songs of his native land, stopping now and then to bellow with glee at Tom and Harry's absurd imitations.

In 1915 a growing rebellion against "big business" and the "city fellers" resulted in the formation of the Non-partisan League, a political organization composed entirely of farmers. The League swept the country like a prairie fire. In 1916 it was ready to take control of the state. My father was cheered by this odd turn of events. When he left politics back there in Des Moines, a rockbound farm in the middle of North Dakota was the last place in the world he expected to find it again; but there it was, all about him, on the tongues of everyone, for the farmers were up in arms, drunk with their sudden strength and powers.

"We join da 'Nonpartition League,'" said Gus. "Big business, dey take our money, dey cheat us wid our grain. Ve do dere verk; dey sit behind big desk an' smoke big cigar wid our money. Dey dirty t'ings!"

"But what you 'spect a bunch of green farmers to do in office?" asked Pop.

"Dey can yust be 'onest!" shouted Gus, all six feet of him rising in anger. "Dats vot dey can do!"

That Saturday Pop went to Steele with Gus and Oscar Olson and August Nordland for a political rally at the Farmer's Union hall. Something about Townley, the dynamic little organizer, inspired Pop, set him to thinking. Two weeks later, when Lynn J. Frazier, the League's gubernatorial candidate, came through Driscoll campaigning, Pop was the first to shake his hand. "Remember me, Governor, when you get to the capital. I'm Tony Thompson." The big, pleasant-faced man smiled and shook his hand.

That night Pop wrote a letter.

Fall was the time of threshing, of hunting, and of cold drizzling rains. As the sloughs and ditches filled, wild game flying out of the North paused to feed in the fields and swim in the muddy water. There were little brown-flecked teals and big green-necked mallard ducks with their gray coats and white dickies; in the grain and high grass were prairie chickens, fat, meaty birds, close kin to the grouse and the pheasant; and far, far up in the blue heavens came the melancholy cry of the wild geese, kings of the sky, flying like silver-arrowed squadrons on their pilgrimage to the Southland.

Each dawn found Tom lying motionless in the weeds at the edge of the slough and heard his old shotgun explode noisily in the crisp morning air. Tom's shooting was good, considering his weapon, which had a habit of dividing into four parts every time a shot was fired. He swore he killed the first duck with the barrel of the gun; said it flew into the air and knocked the mallard in the head. There were no bullet holes in the duck, but the general consensus was that it died from natural causes, that is, old age. Mother refused to cook it.

The next one resembled a sieve. "Just lay the dressin' outside the body," Pop advised Mother. "It gonna come right out them portholes anyhow. Son," he continued, "never mind what I told you 'bout the whites of their eye. Next time, you backup off that duck an' then shoot. This here gravy is plumb full of buckshot!"

As soon as the rains ceased and the fields dried, the threshing season began. Pop engaged his brother; then, with difficulty, broke the news to the family. "A man couldn't hire somebody else when his own brother had an outfit, the biggest outfit 'round here. What else could I do?"

"You won't have nothin' left, time you pay him," Tom warned. "You know how he charges. That brother stuff don't mean a thing to Uncle John when it comes down to business. You ought to know!"

"But what must I do? Somebody got to thresh the grain!"

"Kill the fatted calf, get out the velvet carpet, and bend low, chillun," shouted Harry from the window, "'cause here comes Massa John now!"

A thin string of smoke moved slowly over the prairies as John pulled his crew out of Knudtson's field, heading for us. Suddenly Sue rode up out of nowhere and ran into the house. "Hello, Aunt Mary, Uncle Tony, kids. Papa sent me to tell you to get ready. We're movin' over now. About thirty men'll be here for supper. Papa told me to tell you." She patted my cheek, gave a poke at Tom, and was on her horse and gone.

"Tonight!" wailed Mother. "Tony, you said next week they'd be here, you said John told you next week! What will we feed them?"

"Oh, my Lord! Oh, my soul! Comin' here this time of night, with all them hungry men. John know better'n that. Whyn't he stay where he was 'til mornin'?"

Tom rode into town on Major and brought home a gunny sack full of groceries. There was a preponderance of pork and beans not included in the list Mother had given him, but Tom loved pork and beans.

Uncle John presided at the first table. He quickly scanned the food, then used his short grace, the Methodist one about the nourishments of the body—if he could be permitted to call cold boloney nourishment. Food at the second table showed decided evidences of having been tampered with, stretched, but the hungry threshers never hesitated. They didn't expect too much in the way of "vittles" from new folks, especially city folks.

I don't think my mother and father got any sleep that night. They peeled vegetables, baked bread and cakes, and set the table up for five-o'clock breakfast. I was up before dawn with the rest of them, thrilled and excited by so many people, in everybody's way. Breakfast over, Pop and Harry took the wagon into town and got enough food for three more meals. There was less than a day's work, everything going all right. But everything didn't.

At ten o'clock the engine broke down. The men came in from the field and sat around the yard until it was repaired, then, on the first round, Slim's pitchfork went into the separator. John swore and raved, and the men came back to the house to pitch horseshoes until suppper. Slim was an I.W.W.

The next day broke cold and cloudy. It began to rain at breakfast, a hard, driving rain, tapering off to a slow, chilly drizzle that lasted throughout the day. Pop bought more food for the men. Pop bought more oats for the horses. Tom and Harry went out into the rain and hauled in more of our precious hay.

"I'm goin' home," said Ben. "It's a damned shame, all of us hangin' 'round here eatin' you folks out of house and home, Uncle Tony!" There was true love in Pop's eyes as he waved good-bye to his nephew.

John soon followed, taking some of the men with him. The farmers in the crew, those who lived near by, also went home, but we still had thirteen pie-hungry hoboes. Tom and Gus went hunting, and that night there was roast duck and dressing and sweet-potato pie. The men sat around on the floor after supper, telling stories and singing until late into the night.

Mother's heart went out to those men, some mere youngsters away from home for the first time. A tall, clean-faced kid, not much older than Harry, a kid from somewhere in Ohio, helped her with the supper dishes. He asked to help. He didn't talk much, just wiped the dishes, then sat watching Mom work down the bread and set the rolls for morning. After awhile she gave him pencil and paper, and, while she peeled potatoes, he leaned over the kitchen table and wrote a letter to his mother in Ohio, telling her he'd be home soon—in time for school. Even among the older men there was a feeling of fellowship, a natural affinity to us and our pathetic efforts at hospitality. Pop, who hadn't smiled since the threshers descended upon us, joined in the storytelling that night. Slim taught me the signs of the hobo language, and I hitched my wagon to the open road and gave the Indians a rest.

By noon of the third day, the rain ceased and the sun came out. Uncle John finished our threshing!

What little of our share of oats was left after the men had fed their horses, we stored in the granary; the rye, the flax, and the blighted wheat went into town to be sold and divided with Hank Hansmeyer. The few dollars we realized from the year's work was outnumbered by

creditors three to one! To Carl Brendel went the first
check and Harry's services (gratis) for as long as he was
needed. Because we had to eat and because we had
to—Old Lady Anderson and Uncle John were paid in full.
With newly borrowed money, we paid the interst on the
mortgages and then gave the banker a new note covering
the purchase of a couple of cows. We were still broke
and further in debt then ever. There was nothing left to
buy a farm of our own, not even money for clothing
and food to tide us over the dreaded winter; so, with a
definite lack of enthusiasm on Pop's part, it was decided
that he and Tom finish the season with John's crew. A
man and team could earn seven dollars a day, and there
was nearly a month's work left.

Mother filled two gunny-sack mattresses with fresh
straw and rolled up the heavy quilts inside them for the
cold nights on the frosted ground. Arrayed in new
harness and hitched to the smallest rack, Dixie and Buck
bore Pop proudly off into the cold dawn, Tom following
close behind.

Four days later Pop came home, Dixie and Buck
preceeding him by fully an hour. Pop was limping
noticeably, elaborately. He was home to stay.

Every Saturday night we waited for Tom. "He's
coming, Tom's coming!" we cried when we heard the
faint rumble of his wagon far away over the prairies. As
it grew louder, came closer, Harry and I raced down the
road to meet him. We wouldn't eat on Saturday nights
until Tom came home; then we sat in the kitchen around
the warm range, eating hot rolls and butter, drinking the
thick, freshly churned buttermilk, and listening to Tom's
tall tales of threshing.

The catalogue is the farmer's Bible, his literature, and
when it has passed its usefulness in that capacity, when
it no longer is current, it becomes a salient accessory to
the outdoor plumbing, where it is further and more
deliberately perused. On Sundays, with Tom home, we
gathered around the table after dinner and made out the
fall and winter order, each one making out his own lists,
selecting his clothes and Christmas gifts from the slick,
colorful pages. My lists invariably included a saddle and

bridle, but I settled for a box of chocolate bars—without almonds—and things like woolen sweaters and long fleece-lined underwear which lost its fleece at the first washing.

Everyone helped on the food order. It was fun for us, buying in such large quantities; but to Pop the cook it was the old restaurant routine, old and dear to his kitchen heart. We picked out choice cans of fruit, favorite vegetables, and always the little wooden buckets of white fish. The fish had to be thawed and soaked to remove the salt, but the brine was good for Father's feet, so we ate white fish steadily for four years.

Tom gave half of his threshing money to the house; the other half he spent on his secret list, laboring arduously and mysteriously over the order blank, throwing out strange hints, asking odd questions. Long after dark, Mom and Pop worked over the lists, cutting them down, substituting good for not quite so good, fitting the order to our limited budget, and preparing for the terrible winter days ahead.

Mother and Father shuddered at the thought of the approaching winter, those days and weeks and months when we would be marooned from the world by an arctic wall of ice and snow. Twice they put a heater on the list, and twice they replaced it with food and clothing.

"We can git along with the stove we got for one winter," said Pop.

"But, Tony," Mother protested, "it's only a laundry stove, a two-hole laundry stove! We can't heat this old house with a laundry stove."

"What's the reason we can't? I won't have nothin' to do all winter but keep it goin'. Besides, we got the range in the kitchen."

"All right, then, but remember they burn lignite here, not Iowa hard coal. You know what a time the Evanses had with that stuff last winter."

"I told you I'd make it burn, didn't I? Never saw no coal yet I couldn't make burn."

"Tony, if we can survive this winter, we'll make it; I know we will. Next year we'll have a bigger and better crop, and we can buy that land across from the Widow Weiss."

"That'll make a good farm, Mary. It's high and smooth like a baby's skin. Ain't much rock on it either; I been all over it on foot. I want that land, Mary. We been through one year out here, and we ain't none the worse off 'cept for a few more debts. If we can just make it through this winter, we'll belong here. Lord, we'll be farmers, sure 'nuff!"

"I Intend to Stick"
Hilda Rose

In the introduction to Hilda Rose's letters, the editors describe the unusual circumstances that led Hilda to write letters and thus record the story of her heroic life as a farm woman. During the long winter months she needed books to maintain her sanity, so she wrote to the Chicago Tribune *office, asking if they had books that they could send her. This contact led to a correspondence with several women. The letters she received from these women were her link to the outside world. But her letters to them did much more than simply maintain the connection. At one point she says, "I have no women to talk to, so I will write to ease my brain." Putting words on a page helped her cope with hardship; eventually, when the mail carrier came, the words were posted to one of her friends.*

Her letters begin in 1919. There had been a three-year drought in Montana, where she had been living since 1906. She married a man who was 27 years older (referred to as "Daddy" in the letters). She has an infant son ("Boy"), and she is also taking care of two orphans.

Hilda's letter of 25 March 1925 marks a turning point in her sense of self. Crops have been good, "Daddy's" health has improved, and even though her life is "full of work" she has the time to evaluate the past 12 years. She says, "I have found my life work." She no longer dreams of the day when she can return to a town and teach and enjoy cultural events; she recognizes that she has a mission to improve the lives of women in her sparsely settled community.

In the summer of 1925 most of the neighbors are leaving because of the drought. Daddy wants to go to

Alberta or British Columbia. Hilda says, "I don't want to go. It's so beautiful here. I love it, and I dread the unknown." Nor does she want to go to a city: "Better to die fasting with a flower in my hand." Eventually Hilda chooses a homestead site in Alberta, north of Edmonton, where the soil is rich and gardens are fed by regular rainfalls. Once again she must endure the deprivations of frontier existence. Nevertheless, she writes that she "intends to stick." In her last letter, dated 31 May 1927, she vows to show the fur traders that she can stick it out in their wilderness longer than any other white woman has.

Source:
Hilda Rose. "The Stump Farm: A Chronicle of Pioneering." Atlantic Monthly *February 1927: 145-52; March 1927: 334-42; April 1927: 512-18.*

---. "The New Homestead: Letters from Fort Vermilion." Atlantic Monthly *September 1927: 289-300.*

We are friends now, so we won't stand on ceremony. At last! At last! I am going to have friends who will be glad to see me when I go back to the world for a visit or to stay. Time will tell, but I presume that it will be when I am old and gray. I can see one farmhouse from here, but it's about a mile off and the inmates are impossible. The nearest "shack," about as big as a henhouse, on the east, is inhabited by a crippled grandmother and her son. I tramp through the woods to see her once in a while. She is very poor and ignorant, but I like her, and she treats me like an equal. On the west I am bounded by the woods, and also on the north. So there isn't much to see, as we live in a depression, or small valley, on this shelf or bench. I can't go anywhere very often, though I do get out for at least one picnic every summer, given by the Farmers' Union. I belong to it, but I have to go alone, as Daddy is so old he doesn't like to go anywhere any more. So whenever I can, I take the boy and go. But it's the winters that are trying. That is why I had to have something to read, or go crazy. You don't know how anxiously I look in the glass as the years go by, and wonder if I'll ever get to look like the rest of the natives here. You have seen overworked farmers' wives, and weather-wrung and sorrow-beaten faces, drooping mouths, and a sad look.

I want to go back, I don't care where, and have friends once more. I must not look like that--No! No! I want to be elected president of a club, and go to socials,

and I want to eat ice cream. I also would love to live for
a few years in a college town. Wouldn't that be grand?
And then I'd teach kindergarten a few years, and join a
card club. But the truth of the matter is that I'll
probably spend the rest of my life right here. But dreams
don't hurt--nor do air castles, and maybe they'll come
true.

For the third year we are having a drought. Each
year has been a little dryer, until this summer, and I
don't believe we'll get any hay at all. Daddy and I
thought we were getting along well until the dry years
came.   Then we sold the old cow and bought feed for
the calves. Last summer they went, all but a few head,
to buy feed for the team, and food for us, and we got
into debt besides. I couldn't stand it. Daddy was nearly
beside himself with worry, so I wrote to the *Tribune* for
reading matter. All winter I have read aloud to Daddy
and helped him to forget. We went through a siege of
the flu also this winter, so our dear Daddy is practically
an invalid. He may get stronger after a while. Ruth and
I do the chores, which are not many. What we are going
to live on this winter I don't know. Something may turn
up. We may get a rain before it is too late. By religion I
don't know what I am. I never could decide. Daddy says
I'm an atheist, but I hope not. Sometimes I doubt if
there is a God. He seems so terribly cruel to his children.
And what is he and where? My brother says I am an
agnostic. They don't believe anything, you know.

                                          December 12, 1919
I imagine you are in a garden, and roses are in
bloom, and calla lilies as tall as a man. That is California, I am told, even in winter. It is nice to dream about
it, and forget for a while that the thermometer is thirty
below, and it seems next to impossible to get my feet
warm even when I put them on a piece of wood in an
open oven.

I undress the children and then I dress them for the
night. I have plenty of comforts, but still they'd be like
ice in the morning if I didn't dress them up warm. I put
one of Daddy's old patched shirts on the baby, then an

old pink faded eider-down dressing sacque of mine, then a crib blanket over his shoulders for a shawl, and then he is wrapped up on an old wool shawl that belonged to his dead grandmother.

I expected cold weather, though not so early. The drops of water I spill on the floor freeze at once. Why, my milk freezes on the table with the hot stove going. But this bad cold spell will let up soon, I think. It seems unusually long, though.

The drought was broken after fourteen weeks, but it was so late that we didn't even get a spear of hay, and had to buy straw. That is poor stuff to make milk on, and I am quite short, having butter to use only one day a week. And the horse is very poor indeed. My riding pony, who is used to good feed and is getting old, will hardly survive the winter, though Daddy is doing his best by giving her the chaff.

I never thought that I would go through the horrors of a drought, but this is the third year now. Last year I helped Daddy take the straw that had bleached for ten years on an old log henhouse, put there to keep it warm, and we fed it to the starving horses. I lay on my knees many times in the empty hay barn, after scraping the ground carefully for one more forkful of blackened old chaff to give the poor animals, and I prayed as I have never prayed before, as I looked up at the stars that shone through the roof where the shakes were gone. They looked down on me so cold and pitiless that at last I couldn't see them for tears and I went back to the house, washed my eyes, and tried to smile, for Daddy had the flu, and Ruth and Boy were just getting over it. Daddy would get up and try to work, and then get sick again. He's only sixty-six, but already broken in health, and isn't well yet. I have straw enough this winter, but it's not paid for, and I don't know how it will end.

Another drought and we leave in a wagon, if there are any horses to pull it. Very likely we'll go on foot. Where to? Daddy says Alberta, Canada, to take up a homestead. I can just see him, feeble and gray, with a frail wife and infant son and two orphans, starting life anew on the frontier.

Don't worry about us this winter. I have beans and
five sacks of potatoes and lots of berries canned up. You
see, when the cupboard was getting bare last summer, I
slipped away and picked berries on an irrigated ranch,
and took my pay in vegetables and berries. I'm not very
big, and I have to jump around quite lively with my big
family so sort of helpless on my hands. Sometimes I'm
too tired to sleep. Am I an atheist? Well, I don't know. I
believe I would be happier if I felt nothing, feared
nothing. Hoped nothing and believed nothing. Life is
breaking me on its wheel because I have wanted so much
of life.

                                        Spring, 1921
Thanks for the package. Daddy and I are enjoying the
literature immensely. And the children will love the
"pretties" you picked up for them.

Since my last letter to you girls I have had my
parents come to live with us. I went down on the prairie
and borrowed a cow for her milk. She gives about six
quarts a day, and that is luxury for us.

Potatoes are plentiful, and there is no sale for them.
They sell for twenty-five cents a hundred pounds, and
last year I had to pay ten dollars a hundred for them. If
there is no change in conditions the farmers will be sold
out, as nearly everybody is in debt up to theirs ears out
here too. I'm in debt for seed and taxes for last year and
there will be seed and taxes for this year added to that.
Then if we don't get a crop you can send for the
undertaker.

But if Daddy can stay well and work,--he's a dreadfully hard worker for his age,--and if we get hay, and
if we get that pig fat enough to butcher, and if we have
good luck with the cows so we get lots of milk, and if
our vegetables grow, we'll have enough to eat anyway
next winter. Daddy wants to hew out some ties for the
railroad and I wrote to three roads, but they all say they
are not buying any, but maybe they will later on.

I have a lovely flower garden. There are three rose
bushes, a peony (red), some jonquils, a bleeding heart, a

pink tulip, some flags, London pride[1], a lemon lily, Shasta daisy, sweet Mary, sweet William, southernwood, pansies, a lilac, and a bush honeysuckle. Only the jonquils are in bloom yet. I take much comfort from my flowers. We have a square bed 20 x 20, and it's only pretty until August 1. After that it is a brown, dusty, dry patch, but it always revives with new green every spring. I spend lots of time on it; odd moments when my soul is weary.

It has taken me years to collect these flowers, a root here and a slip here, and each has a story of its own. A robin is building a nest in a bush, a wren has rented a coffee can I nailed to the house. I made a hole in the cover. A pair of martins (bless their hearts) rented a flat I made of an old cigar box by putting a roof on it and nailing it to the house too.

So I have lots of bird neighbors. The bluebirds are occupying their old house on a post, and the swallows have already new babies in their clay house, under the eaves.

July, 1921

At last I have found time to write to you in answer to your many beautiful letters to me. I have read the three religious papers and was surprised to find them interesting and worth keeping, too, to read over again next winter when I'm snow-bound. Another little paper that comes regularly is the *Cheerful Letter*, and it's fine. The *Good Housekeeping Magazine* came, and it was such a treat. I've read it even to the ads.

The nomad life you speak of in your letter would suit me, but with the bunch of invalids, or what you call semi-invalids, that I have to take care of it is impossible. My father (76) and mother (74) and Daddy (68) are too old to travel, and I dare not take the risk of moving anywhere just now. Father is partially paralyzed, but not in his legs, so he can walk yet, and Mother is

---

[1] A hardy perennial which is native to Ireland; cultivated in English gardens. *Saxifraga umbrosa.*

too feeble to be up all day, so she lies down after each meal for awhile. And Daddy is so tired he goes to sleep if he sits down anywhere, so you have a picture of my three old darlings, and can readily see that as long as I have a roof over their heads I have to stay there.

You think I still believe in God, but I don't. Three winters ago I gave him up. It was on a cold winter night, and Daddy was in bed with pneumonia. This was in February. I left Ruth to watch him while I went out to feed the stock. I gave the horse some straw that I got on the floor of an old log henhouse. There was no hay, no straw, and the poor cows got nothing. I knelt on the dirt floor of the old barn. The roof was old and broken and the stars looked at me, bright and cold, and I prayed for help. I begged and prayed and cried until I was cold. There is no God. That was the beginning of the end. Twelve head of cattle died and the rest were all but dead when spring came.

The earth is beautiful and life could be so pleasant if it were not for the terrible struggle for existence.

Two weeks later.--I could almost believe in God. I wish you could have seen Daddy out in the rain doing up his chores this evening. With his white beard flying in the wind, and his old white dog, he reminded me of old Rip Van Winkle. Are we happy? Did you ever go through a drought on a farm? If you have, then you'll appreciate rain. So we're all happy, too happy. Yesterday we were blue and worried. Daddy looked so tired, and I knew he was worried, and he helped me to water some of the vegetables. I was so tired I couldn't sit up to write you even a line and I'm glad I didn't, I was so blue. I set out four dozen cabbage plants a week ago, and carried each of them a pail of water. It was so dry and dusty, and the hens got in one day and ate up all but four of them. Well, I finished replacing them yesterday, some way, and carried water to them until I was too tired to talk.

Since the rain came there is sure to be a crop this year and I can't tell you how good it seems. It is July now, and I have onions and lettuce on the table every day, and green peas will be on in a week. My garden is small, but ample for our needs when it grows.

And what do you do in California all summer long? Do you read and tatt and go to the movies? What a life! Or do you do things and keep moving? I can't sit still. I love to work, but this God-forsaken country gets me discouraged.

Just now it is a little taste of heaven. I heard a lecture at our little school-house last Sunday entitled, "Millions now living will never die." It said the Millennium would start in 1930. Have you heard about it?

December 27, 1922

I think of you often, and of your kindness to a little unknown mortal up here in the hills. The "thing" that I feared has got me. I'm afraid I wanted to keep up with the world outside, wanted still to have ambitions and dream of better things; but the never-ending struggle for existence and the lonesomeness are telling on me, and I feel so old, so drab, and so hopeless. I quit writing, and yours was the only Christmas card I have received. The girls, N. and her friends, must think I'm terrible and ungrateful, but I'm not ungrateful, just too tired of life and living to write.

Daddy is more and more feeble, so I have more to do than before; getting wood and water is hardest, and I must do the milking too very soon. I planted and raised a good garden, and potatoes too; dug them and put them in the cellar myself, about one hundred bushels; but they are not worth ten cents to sell, so I am feeding them to the cows and the hens. I sold all the old hens in June, and bought a good hand pump and pumped water on my garden from a spring, so this year I have the cellar full of vegetables, thank God. Daddy has been going to make a pump for years, but I saw plainly that I must take the helm and work.

Ruth, poor child, died in April, at the Home. Then, as if I didn't have enough to bear, the father who deserted the two children about eight years ago appears, and takes the other one away, and disappears into the big wide world. So once more I am alone with Daddy and Boy.

Daddy talks every day of his birthplace in Canada. He wants to die on Canadian soil among the Indians. It doesn't matter to me where I go, or when I die, and I have told him I'll go to the end of the world with him whenever he wants to pull out. I would do anything to make him happy, my sage and poet; and if a tepee will do it, he shall have it in the land of his birth. So some day you may get a letter from a village up North among the "Yellow Knives" or some similar hair-raising name. Perhaps I'll start a kindergarten for fat brown babies. I took Boy and went to the Christmas tree at the little schoolhouse up here in the woods. Boy spoke "Little Jack Horner" for them. The first thing he did was to bow till his head almost touched the floor and then throw back his head and laugh gleefully. Then his voice rang out loud with the four lines of the rhyme, and the lumber-jacks nearly raised the roof with their noise. It was Boy's first appearance, and he won all hearts, he was so dear.

I was snowed in for about seven weeks; it was only about five feet on the level, but it drifted terribly. A horse couldn't go through at all. Then two days before Xmas it changed suddenly from ten below zero to forty above, and started to rain, something very unusual, and it is still raining. I hope it continues, so the snow will sink down to something reasonable.

Daddy's only sister came to see us this summer, a very prim old lady who is determined to have Boy. This is the second visit for this purpose since Boy came to us, and I can't give him up. Boy is getting braver than he was, and in time his fear of the woods and the creatures that inhabit them will wear away, I think. I speak of the "good wolves" and "good cougars" and "pretty deer" and weave his bedtime stories about how they feed their babies, and so forth. He didn't seem a bit shocked when a man told us that a large cougar had crossed our place a week ago following a deer. A year ago it would have terrified him so he couldn't go to sleep.

December 28.--I just heard from a man who went by that a Rural Delivery is almost certain to go through the coming year. Won't it be wonderful to see every day? And to run out to see if there is a letter in the box!

When I was snowed in I didn't see a soul except a neighbor woman in a small shack near by. I wallowed over there every week to see if she was all right, as she was alone with two babies under two. Her man is a lumberjack, and got stalled forty miles north. He just got back.

January 24, 1923

You surely have accomplished what I thought was impossible. I had given up hope of ever feeling real cheered up again. Life is so hard on a stump ranch when things go wrong. How lovely those violets must have been when they were picked! They still retain a little fragrance. They reminded me that summer would come again if I only have patience.

Boy goes out to play with his sled every day now. It is hard to keep a lively child in the house all day, but I have to when it's from ten to twenty degrees below.

His aunt lives in New Haven, Connecticut, so it is quite a trip for her. I'll never give the boy up as long as I can work for him. She offers him a college education if I give him up. I tell him he must work his way through college, and perhaps, now that hope springs again in my heart, I may get to be a writer and help him.

I was not joking about going to the ends of the earth. That is, the civilized part of it. It's a grim reality that is steadily coming closer.

You know that one's childhood is a happy state of mind. Nothing you eat now tastes half as good as the same things in childhood, nor is anything half as nice as the place where you were born.

That's how it is with Daddy. He is seventy, getting older every day and a little slower, and just a little dearer to me as he depends more on me. He got what you call second sight this year, and reads without glasses now. But he doesn't live here any more. His body is here, but his mind is in Canada, where he was born. Land in Quebec is sky-high, so we must go far to get a free homestead, you see. Maybe we'll never get there. He has talked about it for the last four years. If we go it doesn't matter, for it can't be harder than here.

I can't teach school and take care of Daddy too. So I
thought I would get some traps and try for some furs up
there; live like an Indian; shoot and fish and trap. Boy
will soon be quite a lad and able to help me. His
education won't be neglected, for one of my greatest
pleasures is teaching him. I have a map of the world
pinned up on the wall, and he is learning geography
from it. I have *Gray's Anatomy*, and he just loves it.
That is his best picture book. At the table when I have
cooked a hen he gravely tells Daddy to give him the
femur or the radius and ulna. The old white dog is lazy
and won't play with him, but a stray pup about ten
months old came Christmas week. Boy is sure Santa Claus
sent him, and they have great romps together. I named
the dog 'Bonny Lad,' but Boy shortened it to 'Barney.'
So Barney is his name now. He is a beautiful black
shepherd dog with a wonderfully kind disposition, and I
hadn't the heart to turn him away after Boy welcomed
him so joyfully.

March 22, 1923

I have been ill, and it is hard for me to write, but I
must thank you for the reading matter which you so
kindly sent. I can't tell you how much I appreciated it.
First I had flu and then quinsy. I am writing this down
on the prairie. At home I couldn't write. I had no peace.
Daddy is poorly, and I'd drag out and milk and feed up,
and I'd get so tired I was all in. I've run away to-day
and left it. The cow won't be milked or fed, poor thing,
till tomorrow. The roads are so bad I can't get back the
same day. It is six weeks since I have had any mail, six
long weeks, and we had the worst blizzard in forty years
in this six weeks. For three weeks we couldn't get to the
barn. It drifted as high as the second story of the house.
The north and south roads are muddy and heaving; the
east and west roads I could[2] hardly get through, as the
drifts are piled up so sidling.[2] I slid and tumbled once in
a while, but managed to arrive at last.

---

[2] Sideways.

March 23.--After a good sleep I feel more like tackling the road back than yesterday. Last Saturday we-- that is, a dozen women who live in the woods around me and on the slopes of the mountains--gathered at the schoolhouse. I wrote the posters and sent them out to be tacked on trees on trails that I thought would catch some eyes. For the first time we have a teacher with a vision. Why couldn't we have had one before? She is forty-five, I guess, and born in Ireland, which accounts for it. She called on me and we warmed up to each other and she said, "Let's start something." "Call a meeting of the mothers and I'll come and talk to them," I said. She did, and we organized a club, and they made me the Queen Bee, as none of the others had ever belonged to a club. We decided on a box social to raise some money. In a poverty-stricken community a few dollars can do much when there are births and deaths, or forest fires wipe out a homestead. So Saturday we had our box social. We each brought a box with food in it. We made coffee. I brought cream, as my cow is fresh, and the teacher brought coffee. One woman brought bread, another meat, and so forth. The lumberjacks poured in till the little room was crowded (even the standing room) and you couldn't get in. The programme was just stunts. The teacher played the organ, and anybody in the audience who could sing a solo came up and did his best. Some of the men had good, though untrained voices. Everybody brought a lantern so we had plenty of light.

The teacher sang "The Wearing of the Green" till our hearts were breaking, and then men stamped and whistled till she had to do it all over again. One fellow did handsprings and one played an accordion with his back to the audience, he was so nervous, but he played "Marching through Georgia" real well. It was not a critical audience.

The programme lasted three hours and then the boxes were auctioned off. The auctioneer would hold up a box trimmed with a bit of colored paper. I cut clover leaves and pasted them all over mine. And he'd say, "Only a dollar for this box! Why, just see the purdies on it!" And somebody would offer a little more and get it. Those that didn't get boxes could buy a plate with a sandwich, a piece of cake, and coffee for twenty-five cents. We took in $28.75 and I thought that was pretty good. You'll wonder why I did it. Just one instance. In a shack a few years ago a dainty, well-educated woman gave birth to twins. They had had bad luck, there was no doctor, there were three other little ones, and the neighbor woman who stepped in had to wrap the babies in a dish towel. One died. I'm sick of seeing it and doing nothing. These I. W. W.'s who work in the camps are hungry for a good time and won't miss a dollar or two. We are going to repeat it later in the spring maybe. I must close now, and walk back again. Daddy and I enjoyed the magazines, all of them, but the *Atlantic* the most.

October 11, 1923

I am sorry to have delayed so long answering and thanking you for the good reading you sent, but I have to work all the time. It's work, work, until I feel as if I had only a body and the soul is gone. Then night is the happiest, when I can lose consciousness for a short time. To-day I cut cornstalks for fodder. They are very short, but there is an acre of them, and I'm glad I had them to cut. Winter is almost upon us. I am worried about the prunes. They are so nice this year, and a black freeze is liable to come any time. Shall or shall I not get them picked in time? I picked one pailful to-day, but will devote every spare minute to them from now on. We have never seen a year like this since we came here. It has rained and rained. I have never seen such prunes before and I'm almost sick with fear I won't get them in on time. Winter will be here any day, and I still have some carrots and potatoes out.

October 28.--Since writing the above I have dried ten bushels of pears, slicing them by hand and drying them around the stove. I did a bushel a day. Then I picked ten bushels of prunes. They are safe now, and now my work begins on them. This is the third time in twelve years I have had prunes ripen. Usually they freeze.

November 10.--The prunes are well under way. Two more weeks will finish them. Boy and Daddy are both sick with the whooping cough. The ground is frozen a little, not deep yet. I keep digging away at the potatoes, and get a sack most every day. I have fifteen sacks in the cellar now, and I went over to T.'s and picked apples and have ten sacks in the cellar. Culls, but good eating.

One night I worked four hours on Daddy, putting compresses on his chest until he could breathe properly. Twice I have smoked both my invalids so they could get a little rest.

Monday.--Boy is still in bed. He has bronchial pneumonia now, and Daddy is worse. I am more afraid for Daddy than for Boy. I was up nearly all night, but got a little rest in the morning. It would be a comfort to have a doctor, but that is impossible with six months of winter ahead. Queer that doctors are prohibited to the poor. Out here the women get their babies without them, just their husbands doing for them. I have several sad stories laid away in my brain about them, and now I am in the same class. I must struggle on. I have no woman to talk to, so I will write to ease my brain.

Conditions are very hard. The struggle for bare existence is awful, but one gets used to it. Every penny should be used for at least a dozen such urgent needs that I have carried a dollar with me for days, laid it in front of me when I ate, debating what it should go for. Time passes, we live on, and get through somehow. If I accept money it burns me, it seems to lower me somehow. I will never accept any of it any more, for now I see I can never pay any back. This is my diary. It is true and not written for money. The brain forgets, so I will write down each day.

November 17, 1923

Boy is better and sitting up in bed. Daddy's cough is worse. I cleaned part of the henhouse yesterday. It is very dreadful, and the dust is annoying and makes me feel sick, but I'll finish it to-day. It's a big henhouse, 24 x 16, and has a loft where I keep my small late chicks that the hens are mean to.

December 21.--Boy is almost done whooping, and two more weeks will see him well. Daddy is better too. There are still six sacks of potatoes in the ground, and I have given them up. I dressed up in my best dress and wrapped up warm and sat down on the fence to-night for an hour in the moonlight, hoping that someone would go by that was going to the Xmas entertainment at the schoolhouse. The teacher was going to have a tree. I didn't dare go alone, as I am afraid at night. Nobody came, so I went in, and Daddy sang some old Scotch folk songs, and Boy and I were happy again.

December 23.--It is snowing. So old Winter has come in earnest. I am going down on the prairie to-morrow to get the mail, and mail some letters. My calves are home and look nice. They have been on the range all this time, and just came home this week. I tried to sell four of them, and sent word to seven butcher shops, but they have quit buying of ranchers, and I will have to peddle to the camps that are logging in the mountains. Dressed veal is eight cents a pound, and I may get enough to pay the taxes. I have counted so much on them, and am so disappointed, as my taxes are a year and a half behind already. Eggs are thirty-five cents and my hens barely pay their feed bill. Boy is trimming a tree for me. He is busy cutting paper, and I have sent for a box of tiny candles that should be in the mail. I have a ball, a tin horn, and some peanuts for his stocking, so he'll have lots of fun Xmas morning. Dear old Daddy is stargazing again. He watches the stars and wonders about them, why and wherefore they are.

December 26.--Seven yearlings, a few almost two years old, are missing. Where can they be? It has turned so cold, and it is snowing from the north. How I hate winter! I have just pulled in some fence rails into the kitchen, and when I get rested I'll saw them up for wood. The wind is rising again, so it will be a penetrating cold to-night. I don't keep a fire at night, as I can't saw the wood fast enough, but we are very comfortable, even when it is twenty degrees below in the house and a drop of water freezes instantly.

January 7.--Daddy and I and Boy drove ten miles east into the heart of the ridge of mountains. We went up a gulch, but we were halfway up the side of the mountain on a trail cut by the Forest Reserve men. A blizzard came up behind us, so it got pretty fierce, but we had to go on. Daddy drove the old horse, and we sat on some boards nailed on the front bob of his old bobsled. You couldn't take a whole sled in there on the sharp turns on a trail cut barely wide enough to get through. We got word on Sunday that the yearlings were at a logging camp on the Reserve. One of the loggers came down and told us they had been there about two months. It was after dinner when we arrived in camp, but the cook fed us well, and stuffed our pockets with real dandy cookies as big as saucers when we left. The men had been good to the stock and had thrown out feed for them, so they looked good. For shelter they were allowed to sleep in the blacksmith shop, and the men all liked them, for it's lonesome up there.

We started for home, and I drove, and Daddy and Boy walked behind the yearlings, who followed me. I had to go so slow and faced a blizzard all the way. The horses had to pick their own way, as I couldn't see. Boy thought his eyes were frozen, but it was only snow on his eyelashes. It was after dark when we got home. I can't tell in words how glad I was to get home. I pulled off Boy's and Daddy's coats and got them into bed, and made a fire, and went to bed myself until it got warm. It's the only thing to do when you are chilled through. Then I warmed up some soup and waked Daddy and we ate a hot dinner by the stove, using the sewing-machine drop leaf for our table. It was no use to try to thaw the kitchen out--it was too cold. When it storms I read aloud to Daddy, and the papers you sent last year I am reading over again, and find much in them worth reading over.

April 14, 1924

I am down on the prairie for two nights. I walk back Wednesday night. You see, the University Extension Department of Montana sent teachers into the country to teach various things, and I wanted so much to go, I've planned for weeks on how to manage so I could get away. Not so much to learn, although I'll be glad to learn anything, as to meet the teachers and see and talk to a bunch of women once more, for it almost drives me wild to be alone, and it storms so much of the time we only see the sun a few times all winter.

I baked bread and cooked beans and put a pail of potatoes beside the stove real handy for Daddy to bake in the oven, and did all I could to make it easy for him, and took Boy with me so nothing should bother him.

To-night is Monday night, and while I'm a bit tired, having walked seven miles, still I'm so uplifted in spirit that I can't go to bed and sleep. The teachers are wonderful, college girls, and have been out of college and at this work for about five years. They talked and demonstrated hats to-day, and we were all taught frame making. Eighteen women came. To-morrow we cover the hats, and Wednesday we trim. I haven't bought a hat for years, and one of N.'s friends sent me a bunch of old, old hats that had lain for twenty years or more in her closets. "lids," the University women call them. I ripped the braid off, and have material. For trimming they will show us how to make flowers and rosettes of the material itself also. That wonderful cape--it's an open sesame wherever I go. I wore it in M--- and the clerk where I sold my eggs opened the door for me when I left. Such deference to a woman from the backwoods! The University ladies planned my hat to match it, and it's going to be very pretty. The crown is brown horsehair braid, which is so sheer my hair shows through. The brim is tiny and faced with bright blue silk. It will have flowers of the silk. My eyes are blue and my hair is pale gold. They thought it a wonderful combination. Forgive me if I talk so much about myself; one doesn't enter paradise very often.

Up there in the woods where I live (I am on the prairie now) most of the women are very crude and coarse. Against Daddy's wishes (he is an old darling, and thinks I ought to keep away from those women and just be on speaking terms with them) I and the school-teacher called a meeting at the schoolhouse a year ago to see what we could do to alleviate some of the worst cases of distress that came to my ears from time to time. About two dozen women came, and we organized a "Helping Hand." To get money we had a stunt night at the school-house, and I made posters and put them up where the lumberjacks and miners could see them. The programme of stunts was most remarkable. It lasted for hours and then we sold boxes of lunch and made coffee. We took in twenty-nine dollars. We bought a spring and mattress for the dearest old grandma I've ever run across. She is over eighty and was in bed for fifteen weeks without being able to sit up, and lying on the dirtiest straw tick on boards. They met with me, and we dyed flour sacks and pieced two of the brightest comforts I've ever seen. We each pieced seven blocks at home, and used the flour sacks for in between and linings. Grandma was so pleased with them; she said they would pass the time away for her, they were so pretty. Maybe I've told you this before, and how when she was younger she helped over one hundred babies to come into the world before any doctor lived close enough to this district. She came to this country over the Oregon trail in an oxcart when she was seven. Her mother and father both died on the trail here. Many the hardships she passed through. I'm glad she has a decent spring and mattress under her to-night. We next met at her shack and cleaned it. I can't tell you all the things this little band of women have done. We are making a layette for a poor woman who has six half-starved young ones. She expects another one next week. Her children are all mentally deficient, but such people breed like rabbits, and babies are so helpless I can't bear to see them abused.

I worry over my debts and twenty-five dollars I borrowed one spring for seed, and haven't been able to pay back yet. I counted on selling my calves when they got big. But I wasn't able to find a purchaser. Times are so hard there is no sale for anything in this Western country. There is an embargo on cattle west of the Rockies and cattle don't sell. I haven't paid the taxes for two years now, and this year's are due this fall again. I hope for better luck this summer. No, I cannot take a crippled old man, sick half the time, to California, or anywhere else. He has to stay here until he dies. He can't live anywhere else. You know they get crotchety as they grow old.

Boy is a great help and comfort, so I shall tell you about Boy. He has always been a remarkable child, odd, yet fine and strong. Just as soon as he gets among other children you notice how different he is. He sings to himself, and two years ago a sister of Daddy was out for a visit and tried to listen to hear what he was singing about. But he was too bashful. I never paid any attention to it, but after she had gone I got a pencil and paper and wrote down his songs. I haven't them here, so I'll write more about them after I get home.

The verse in the Bible about "Knock and it shall be opened" seems to have a special message for me. For you see Boy and I are planning to go to college after Daddy is gone. I have always wanted to go, and that wanting is increasing every day. So some day a little old, old lady and a young lad will knock at some college door. Will they open for us? The message in the Bible says they will. It doesn't say we have to have money, but just knock.

April 20.--Time passes so quickly when you have more than you can do. Since that dreadful day we went after the yearlings I've had to be legs for Daddy all I can. He froze one toe and the varicose veins broke soon after, and he has a dreadful leg. I am going to write to the University and see if they won't come and help the women up here in the hills. It would be such a treat for them.

December 20, 1924

We are right in the middle of a cold snap. I expect it to moderate in a week or so. We had an early winter this year. It was thirty degrees below zero two nights ago, and now it is twenty-five degrees below zero. It wouldn't have been so bad if the wind hadn't blown so hard. I never saw a stronger wind. It uprooted many trees. I could hear the crashing, and the snow, real fine, sifted into the house everywhere. If I spill a drop of water on the kitchen floor, it freezes instantly. The Woman's Club I started up here had three days' instruction from the University Extension. They enjoyed it so much. Now there won't be any more until spring.

In spite of the drought, we got a big load of ripe wheat hay off of five acres. This has been the driest year we've had, but my little garden did well and I canned 125 quarts of green vegetables off it, besides the roots I grew for winter. Daddy put the hay in a shed and then hitched up the old team and drove them round and round until it was threshed out. The horses were eating big mouthfuls of it, and I told Daddy he ought to tie up their noses. But he wouldn't, for it says in the Bible, "Muzzle not the ox that treads out thy grain." This Bible verse taught him how to do it also, for he had never seen or heard of threshing grain before in that way. Then we raked off the straw, and on a windy day we cleaned out the chaff by pouring it from one pan to another. I grind it in an old coffee mill and cook bread out of the fine meal and gruel from the coarse. A scone baked in the iron spider, from sour milk and soda and this meal, is just fine. I bake one every day. The reason I use the spider is because it requires no greasing. But last month she began to stick and it was so provoking. Daddy joked about it and said the old frying pan got hungry. We were all hungry for fat, for the old cow dried up when the drought came. I get just a little bit of milk to cook with. Taxes had to be paid, so I helped Daddy butcher Blue Bell, a small cow, and then we drove to town and tried to sell her. The butchers all told us they were buying only of the packers, so we went home again. It was bitterly cold, the roads were bad, the horse slow, but I had two bricks (hot) at our feet and we got along fine. Now we are eating the cow and it is certainly grand to have both meat and fat to cook with again. Daddy feels so cheerful that he sings after meals. He can't carry a tune, but it's nice to hear him sing. So far he has been well.

We have a new mail route. It starts on the sixteenth of July this summer, and my Woman's Club up here is what did it. I am so proud of my club and the way they work together. We have twenty-two members now and some are foreigners. A few objected to the foreigners, but I told them these women needed to be Americanized, and that settled it. One of them, an Austrian, is beginning to eat with a fork, and that shows intelligence and desire to be like others. So we get to know each other better, have a community spirit and grow more charitable toward each other. I picked berries on the prairie, and apples in the fall. I broke a finger on my right hand and sprained the joint on it, too, by falling off a stepladder the first day I picked apples. I tied it up and went on working, because I had to. Winter coming on, there was no choice. It ached fierce and is tender yet and a little crooked, but I don't think it will bother me when it gets strong again. It's next to the little finger and I spare it all I can.

March 25, 1925

The magazines you sent me were very interesting, especially as I am working on somewhat the same line with the women up here in the mountains. They are settlers on the cut-over land, and homesteaders, and the land is sterile and frosty, but those that have men that are able to work get along fairly well, as there are logging and construction camps here and there and they can get work.

I started a club two years ago and have now twenty active members, and they are so active and full of life I find it hard to give them enough to do. I should like to join them up with some state organization of women's clubs. They have hard lives, but have big families, and it's an education to these women to get together every other week and discuss welfare work and do things together. Having nothing else, the club is absorbing to them, and the way they tackle the work and obstacles in the way is certainly inspiring. We have started a debating society at our schoolhouse, which meets every other week. Sometimes we have a spelling match for a change, and sometimes just sing while the teacher plays the organ. It is a sparsely settled community and we have small one-room schoolhouses, so three school districts have to get together for any kind of entertainment. Our school is central, so we always meet there.

I have lived here now, on the prairie and up here, nineteen years altogether and I am behind the times in many ways. It was so good of you to send me such nice things. You can never realize what they mean to me, for I stay home from the prairie club many times because I'm not presentable. If it's a nice day, I'm going to a meeting there to-morrow afternoon and wear the new voile dress you sent. It fits as if you had fitted it on me.

I am forty-five next October and I weigh eighty-six pounds, but I am well. Restricted by nature and circumstances to a simple and wholesome diet, I can't help but be well. Because I am so small, I resolved to raise a Better Baby, and my small son is as large now as any ten-year-old in this part of the country. I planned for a baby all my life, and I picked the best Daddy for him. My only regret is that he is so old now, but I am trying to take good care of him so Boy and I will have him with us many years yet. Daddy is a treasure. I don't know what life would be without him. He calls us his two children, and he's never cross, no matter how tired or ill. He was seventy-two last month and has a white beard like Burroughs.[3]

I can't raise many chickens because the coyotes are so bad. They seem to have increased at a most alarming rate lately. Next winter I'm going to have a line of traps for them. I shall work on the places to set them this summer. They are hard to trap, but I may be able to get enough skins to buy shoes and clothes for the boy. He is eight this spring and dreadfully hard on clothes.

It will soon be time to put in garden now. I plant about an acre altogether of garden stuff and potatoes. It's all I can take care of myself, but Boy is getting big enough to help me now and I have rented an acre of irrigated land on the prairie--very rich land which I will put into mangels[4] and beets for the cow. I get two thirds of the crop, but I have to weed and water it. I see I have to have something besides straw for the cow, in order to make milk. Sometimes Daddy is able to work,

---

[3] John Burroughs. American naturalist, 1837-1921.
[4] A large, coarse beet used for feeding cattle.

and sometimes not; so I have learned to go ahead, and if Daddy feels able to help I am very thankful, but I never count on it. I think he feels better this spring than for several years, as he had a good winter; the way he puts it, "I wintered good." Mostly due, I believe, to the fact that he had greens of some kind at every meal.

The University Extension for the Rural Districts has been a great help to me the last two years. I have learned so much from them. The coming year they will teach us more about foods and their effects on the system. What I have already learned has been a benefit, but I am looking forward with much interest to the classes this summer.

March 25, 1925.

You are certainly the best and dearest to write to me when I neglect you so. But my life is so full of work I can't write, at least as often as I would like to, and I do love to get letters.

I was delighted to get a new friend and I clasped my hands with joy, and then Daddy said, "Go slow. If Mrs. T. and this club lady know what sort of women you have taken up with, they'd have nothing more to do with you."

So, now, Mother Superior, I come to confession and I need advice. On only one subject are Daddy and I out, and that's my new club up here. You see it's this way. At heart Daddy is an aristocrat. He'll quote Bobby Burns about "A man's a man for a' that and a' that," but he doesn't practice what he preaches. He considers me so fragile, so nice, so dainty and everything, that I mustn't have anything to do with anybody who has the least blemish on her reputation.

So for twelve years I have minded him, and then I couldn't stand it any longer. I started this club. It has twenty active members and they are all living straight now. The club is keeping some of them straight, they are so anxious to belong. Here is what some of them are: (1) Mrs. C. has two children and almost kills herself once a year to avoid a baby. (2) Mrs. T. is not married, but says she is. We all know better. She lives with Mr. T. and has two children, and does what Mrs. C. does every year. She has wretched health like Mrs. C. (3) Mrs. S. left her husband one winter and lived with the hired man several months. Her husband told her to get a divorce, and she did, but married, not the hired man, but the Greek cook at a railroad construction camp east of us last fall. She is fifty and he is thirty, and it is a poor match. (4) Mary has an illegitimate child, eleven years old, but is a fine woman, and has a good husband now. (5) Mrs. N. is an Austrian and can't speak good English yet, but she has three nice children and a good reputation. (6) Mrs. M. kept what we call "two husbands" up here. It's hard to make a living, she had many children, and an extra man to work was a great help. When I moved up here fourteen years ago there were seven women who lived with two husbands. Mrs. M. was put out of the Farmers' Union because she kept two husbands, but she is living straight now. (7) Mrs. A. is a coarse type that you find in logging camps. She is used to fighting and hair pulling, but has become very sedate and peaceful now. (8) Mrs. W. has spent twenty years as cook in logging camps. The hard work has refined and aged her.

I could go on like this all night. These women have many children, swarms of them in some homes. Daddy claims they are not in my class, that he who touches pitch will be defiled. Then something heart-rending will happen and he'll say, "You'll see the nice women on the prairie won't speak to you when they know who you consort with." And I tell him it isn't so. The women on the prairie are too busy painting their complexions to worry about me, and the University Extension ladies just love me and tell me how much I'm helping them.

Maybe Daddy is right. I'll confess this much. I don't feel the aversion I used to to a fallen woman. This aversion was the result of my mother's extremely Puritan ideals. One day a girl of sixteen came to a school entertainment in our schoolhouse here and she had in her arms a six-weeks-old illegitimate child by a married man. She was there on a seat all alone, and I just picked myself up and went and sat down beside her and held the baby for her. I would have done anything to bring her to lead a good life, but she went to the dogs just the same, and is so miserable now. If I'd had my club this wouldn't have happened. But it was years ago. Now in the city you'd cut dead these women with a past. I know it. A nice woman on the prairie had made a misstep in her youth. She came West to start a new life. An old neighbor saw her and told about her. Nobody goes near her now. That's what Daddy goes by. I used to feel that I must read, study, to go back into the world some day and be broad-minded and take my place and associate with cultured people once more. You said my last letter was cheerful, and I'm glad. It's because I've found my life work. This section has a bad name, and it's because it's poor and hidden in the timber and mountains. I shall change the bad name to a good name if I live long enough. It's uphill work.

Well, I tell Daddy I'm in now, with both feet, and as long as I'm true to myself it doesn't matter what other people think about me. As far as I can see, it doesn't make any difference. The prairie club insist that I must belong to their club down there, and I try to get down there once in a while. There are fourteen members--it's limited to this number. They dance and play cards and meet twice a month. They are very exclusive, up to date, and I haven't the clothes to attend in, so I haven't gone much of late years. Every summer when my garden is ready, so I have peas and lettuce and new potatoes, I stuff a couple of hens, and have the club all up for dinner. Then the vines and bushes cover up the tumble-down looks of the place.

Every summer Boy and I make bird houses. They are rough and crude, but the birds don't care, and so every year we add new folks to our bird village, for that is what the garden looks like. Last year two pairs of wrens moved in, and we already had a martin, several blue-birds, and three wren couples, besides the birds that build their nests. I have learned to make the holes small in the bird houses, for sometimes I've had trouble with the pine squirrels who go in and eat the eggs.

One day about four years ago I went down on the prairie after my mail. We didn't have a R. route up here then, you know. There were several mail boxes down there, and a large dumpy woman was getting her mail too, and I saw that she had been crying. I knew who she was, but had never met her; but I started in to talk to her, and as everybody tells me their troubles it wasn't long before she told me. They were dreadfully poor, trying to pay for a place, and she was going to have a baby. She had three nice boys, and she wanted a girl, and the tears ran again, she felt so bad. You see, Mr. C. didn't want the expense of getting a doctor or even a woman. He said he had always tended to stock and never needed to call a doctor and he guessed he could tend a woman all right. Well, I happened to run into a woman down there who used to be a trained nurse, but is married and has a family. I told her about Mrs. C., and she said she'd look after her for me. She did. She told me about it one day. A few days before Mrs. C. would be confined she walked in with her suitcase and said she'd come to stay awhile. And she sent for good old Dr. H. and he had to take the baby; but it's a lovely little girl, and the mother just adores it. So now you have one of my baby stories.

It takes money to run the club up here, there are so many in trouble, so we pieced a quilt and raffled it off at the schoolhouse last week, and took in twenty dollars. We found an old woman living in a shack with her son, and she was nearly ninety. We sent her a potted plant, and she cried, and said she thought nobody knew about her and everyone had forgotten her. The old woman who came out in an oxcart over the Oregon trail when she was seven died last summer. Well, we made her last days comfortable, anyway. I met a rough lumberjack one day, and he says to me, "I didn't think much of your club when you started it, but my hat goes off when I meet any of youse now."

July 3, 1925

My club up here had one meeting in our little acre cemetery, and we fixed up things real nice. Some raked and burned up the accumulation of years, while others lettered names and dates on white-painted headboards for the baby graves. We put up eighteen of them in the afternoon. It was a busy day, but everybody seemed happy. The happiness that comes from doing.

July 19.--The garden is burned up by the sun, and not a drop of rain for weeks. The peas dried while in bloom, except the early ones, from which we had a few messes. The potatoes held out the longest and we have tiny potatoes like small nuts, but real good, and I'm using them as long as they last. Such a nice garden as it was in the spring, and to look at it now! While pulling up the dried pea vines for the cow, I thought hard. If you think hard enough and long enough on anything, it will finally come to you. Down on those irrigated tracts there was garden truck nice and green, and I had no money. But I made a proposition that had "come" to me and the result is I get canning to do on shares. I have finished the peas and have seventy quarts for my share and am working on string beans this week. I pick them before it's hot and get up at four o'clock to do so. Shelling so many peas was trying, the days are so hot, but it's over with and I feel good when I look at my jars of peas. Boy goes with me and we walk, but it's nice and cool and we never start for home until after seven. After the beans, there will be squash and corn to can. It has made me very happy. In a dry year, I must have more provisions, so I must reckon on enough to last nine months at least. I divide up my supplies into nine parts and as I come to each month's allowance I divide it into so much for each week. Early settlers in New England used to do that and Daddy chants a line (when things don't hold out and he has to go short in the spring) that says, "Only five grains of corn, mother, only five grains of corn." He varies the number of grains each time; sometimes it's six grains, and sometimes seven. But I'll get through to grass nicely this year, for I'll have milk. Other years the cows dried up on the poor feed, but this year they are going to have beets, a pailful each twice a day. That's why I work so hard on my acre of beets. Last year we did not have a drop of milk until spring, and determination to have milk another winter helps me to weed and water the beets on the prairie.

Daddy and Boy help to water them and they are looking fine.

'Be a living question mark,' my old professor in physics used to say, "and you'll never grow old."' I believe I live up to it, for I question the why of everything and get no answer. There are so many things that would make this life happier, why must I go without? These are questions I ask of life and get no answer. If it weren't for "make-believe" I'd give up and become an old woman, tired and discouraged. But Boy has named me Jenny Wren, and who ever saw a mother wren tired? She's busy, busy, busy all day long hunting grub for her nestlings, and so am I. But I take time to swing in Boy's little rope swing under the old apple tree and we have a teeter-totter in the barnyard and we do have fun. When I play, I'm Jenny, but at night I am just "Mother." If you ask Boy what his mother is, he'll tell you: "She's just a little girl." The other day he was out in the barnyard with Daddy and he saw me in the garden. He turned to Daddy and said with a grin, "I wonder what that little rascal is up to now." It amuses Daddy. But I have always loved children and one must have love and infinite patience with small children. Which reminds me that I was reprimanded once by the principal because my kiddies made so much noise at times that the room above was disturbed. We were just having fun and playing games and I toned them down, but that principal did get a good jolt a bit later. There were twelve rooms in the building and I had the primary with sixty babies in it. A much-traveled woman, who was a member of the school board, went around visiting the schools and dropped into my room one day. I didn't know her, but my children treated her fine. She liked us so well she stayed all afternoon and became one of the family. Later she addressed a principals' meeting (nineteen big schools in our city) and this is what she said, I was told: "I have journeyed in many lands and have visited schools in this country and in Europe, but I have at last found the perfect school right here in my home town, in Room 1, at the Jackson School."

You see, the old superintendent and I were chums and he gave me nearly everything I asked for. When I wanted a kindergarten table and chairs, he hunted them up in the garret of an old church (the Sunday school had discarded them) and he let me teach in my own way, which was original to say the least. I was the mother and they were my children. They answered the door and seated visitors and talked to them. We did the regular kindergarten work and first primary combined, but that didn't take us long and we had games and stories the rest of the time and visitors nearly every day. I had no rule except to be kind and not too noisy. They were free to walk and talk to each other, and everyone was so busy and happy the time just flew and soon the gong rang to go home.

July 6, 1925

The weeds in the acre on the prairie took me longer than I expected. I'm not used to that kind of work. . . . I experimented, first one way and then another. First I straddled the row on my knees, one knee on each side of the row and with a hand weeder in one hand, hacking at the weeds, and the other hand pulling out plants where they were too thick. I got along pretty good, doing a row in about two hours. But then burning pain came on my knees and I found them red and swollen and some big blisters. That would never do, so I walked to the nearest house and borrowed two gunny sacks and some sack twine. No one lives on the acre I have rented. I rolled a sack around each knee and tied it, and started the second row. I finished the day that way, but it worried me to find that I had slowed down instead of speeding up. As the sun rose higher and became hotter, it was all I could do to keep up my morale and stick her out. I tried all kinds of ways to amuse my mind. I pictured you and the girls drinking iced lemonade on the deck of a beautiful ship, and J. fox-trotting with a handsome lieutenant, going out to the islands. My water jug didn't taste half so lukey after that. The rows were so long they looked like railroad tracks coming together at the far end. It brought a long-forgotten picture to my mind.

Many years ago I saw Mansfield.[5] I don't remember whom he played with, but I think it was Julia Marlowe[6]. There was some misunderstanding and the heroine went back to her humble life in the country. The hero hunted her up and found her in the "lettuce fields of France." Those long rows of lettuce looked just like the long rows of beets. So after that it wasn't in the beet fields I was weeding, it was in "the lettuce fields of France."

I stood it three days on my knees and then they were so bad I sat down and moved along like a frog in little jumps. In two days I didn't have any seat in my overalls and nothing to patch them with. "There's always something to take the joy out of life," as Daddy says. Then I took the hoe and walked stooped, and hoed and pulled, and next day I could hardly get out of bed. My back seemed to have gone back on me. I made breakfast and washed the dishes three times a day for my board, and I planned to write letters nights, but was too tired. I talked to myself all day; it helped me to forget the blazing sun overhead and the dust and the long, long rows. The utter hopelessness in Daddy's old eyes drives me on. I have thought how nice it would be if we had old-age pensions. Nothing to dread any more. No hunger, no cold. It would be heaven here on earth.

Boy and I have been reading *Alice in Wonderland*. He wants my little "22" so he can "get" that March hare who was so mean to Alice. That March hare lives in the woods just east of us--he's seen him lots of times, he says. But out in the beet field the song the Mock Turtle says rang in my head day after day, but the words were a little different. I tried to get rid of the jingle, but it persisted: "Will you work a little faster?" said old Summer to the snail. "For Old Winter's just behind me, and he's a treading on my tail."

---

[5] Richard Mansfield. 1854-1907. Considered America's foremost actor from 1886 until his death.
[6] 1866-1950. Respected as an actress in American theatre because of her competence as a performer and the morally uplifting roles that she played.

It hustled me up all right. I had another acre of vegetables and beets at home and I couldn't be at it all summer. Well, I finished it in seven days and came home to find my garden choked with weeds and drying up badly. Have been at it ever since. Except for two days when I loused chickens on a hen ranch down on the prairie. Gee, it was hot in that henhouse. I shed everything but my overalls, and I got thirty-five cents an hour, and we, another woman and I, did a hen and a half a minute. That's ninety hens an hour, but experienced workers do a hundred an hour. My job was to catch the hen with the miniature shepherd's crook that caught the leg, put a ring on the right leg, and pass her to the other woman, who put on lice poison and threw her into the hen yard.

The Spokane paper said the heat broke all records, going to 102 in the shade. There was no time for dreaming, or even thinking. I was glad I was little and thin, and my little crook was flying every minute faster and faster. Poor frightened hens! But I was happy, for I was earning a pair of new shoes for Daddy and a sack of flour. Daddy's wheat is all gone and we have been without bread some time. It's been hardest on the boy, but we'll have plenty from now on if I can pick up a day's work now and then. The future looks much brighter.

If I were to put down on paper one half of the struggle, one half of the hardships, or picture one winter, day by day, you could hardly believe it to be true, and yet my life is not half so hard as many here, up in these hills. I can plan ahead fairly well; I know food chemistry and what is needed to keep healthy. When winter comes, I'll have about the same amount of wheat for Daddy to thrash out with the old team, enough potatoes and vegetables and sugar beets to make molasses, which will give us all the sweets we need. Fruit is scarce, but I will have crab apples and rhubarb to can, and that will furnish the acids. A cow to make soups for Daddy and Boy. As Daddy says, "We have taken our noble President's advice and are trying to raise everything we need on the farm." If everyone would try this, it would be better for them. Every month some family is pulling out because they can't make it. M.'s have gone to live in a logging camp where he can work. S. went back to Oklahoma last week. B.'s lost their place because they couldn't pay the interest on the mortgage. L. pulled out with his wife and four lovely children. I asked him, "Where are you going?" He said, "God knows." They lived closest to us, and how little we know even our nearest neighbors. When they left, Mrs. L. and the children walked on ahead and stopped to say good-bye to me. It was exactly twelve o'clock and I had a kettle of soup waiting for Daddy, as he hadn't come in yet. The soup was made from field peas and a piece of pork and it was "licking good," as Boy says. "You're starting early," says I to Mrs. L. "Have you already had your lunch, or are you going to picnic along the road?" She startled me by saying quietly: "We haven't had anything to eat to-day and there's not much show of our getting anything very soon." I said, "Come right in. There's soup and bread and butter and rhubarb sauce, lots of it. I'll tell Mr. L. to tie his team and come in too." I never saw youngsters so hungry in all my life. The little four-year-old girl stood up in her chair and screamed with joy at the sight of the food I put on her plate.

I watched them until they were out of sight over the hill and it was with a feeling of insecurity that I came back into the house. Perhaps it will be me next. There are empty farmhouses all over the West, and each one has its story.

Daddy says every day that he's going to pull out and go to British Columbia. "Why," he says, "it's better than a stump ranch; there'll be grass for the cows and the boy will have a better chance." I don't want to go. It's so beautiful here. I love it, and I dread the unknown. What could I do there with a feeble old man and a young child?

July 26.--I'm worried to-night, not so much for myself as for my neighbors north a couple of miles. The smoke is rolling up fast, big billows of it in the sky, and one by one the settlers have gone by and none have come back, which means there is a big fire and help needed. I hear S. has been appointed fire warden for this district, and a better man couldn't be found, even if he is a bootlegger. A big, clean, helpful man, he was quite downhearted when he got arrested and sentenced to six months in jail. "I oughtn't to have done it," he told me, "but times are so hard." "Cheer up," I said, "no use to worry about it now, but do keep out of the real penitentiary--it's so disgraceful to your family!" Daddy and I don't believe in bootlegging nor lawbreaking, but you can't do anything in a community if you antagonize people. I wouldn't sleep nights if I had helped to put anyone in jail. I love freedom so much myself.

July 30.--Mrs. F.'s house is gone. She lost everything, which wasn't much, but all she had. More work for our Club. All the men except Daddy are gone there. He can't go any more. A strong wind is blowing the flames north, but if it changes, it will be so thick with smoke one can hardly breathe. We are not in any danger, as there is a road between us, and that's a fine firebreak.

There's about a hundred settlers fighting it, and the logging company just sent down as many more to help. Mrs. L. got out in time. These fires roll awfully fast when it's dry, and there's plenty of slashings to feed it along. I see the smoke clouds rolling faster and faster. And what do you think started it? An orphaned boy that's been working around for his board set fire to a yellow jacket's (yellow hornet's) nest in the woods. Those yellow jackets are pesky, but that orphan had better vanish from this neck of the woods or he might get strung up. We consider anyone that starts a fire as worse than any other criminal. It's looking bad. I go out to look at it every few minutes. It looks awfully close. There are several families that will have to get out before very long. It seems to be only a city block away, but that's on account of the hills and the dense smoke. I can tell when the fire strikes into green timber and when it's in slashings. The smoke is so different. It's interesting to watch it, but I feel bad over the homes that are going. Nothing much in the way of buildings--just shacks mostly--but they sheltered from the storms and each was a home.

Latest reports from the fire: A man just came by and says the Forest Reserve has sent help and that the L. home isn't burned yet, and it may be saved; but they are all out, in case the wind comes up.

August 2.--The fire is still bad and cars are running back and forth all night with men. The wind has changed and it's racing up into the mountains on the reserve. It gives the settlers a chance to back-fire before the wind changes again.

You have reason to be proud of your children. When I see fine children, I know they have pure-bred parents, speaking in stock terms. Many times have I wondered why I married an old man, but I'd do it over again to get my boy. Daddy's ancestors are the finest in Scotland and England. I believe in blood and good breeding and I love Daddy for the beauty of his mind, which is the result of generations. What I mean is this: Leisure is needed to cultivate the mind in music, literature, and so forth. Therefore my boy is more receptive and by instinct chooses the better things because I chose for him a father of that type. There are members of the family still living in the ancestral castle in Scotland. His grandfather was a captain in the British navy and we have his old telescope and several other old keepsakes.

I told Daddy to-day that I was ready to pull out any time he was. If he thought it best to go, I was willing to follow him and work for him. If things get much harder than they are, we can't even exist here and we must go like the others, but never to a city. I'd take up a homestead in British Columbia before I'd live in a city. The country has got into my very bones. I love it--the trees and birds and growing things. And city, what would that give me? A little comfort and starve my soul. Better to die fasting with a flower in my hand.

Fort Vermilion, Alberta
July 14, 1926

It did take grit to go to a strange land and my courage almost failed me many times, for I didn't know a soul here or anyone who had ever been here. There were only the government statistics to go by. But when

you're down and out there's not much to lose, so I staked
my all to get here and I'm not sorry yet. The captain of
the steamer was surprised when I told him to land us at
a certain point and he told us there was only one white
settler there. But he said it didn't matter to him, and he
dumped my belongings off on a mud bank where there
was no sight of human habitation. I felt like Robinson
Crusoe as I stood on the shore of this mighty river and
looked at the swamp that edged it, so dense and luxuriant
that I had never seen anything like it. The mosquitoes
soon put an end to dreaming and we all got busy gathering sticks for a nice smoky fire. The potatoes and bacon
cooked over it tasted good in spite of the cinders that
got into the pan. We rolled the boy up in a blanket so
even his nose couldn't be found by the singing chorus. It
looked like rain, so we covered our boxes with the tent
and spent the night by the fire. Daddy fell asleep and I
covered him up from the mosquitoes with a piece of old
canvas. A hard bed for old bones, but the best I could
do for that night. I sat there alone, thinking of all that
lay ahead to do. No home, no shelter, and a long winter
ahead. Two o'clock the heavy dew quieted the mosquitoes
and I turned the three old horses loose to feed in the
swamp. Following them, I was soon lost in the heavy
undergrowth, higher than my head, and I called and
called, getting more frightened every moment, and at last
I heard Daddy's halloo and he came to meet me through
the brush. I was trembling all over when he found me
and put his arms around me and held me close. To get
lost is a fearful thing here. The captain, the purser, and
the cook all warned me to be careful. Then we sat and
watched the sun turn the twilight night into day.

The white settler lives a mile inland on a slight rise
of the land, as this river sometimes overflows and covers
the river flats, but only for short periods and very
seldom. This bottom land is very level and from one half
to two miles wide only. The soil is very heavy, black,
and rich. Above this the land is higher, not so rich, and
lighter.

July 16.--The white settler has given us a bedroom
where we sleep--but we eat at our little camp by the

river. The river is wonderful, over a mile wide and flows north. The banks are very low the farther north it flows. . . .

July 17.--We have picked out our homestead and will move on to it as soon as possible. It will be tough until we get a cabin and get through the first winter, but if we survive that we'll be old settlers. The more I see of this country, the better I like it. Coming from a dry country with a blazing sky all summer, it is pleasant to see the fleecy clouds go scudding[7] by, and there's seldom a day that we don't get at least one shower. The rain isn't even cold and I go out in it just to get my bobbed head wet as when I was a child back in Illinois. The gardens just love to grow here. Mrs. L. is using green beans, peas, new potatoes, beets, carrots, and lettuce on her table and has radishes coming on new and crisp all summer long. Ever since Daddy begged to die in Canada, the country of his birth, I have studied it, and chose this spot as the best and most available in my meager circumstances. Daddy will die happy and contented; we'll have a home without being afraid of being forced to go into some city to die in the slums, and Boy will grow up like Lincoln, in the wilderness.

The "fur" is pretty well trapped out here along the river. But there will always be some. Dogs are used here all winter and our big black-and-white shepherd dog is very much admired by the Indians. . . . Well, I have found the place where hay and potatoes never fail, thank God. Once more I can say the Twenty-third Psalm when I wake in the morning as I always used to do.

Sunday afternoon.--Mrs. L. gathered her children around the old organ for a few hymns. Each one of us chose a hymn, even the three-year-old baby boy. The young married daughter, home with her wee babe, chose a song about love from the songs of matrimony in the English Prayer and Hymn Book. Her father said, "A good hymn." We sang "Onward, Christian Soldiers," "Rescue the Perishing," and many others. It gave me hope and

---

[7] Running or moving swiftly.

strength to carry on when I looked at this wonderful family singing so earnestly alone here in this vastness. I don't know yet just how I'll get a home built. If winter comes too fast for me, I'll have to dig out a room in a small hill on one side of the homestead and put a long front on it. If I have time, we'll build a room entirely of logs. We have an old mower with us, but no rake, so we'll have to rake what hay we cut by hand. . . .

But nothing matters, so we get some kind of a shelter before winter comes. The lowest has been 78 degrees below, but it generally stays at 40 degrees below, which isn't so bad. But the winters are very long.

How beautiful it is and how happy we will be in our little home! I found an old hymn in the Prayer Book that appealed to me and expresses what I can't say myself.

> Some humble door among Thy many mansions,
> Some sheltering shade where sin and striving cease,
> And flows forever through heaven's green expan-
> sions
> The river of Thy peace.

There isn't time to write to Mrs. W. and you will pass this letter on, for I am working very hard and one letter must do for all. Love to you all and write once in a while. The mail this winter comes up by dog sleds when no other way can be used. So we aren't entirely isolated from the Outside.

August, 1926

I have just received your letter and the boat isn't back yet and I'm writing in a hurry to thank you for your letter and the things in it. Next two weeks I will write you and Mrs. W. another letter of the events that come and my impressions of this place. I don't know the date; time means nothing here. I am glad Mrs. W. liked the two adventurers she met in the railway depot for forty minutes. I was very tired, worried, and depressed, so I didn't look my best, but I surely felt good when she actually kissed me and Boy good-bye. She did like me a little, and me a perfect stranger too. The white settler's wife is a college woman and she teaches the children and conducts a real school in a log cabin. Two daughters are home from college and one will teach this year and give the mother a little rest. I'll tell you more about them later, as they are indeed a very interesting family. And these woods and wilderness have human souls buried, I am finding out. That's my specialty, digging up the half dead and helping them to find themselves again. Queer, isn't it? They tell me their troubles and I lay them on you. I am still happy. How wonderful it seems to know I will never starve any more. To always have potatoes and hay for the cow. No "straw horses" any more. Never to hear Daddy say, like Little Claus, "Get up, all my straw horses," and then see the poor ribby creatures try to pull a plough. I have four wool blankets, all heavy, besides quilts. The winter is long and cold and I am trying to prepare for it. I have fifty-six traps and a good location to trap muskrats and also fox. I'll just make it, I figure, and by next fall have a good vegetable garden and what grain I need for bread. I have a grubstake [8] for the winter and spring of beans, dry peas, rice, flour, and vegetables already cached away. The only thing I'm worrying about is a place to live in and I have a month to do it in. No need to worry. Hay for the winter, plenty of milk, fish in the river, and wild game and deer to shoot for meat. I'll make it. "The Lord is my shepherd; I shall not want."

September 5, 1926
The silence almost gets me and I have to say to myself that the same sun shines on you. You see the same stars and moon and it's the same old earth, only I am farther north. It helps some as I stand on this bend of the river and gaze in awe on the northern lights as they play and shake their shimmering curtains. . . . The past two weeks I have seen only two breeds, one Indian,

---

[8] Money or supplies advanced to a prospector in return for a share in his findings. Money advanced for any enterprise.

to see even that many in a month. The boy is changing
even in the short time we have been here. He is more
like a man and takes his responsibilities very seriously.
He is allowed two shells each day for the "22" and is
supposed to bring in one prairie chicken or rabbit each
day. It usually only takes one shell. How proud he is
when he comes in! I hear him whistling long before I see
him and one day I heard him say to Daddy, "I guess I
can keep the pot boiling for Mother." He gets lonesome,
too, and I have to play with him. There isn't a breed or
Indian around here but what he knows their names and
all about them. They have named him "Jabbering Colt"
and he thinks that's a fine name. These silent folk find a
little white boy quite amusing. Boy has another friend in
the Mounted Police who is nicknamed Baldy. He has had
many adventures and Boy is a devoted admirer and
listener. To live up here far from the madding crowd,
automobiles, and movies gives us a saner view of what
life is and time to reflect. There is time to look at the
stars and wonder at their stillness. I have been reading
bedtime stories to Boy and we enjoy them very much.
And in the night I sit up sometimes and listen to some
of the "little people" that hunt for crumbs in the dark.
Last night one that we call Mrs. Deer Mouse fell into the
water pail. I heard her swimming frantically and butting
her head against its side. Poor little thing! I rushed up
and emptied the pail outside on the grass and went back
to sleep. . . .

   This is but a short letter, but the winter will soon be
here and I'm far from ready for it. I had intended to get
us each a warm wool sweater but decided to get two old
ewes and a spinning wheel instead. I have Grandma
Rose's old cards to comb the wool with and next year
we'll have good warm sweaters that I shall knit as soon
as I have the wool. Besides, I'll have the lambs. We can
get along with what we have this winter. I have to look
ahead to the many winters that are coming. There is
plenty of hay and I'm going to utilize it. The tent is

already cold at night, so I can't sit up any longer, as my feet get so cold. My tallow candle is getting low, and so good night.

Lovingly, Hilda Rose

January 18, 1927

. . . . Just think, I've been to a party. A real party, and it seems just too good to be true; and a year from now there'll be another one. But first I must tell you about the Preacher, because he enters so much into our lives. The English Church sends us one missionary and we call him "the Preacher." The old one was pensioned and sent to England the week we arrived here. He thought he could ride his circuit as usual and the result was he was found wandering in a muskeg[9] by the Indians. He had started out with a sandwich in his pocket and no mosquito bar, and when found was out of his head. It's no trouble to get lost here at all. I never venture over a quarter of a mile from home without the dog. When I want to go home I tell him to go ahead and show me the way. Our new Preacher is just out of college. He's a dandy--real good-looking, young, jolly. Can sing a rollicking college song or dance a jig. He is very modern, immaculately dressed, and rides like all Englishmen--bumpety-bump. It looks so unnatural. We enjoy his visits very much and he has called four times already. There are so few here that it doesn't take long to get around.

No, the teacher got cold feet at the last minute and wouldn't come. She was a strong, husky Scotch woman, and if she'd come we'd have got along fine and got our cabins built. Yes, I read your proposition of the irrigated land; I know all about truck, fruit, and apples and the marketing of it, too. It sounds nice, but when you can't sell what you raise, what then? Freight rates are so high that the selling price of the stuff won't cover it. There are no markets in the West. Some day I'll tell you of five years spent on an irrigated ranch. I'm grateful for the offer, but never again will I crawl on my belly for nothing. . . .

---

[9] a bog or marsh

February 11, 1927

These civilized people are scattered over a couple of thousand square miles. Many live in teepees and the rest in log cabins, except two or three who have board cabins. Mr. L.'s house was built by his father forty years ago of boards sawed with a handsaw. Some labor. He gives a party once a year after Xmas. The Preacher was so afraid we wouldn't go that he came after us. It's hard to find the trail in the snow and it's a perfect maze to me, but we arrived at 7 p.m. and after a hot supper the L. children gave their school programme of music, recitations, songs, and dances. They have a big schoolhouse in the back yard and the eldest daughter teaches them. After the programme the dining room and big kitchen were cleared for dancing. Everybody was there except five and the Catholic Mission.

The white women were elderly--wives who had followed their husbands in here. Old-fashioned, unbobbed, and with long skirts. But it was like coming home, so warm was the welcome I received from this lonesome sisterhood. They held my hands so long; they didn't want to let them go. They were nearly all from the States. One had gone insane--not very bad; you could see her mind was shattered. You know it takes some mental calibre to come in here and live alone and not see a white woman more than once or twice a year. If you haven't much in your head the lonesomeness will get you. This woman is poor white trash from the cotton fields of Texas. She knows nothing but work. I questioned her about her life here in order to learn what I could of the loneliness that makes insanity among sheep herders and farm women.

I see by one of your letters that you have no conception of how far north I am. Calgary is a large city crowded with cars. Farther north is Edmonton, also a big city. Next comes Peace River, a small town at the end of the railroad. It has some autos and two wooden hotels. Each hotel has a bathroom in it, but you have to carry your water up from the creek and heat it on the kitchen range if you want to take a bath. Then I went on a steamer that holds thirty carloads of freight in the bottom. We went north all the way until we came to the

Great Slave Lake Region. We got off just this side of it in the wilderness. There are no autos in here. There are nine white people at Fort Vermilion, the Governor, doctor, Mounted Police, Hudson Bay man, and so forth. Get a map and find the Great Slave Lake. A little south of it--that's here. Boy has already had two invitations from Indians to go trapping with them there when he gets a bit older.

The Calgary, Edmonton, and Peace River Town districts are settled with farms till it looks like a checkerboard. Here is the primeval wilderness. Unless I have the dog with me I never dare go out of sight of the house, as I get lost so easily. The white settler's wife and children have to climb a tree quite frequently when picking berries to see in what direction to go home. As there are no roads in the sea, so there are none here.

February 12, 1927

I have now been in bed one week. Last night was a good night and I feel rested and easy to-day. Just a week ago I fell, striking my back on a small bag of frozen salt in the tent. I walked back to my little house, undressed, and crept into bed, and there I've been ever since. It will be two weeks yet before I can walk. I found the hurt place in the Anatomy. The hurt is on the right side.

I lie on my left side. To-day Daddy raised me up in a reclining position, which feels very nice. Boy is the cook, and by following my directions does real well and bakes good bread. Sets his sponge at night just like any good housekeeper. There doesn't seem to be anything out of joint and we're so far from a doctor that at a dollar a mile the price is prohibitive unless something is really broken. The Indians are doctored free, but not white people. Doctors should be free to all people. I'll never have another doctor's bill hanging over me if I can get well without. So tired I won't write any more now.

March 1, 1927

Still in bed, but better. Next week I'll be up again. It was a slight sprain and much bruised. Daddy is baking meat and potatoes for our lunch. Boy is in bed with

acute bronchitis. Running out while warm into the cold
without a coat must have caused it, but Daddy is bringing him around in good shape. He smokes him every day
for the cough. Pours oil of pine tar on hot coals and
makes him breathe the smoke. It loosens the cough up
fine. . . .

My little house. I love it. There is only one room in
it, but I wouldn't trade it for a mansion. I couldn't make
a dugout in the hill, so then I started a log cabin. Eight
logs were laid when the cold came. Such a cold! The
thermometer dropped steadily and we all cut wood to
keep from freezing to death in the tent. We put up the
big heater, but had to wear our coats to keep the cold
from our backs. We lived from day to day. Building was
out of the question. The intense cold just made the meat
on our bones vanish away, and we ate all the time, all
we could.

Thanksgiving Day came, and just at dusk Mr. L.
drove up with four teams and sleds loaded and three
other white men and one breed. They brought everything
with them and, with the thermometer at forty below
zero, put up my little house in six days and had us
moved in. I fed them. They could just get in around the
stove, but they were a jolly crew. They made big fires
outside to get warm by. The icicles hung from their
eyelashes in the intense cold, and they danced war dances
around the fires and whooped to get warm. Mr. L. has a
small saw outfit and saws lumber, and he brought odds
and ends he had on hand. The foundation was logs and
they even dug me a small cellar. I shall pay for the
material and time, of course. But it was queer how they
arrived just in the nick of time. Daddy was in bed for a
week in the little house just from the cold. Nothing the
matter with him at all. The cold grew worse until it was
forty-nine below by my thermometer and sixty below
by self-registering ones. Wasn't I glad we had a shelter at
last!

Been feeling blue because I had no luck trapping,
nearly sick with worry, when like a bolt from the blue
came good news and a check! Look in the February
number of the *Atlantic Monthly* in the back in the

Contributors' Column. "It can't be true," I say to myself a dozen times a day. Mrs. A. sent my letters in to the magazine and they accepted them. I can't believe it. A grubstake for the coming winter; able to pay my debts and buy some clothes for Boy, right out of the blue sky! The piano was never unpacked and the last thing the men did was to set it up in the little house. Perhaps you have already seen the *Atlantic*. I received the February number and the check February 20. I didn't fret any more about staying in bed. Your letter and package came on that day, too, and Boy's book and all the reading for me. You are too good. How can I ever pay it back! Everybody is too good to me.

March 14, 1927

I was afraid you might worry about me, so I'll write a few lines to tell you that the young doctor was out to see me and he examined my back and said it would be all right, but that one kidney was still sore. He left me a heap of pills of many colors which I won't take. The Government furnishes us a doctor and this lad is a dear child just out of college. He is very busy and has a hard row to hoe up here doctoring Indians. I didn't send for him, for I can't afford such luxuries. He came anyway. I guess the breeds must have told him I'd never walk again. I can't walk much yet, but I take a few steps every day now. We had a nice visit and he told me all about college days. It was real nice of him to come sixty miles with a cold north wind blowing, but he said that was nothing. He often went one hundred and fifty miles when it was colder. Some life.

April 29, 1927

I am up and around--not so very strong. Four inches of snow fell last night and it's still snowing, but it will go as soon as the wind changes. As soon as the ice goes out the mail will come in. I hope it goes soon. I am planning a vegetable garden and am going to farm all I can. The summer is short, but it's almost continuous daylight and things do grow. I feel lonesome to-day and wish there were some other woman to talk to besides the

one in the looking-glass. I'm not well enough to be
outside and I'm tired of the inside. The mail will be so
welcome.

Peace River, Alberta
May 4, 1927
We're expecting the boat this week with mail. I feel
better--have it checked again. Spring is here, and birds.
It's so lovely it hurts. Ducks and geese and frogs make
the air noisy, and birds everywhere. I am so happy.

May 19, 1927
The mail came in two days ago and I have a chance
maybe to mail this card as the boat goes back. I'll try,
anyway. Medicine came, and just what I needed. My
back is nearly well. I only feel it when I stoop over. I'm
late with my garden and so busy. Had a heap of letters.
Books and papers all arrived. The B. cape kept Daddy's
head from freezing all winter. He even took it to bed
with him. We have a fresh cow this month and lots of
milk.

Fort Vermilion, Alberta
May 21, 1927
Spring is here at last and the grass is green. Flowers
are springing up everywhere and wild strawberries are in
bloom. There was quite a severe frost a couple of nights
ago that may have injured them. The mosquitoes are also
with us now. If this land ever gets settled up they won't
be bad, but as it is now they are fierce. We sleep under
a mosquito bar, at night, made of cheesecloth so the little
ones can't crawl through. They will stay with us now
until fall comes with sharp frost. But they are bearable.
Summer seems to come as if by magic. There really is
hardly any spring. To-day is Sunday, I believe. I am
never sure of the days in the calendar. I studied the
Bible a bit and found that the word "hell" means "the
grave" in many places in the Bible. I have heard people
call this north country by both these names, but I need
never do that now that people outside know I'm here. I
feel as if I have known all you folks all along, but you
didn't know about me.

The weeks and months and years slip by and the old struggle for existence goes on. It's been a fight to keep the intellect alive. Do you think I'll ever be able to write for a living? I can devote a little time every day to study even when I am busy with the garden, and during the long winter there is too much time on my hands. The dark comes too quickly and then stays so long.

What a lovely place I have for a home! The river forms a perfect half circle around us, and there is a hill behind us that shuts out the north wind. The homestead is flooded below the hill until June. It makes fine hay. On one side is a small lake that never goes dry. About eighty acres large. We are all alone.

I was counting on catching fur, and there isn't any and won't be for three years--if I can exist till then. I must write, for, while I hope to grow most of what we eat, we need to buy some things and freights are so high in here.

I find that I am treated with great respect by the men in here. That's because they admire a woman who'll follow her man into the wilderness and stay with him. They look tough, but inside they're homesick for some old mother, and always, of course, with the longing for a woman's sympathy and love, which is the gnawing hunger of lonely men. The trappers are coming out of the bush on their way to the trading posts or to the "outside." Their sleeping bags are filled with duck feathers and quilted. It's really just a large comforter; and they roll up in them and sleep right in the snow even when it's sixty to seventy below zero.

I have gone back to when the world is still young. Civilization is gone and only the little band of lonesome women here remember it. I have a pretty little buckskin Indian pony, but haven't dared to ride yet, as my back is still a little lame. But it is passing away and I am getting stronger every day.

May 31, 1927

Boy and I went hunting yesterday together for the first time this year. He got four ducks, each time he shot getting his bird. The fifth time he shot he killed his duck, but she floated out of reach and the water was too deep for him to wade in after her. He can't swim yet very well, and I can't either. Of those he brought home, two were big mallards, one was an Indian duck, and the other was a spoonbill. It's all the meat we have and it's very good. He is really getting to be a very good shot.

Meat is very scarce here some years and has been so for quite a few years now, the Indians say. It's too far north and the country is so large, and wolves keep it down, too. But ducks are good as long as they last. After a while there will be prairie chickens. There are small deer here, but they are very scarce. I have never seen one. In the muskegs there are moose, but except in winter they are impassable. Bands of large wolves feed on them. It's such a big, wild country--big lakes, rivers and muskegs; no trails and no people. Less than two human beings to each thousand square miles, and that means Indians, too. I won't admit out loud that I'm lonesome, but it's a Robinson Crusoe existence. Like being alive yet buried. Books will save my reason, and letters. Trappers tell me no white woman from the outside can stand it longer than six years. I'll have to show them.

Sincerely yours,
Hilda Rose

"Growing Things from the Soil Is Bliss"
Annie Pike Greenwood

Annie Greenwood and her husband Charlie were newcomers to the land when they bought their Idaho farm. But what they lacked in experience they made up for in hard work and commitment. In the passages presented below Annie delineates her lack of experience in dealing with cows, her pride in growing Golden Bantam corn that looks like the picture in the seed catalogue, and the family's trip to the movies. Most importantly, Annie tackles a subject avoided by most women writing autobiographies in the 19th and early 20th Centuries—abuse. In one excerpt below, Annie describes the men with "the beating habit" and the women and children who were their victims.

Eventually the Greenwoods had to leave their farm. Annie puts it in blunt terms: They were "kicked off by the Federal Land Bank."

Source:
Annie Pike Greenwood. We Sagebrush Folks. *New York: D. Appleton-Century, 1934. 26-27, 35-41, 114-22, 231-32, 270-75.*

I loved Idaho. I loved the vast, unspoiled wilderness, the fabulous sunsets, lakes of gold, and the dreamy, purple mountains that appeared in the sky along their rims; and when these gradually dimmed and vanished, a million stars in the dark-blue sky—a million stars, seen at a breath.

It was not all beautiful. Idaho's wild winds raged for days at a time, lifting the earth in great clouds of dust. Fields were literally transferred by the power of those winds, some of the land having to be sown over again. On everything within the house lay a thick gray powder, like that on a moth's wings exaggerated ten thousand times. Hair was transformed to dun color, eyebrows shelved with it, skin thickly coated, eyes red and smarting, teeth gritty.

The soul of the desert, I used to think that wind, making its last protest against being tamed. Through my kitchen window I could see an enormous cloud of dust pass, two pairs of horses' ears just pointing above it. Somewhere in that cloud I knew was Charley, engaged in leveling a field. When he came in for supper, he was masked in dark-gray powder, the ash of ancient volcanoes, one of whose craters was visible from my kitchen door. At Charley's request, I brushed him down with a broom outside the house. Then basin after basin finally made him recognizable.

I pitied him that summer. He was not used to farm work, and he was so exhausted at the end of the day that right after the evening meal he would fall asleep in painful and grotesque postures in the chair we had bought for our pretty bungalow because it would be so comfortable for him. Jeff and Tony [hired men] were helping to fence the ranch, and so they ate two meals with us and always spent the evening with me, while Charley slept in his chair near us. They afforded a fascinating new entertainment for me, with their wild tales of this wild country. . . .

How we slept that night, after our ride through the brush to the school-house, dancing, and riding back again through the brush! In the night, while we were asleep, the canal overflowed its banks, making a lake of the coulée below our house, and a very deep lake it was, formed of the V-shaped coulée. This was a strip of land very difficult to farm; hence Charley had decided that it was just the place to stake out Jersey. In the night, at the back of my dreaming unconsciousness, I thought I heard a cow bawling. But a cow bawling meant nothing to me at that stage of my life. There comes a time on the farm when you develop antennae of sensitiveness all over your body. You feel that things are wrong out at the barn, or the chicken-house, or what-not, and to hear a cow bawling even in the back or your dreams will bring you stark awake with the swiftness of light reporting a long-dead star—a dart, and you would be running down the hill to that cow, clothes or no clothes.
It was too bad that poor Kansas Jersey had been forced by fate into the hands of city farmers. Of course you know what happened. It haunted me. I thought I should have saved that cow's life, though probably my idea of saving a cow's life at that time might have been to float the ironing-board out to her so that she could cling to it with her hoofs. One thing I did. I vowed that no cow ever again should lose her life on that farm if it were in my power to save her.
I was put to the test late that summer, when Ray McKaig was proselytizing for members to support the

Non-Partisan League. His very lovely wife, Leah, came with him, and I was rejoiced at seeing another woman. She said her feet were hot and tired. Had she paid me this call in the city, I should have let it go simply with expressing my sympathy. But we did things differently in the sagebrush. I expressed the sympathy, and then I went and got a foot-tub, and a really-truly Kansas towel, instead of the beet-seed sacks the men used, and a bar of toilet soap, and she drew off her shoes and stockings and sat there bathing her poor feet while we talked. She and Ray had tried farming in North Dakota. She had been a teacher of English, and he was a young minister when he met her. They had not been able to bear, without protest, the wrongs of agriculture. So they had given up the farm.

We sat there talking together while she bathed her feet. I was so happy in being with another woman that the new cow had a hard time making herself heard, although she was bawling at the top of her voice, and her long, hairy, lugubrious face was almost pressed against the window-pane. Suddenly I remembered my vow, which I considered as sacredly given as that old one of Hippocrates, sworn to so solemnly by my father when he began his practice of medicine. Here was a cow in distress, for some reason. Perhaps I could save her life.

I told Mrs. McKaig the tragedy of our first cow's Ophelian death, though not with flowers in her hair, and asked her to excuse me while I investigated the cause of Jersey II's woes. She said she would put on her shoes and stockings and help me. One look at that cow was enough. I had seen her before, when Charley had treated her for bloat. I could well see that unless extreme remedies were given, and that at once, even slinging her up to the hay-derrick could not save her. I had heard the farmers say to Charley that when a cow is sick and lies down, if you can only keep her on her feet she will not die. So they make a sling, wrap it around the sick cow, and string her up to the derrick, just high enough for her hoofs to touch the ground. If she dies, it means you did not get her up there soon enough. Medical science does so much experimenting with animals for the sake of humanity....I pass on this slinging-up business to physicians, who could maybe save many a life by slinging up all the sick folks so they would have to stand. I leave the details to the doctors, whether they sling the sick people up to the chandeliers or have hay-derricks in all the city streets.

I knew I could not make a sling for a sick cow, for I never had seen one, and had even neglected to find out whether they are made of rope or of canvas. Besides, I have done a lot of things on the farm beyond my strength or understanding, but it seemed to me that stringing up a cow to a hay-derrick was a pretty ambitious project for a woman of one hundred and twelve, or so, pounds. It might leave me strung up on one end of the rope and Jersey on the other end, and what a sight that would be for a husband when he came home from electioneering around the country—his cow made well by slinging up, and his wife half dead from the same cause.

I was determined to use every means short of slinging that cow up to the hay-derrick. A gag, I knew, was the first requisite. I had not noticed how Charley made his, nor how he made it stay in the cow's mouth, so I had to go at the business by the trial-and-error method, the way marriages are made. I took the butcher knife and whittled a stick. Then I tied a rag to each end. With the gag and a big pail I went out to the cow.

This Jersey was of the dehorned variety. I could not imagine how I was to keep the gag in her mouth. If I tied the rag around her neck, she would hunch about until the gag would be out of her mouth. You can't tie anything to a cow's horns when they have been burnt out with acid at the time they started to grow. As I looked at that long, insistent face, I saw there was absolutely nothing to which to tie the rag strings of that gag except her ears.

She did not like this. She probably remembered her dehorning experience when a calf, and perhaps had the idea that I was trying to de-ear her. I managed, by stretching on tiptoe and almost hanging my weight on her ears, to accomplish my design. But I know now that the cow and the giraffe must have belonged to the same

species when our old buggy horse Buttons was a little
Eohippus.

You see, when a cow has eaten alfalfa, she bloats. It
would seem more sensible to me to bloat on dried hay
and a drink of water, the thing that happens when as a
child you eat dried apples and then drink and drink. But
cows are far more sensible, though I think they are like
a great many people whose stupidity passes for good
horse-sense. It should be called cow-sense.

After a cow has bloated, you save her life by three
means, besides stringing up in a sling to the hay-derrick.
First, you must hurry to apply a gag, to hold her mouth
open so she can belch up the gas, because no gas, no
bloat; in fact, if you had some means of degassing a cow
at once, you could deflate her like a balloon. The next
thing to do is to throw cold water on her flanks. This
condenses the gas, I suppose, so that she is not so
inflated, but I cannot see how that alone would be of
much use, for to stand throwing bucket after bucket of
cold water on a cow's flanks for days and days, just to
keep her alive, is one of the few useful things I refuse
to do. The third treatment for a bloated cow is to walk
her up and down. This moves the gas around in her
seven stomachs...or is it five?...and, the gag being properly placed, she then explodes at the mouth, a very interesting performance if it might somehow be used as power
to light a house, or something.

I have omitted one method of saving the cow from
death by bloating, but that method I should fear to
attempt, not being very sure of a cow's anatomy. If
worse comes to worst, you take a sharp knife and stick
the cow in one of her stomachs. You cannot just go at it
blindly, even if Nature has arranged the cow for hoarding
stomachs. Now, when a human being gets gas on the
stomach, he goes to the kitchen for a teaspoonful of
baking-soda. I suppose the reason soda is not used with
cows is because it would take a bucketful. And, too, I
have an idea that someone would have to hold the silly
thing's nose while the soda and water was being poured
down her throat, and did you ever try holding anybody's
nose when the whole face was just one big nose?

A cow may be silly, but after I got that gag in Jersey's mouth by tying the rags to her ears, she learned how to twitch them off, and I spent every few minutes putting them on again. The cow was so interested in getting rid of the rags that she stopped bellowing, so that if bellowing had been what was the matter with her, I should have had her cured. But her sides were still inflated, and though I do not know whether politicians are right in saying that it is dangerous to have an inflated dollar, what I do know is that an inflated cow is cause for thought.

In one of the moments when the rags were staying on her ears, I led Jersey down to the canal, forcing her out into the stream as far as possible without being obliged to go along with her. She stood quietly enough, the rags on her ears acting as a "county irritant," as a doctor from Burley once expressed it when he rubbed the chest of one of our children with some kind of peppy salve. I began throwing pailful after pailful of cold water on her flanks.

When I had reached my limit of endurance on this fire-brigade business, I led Jersey from the ditch, loving-ly and patiently replacing the rags on her ears and the gag in her mouth, and saying a few bad words in an amateurish sort of way. I thought, as I did so, that an hour more of that cow would take all the amateur out of my profanity. Besides, the cow was holding back her gas on purpose. I was beginning to feel sure of that. Just stubborn. She had not belched a belch.

Mrs. McKaig now came out of the house, and together we paced the driveway, the cow between us, looking as though she were laughing, by reason of the gag in her mouth. I felt very solemn, and I managed to inspire Mrs. McKaig with the same emotion. Charley and I could not afford another cow. This was no joke, unless the cow was of the contrary opinion, as I was beginning to believe.

But no! This cow was in the last stages of bloat; I was now sure of that. She should be stuck. I wondered, if she got down, whether I should be able to stick her with the butcher knife, and how far back her five stomachs...or is it seven?...run. Just when I was getting to the desperate point of attempting this sort of tapping act, in through the gateway came Old Buttons with the buggy in which Ray McKaig and Charley were still talking politics.

Upon my explanation, the cow was led to the barn without a word, this being out of respect for Mrs. McKaig, as I afterward surmised. What took place between the two men in the barn, I do not know. But I can tell you that I was hopping mad when Jersey's calf was born the next week. Maybe I was dumb about mixing up the cultivator with the spring-tooth harrow, but I do think the Baron should have told me a few little things like that. I know he did not feel too modest about the matter, and if such had been his affliction, he might at least have explained, under cover of darkness if necessary, that Jersey was in a delicate condition, the way the newspapers always blush in print. . . .

We had five dogs, fourteen cats, and my magpie Pretty. They all ate out of the same pans, together, taking sly slaps at each other if their mother did not catch them at it and make them ashamed. I was their mother, of course. They understood me, and I understood them. The one language understood by all creation is *Love*. *Lady*, says Ruskin, means "bread-giver." Cats and dogs do not like bread, will not eat it if they can get anything else. These dogs, cats, and the bird thought I was their mother because I shamed them when they spatted at each other; because I said loving words to them and looked loving thoughts toward them; because I set out what they liked for food, the big pans of separated milk. The lion and the lamb shall lie down together, and a human mother shall feed them.

I did not mind so much the lack of vegetables and fruits and milk and cream and butter during the very early spring, almost into summer, excepting for two things. Nearly always the pork became rancid, and the potatoes had by that time developed every disease to which potatoes are heir. The pork was well enough for some months; and when put in our cellar, which was just a square hole outdoors, roofed over and with steps, the potatoes looked perfect. Charley dipped his crop in a formaldehyde solution, and our potatoes showed less disease than was general in that part of the country. But by February the black rot had put in its appearance.

I could scarcely bring myself to touch those black-rotted, stinking potatoes. I must struggle up the outdoor cellar steps, a heavy pail full of potatoes in my hand, and pare all of them in order to get enough for dinner. After they were cooked, I could still detect the odor, and I could not eat them myself. In the springtime, before the garden came, I slowly starved. But that made the raising of my garden more of a passion with me than ever, if that were possible. For growing things from the soil is for me a bliss which I cannot adequately explain. Birth. The glory of helping the earth give forth. The glory of watching the miracle of growth, lettuce seed always producing lettuce, and kernels of corn, always corn. How could anything but man come from that norm which was meant to be man? *Who* or *what* meant these things so to be? What is the *meaning* back of it all? And how can we doubt that there *is* a meaning?

Birth meant to the older women of our sagebrush community what some day it would mean to us younger mothers. They had long passed the physical operation of birth, and theirs were now the ineradicable results. Sometimes it meant for them a harvest of pain. For it was their harvest-time, and when they should have been feeling the joy and the peace and the plenty of harvest, they were suffering the tragedy of things gone wrong with their fields, the grain laid low with the scourge of rust, and no more time for growing.

The father of a sagebrush family is its god or its demon. There is no escape for the wife and children. In *The Doctor* Balzac wrote, "Anything may happen on these isolated farms." He meant the farms of France, but no European, nor any Eastern American farm, can compare in its state of isolation with those sagebrush farms of ours, green gems set in the midst of long stretches of desert land.

There are more city women in insane asylums than there are farm women. Statistics tell us that, and we must believe statistics, because men devote their lives to compiling them, and because the figures are all put down there in print. Figures always seem to me as convincing as God. Besides, we all believe what we see in print. "I saw it in an article the other day" is proof convincing enough to clinch any argument. In the case of insane farm women, we need not refer to any article, or even to be overcome by the arithmetic of the statistics (which I always am), for it is a fact that there are more city women than farm women in insane asylums. I was personally acquainted with this truth in one mental hospital, having lived in this asylum for years—in "luxurious apartments," according to the *Salt Lake Tribune*—when my father was medical superintendent of the institution. In that asylum there were more city women than farm women.

The reason mentally deranged farm women are not in the insane asylum is because they are still on the farms. I do not write this to make you smile. The sanest women I know live on farms. But the life, in the end, gets a good many of them—that terrible forced labor, too much to do, and too little time to do it in, and no rest, and no money. So long as a woman can work, no matter how her mind may fail, she is still kept on the farm, a cog in the machine, growing crazier and crazier, until she dies of it, or until she suddenly kills her children and herself. More farm women then city women kill themselves and their children. You read of such cases so frequently that it seems strange to me if this explanation never occurred to you. No need for statistics to prove it.

I was recovering from the birth of one of my babies when the first insane woman of our sagebrush community was removed to the State Institution at Blackfoot. I had been too overwhelmed with work to get acquainted with her, and I never knew certainly the cause of her mental lapse.

The second woman to go insane lived not far from our farm. Her name we will call Mrs. Goodinch. One day, when her entire family of children and her husband were trailing her as she worked out-of-doors—chopping sagebrush, among other things—suddenly she seized a hen and chopped its head off. Then another, and another, and another. She was very agile, and she had no difficulty in capturing the silly fowls. All around on the ground were bloody, flapping, headless chickens.

Her children stood aghast. But her husband was yelling and cussing and hopping in and out among the flopping chickens, all of them together like corn popping in a skillet. He dared not go near her, for she was larger and stronger than he, having done most of the work on the place herself, and there was that bloody ax, brandished in her big, muscular, rough, raw hands.

When the last chicken was done to death, she turned her frenzied face toward her children, pointing with her left hand to her husband and exclaiming, "Go get the old man and hold him while I chop his head off!" And she would have done it, without their help if necessary, but he was through the barbed-wire fence and down the road before she could move in his direction.

He was stumbling down the road, mouth sagging in terror, eyes bulging, when he met two of our good sagebrush women, driving their buggy toward him. At sight of his frantic excitement they stopped, and he related his tale of horror, climaxing it with, "And all them there chickens with their heads chopped offen um!"

Thinking they might pacify Mrs. Goodinch, the women drove on out to the rented farm where the Goodinch family existed miserably; and as they went, they decided that seeing the old man sitting around all winter, with no food and no shoes for the children, probably had something to do with the matter. They met Mrs. Goodinch. She had left behind her ax and her children.

"Goin' t' Burley t' git a job," she told the women.

She was dissuaded from walking the twelve miles to Burley. Instead of that trip, a few days later she was taken to the insane asylum at Blackfoot. I cannot see why. The chickens had nothing to eat. There was no more wheat. It was best to chop their heads off at once.

Maybe the old man needed a good beheading. Certainly the family needed some one to go to Burley and get a job. I think her actions were very sane, though too rebellious for a farm woman. Maybe rebellion in a farm woman constitutes insanity.

"Anything may happen on these isolated farms." There was another woman who lost her mind but was never taken to an institution for mental disorder. She had borne six sons. One after another she had seen them unmercifully beaten by their father until they ran away from home, writing no word as to their whereabouts for fear he would have the sheriff bring them back. It was the last son that did it for her. When she witnessed his brutal beating, she suddenly lost her mind. But she was not violent. She laughed all the time. She had not laughed since she was married. But from the moment she heard the piteous cries of her young son, she began to laugh, and she never ceased. The boy ran away, and she never knew it. She was spared the agony of thinking of those six sons she had borne, out in the world, God knew where. She just laughed all the time.

Her man had money. He had wrung it out of the unpaid labor of his sons and his wife. Why he should have wasted any of it on her, I am sure I cannot imagine. Some twist in his nature compelled him to take her here and there to specialists, always with the same result. She just kept on laughing.

One case came nearer to me. I could not visit my friend Mrs. Howe, though I heard she was ill. I could not walk. I had phlebitis after Joe's birth. The day finally came when I could go with Miss Butterworth and Mrs. Jean in our two-seated vehicle known as a Mormon white-top—I suppose because all the Mormons had them, and the top was covered with white canvas. Ours still had U.S. MAIL in big letters on it. I don't know what its history had been. Charley bought it second-hand, giving what was left of our narrow-gauge buggy to some one more needy than we were. After the white-top came the cart, and after that our second-hand Ford which we called Sagebrush Liz.

We took with us to my friend's home as many dainty
edibles as possible. "These things ought to last Mrs.
Howe a long time," said Miss Butterworth, "but they won't.
That tribe will clean them up within a half hour after
we leave."

"That tribe" were my friend's children. And I knew
what Miss Butterworth said was true. But they might be
excused a little, for they lived on boiled potatoes, lard
gravy, and corn syrup with their bread.

When Mrs. Howe had come to Idaho, she was beautiful, with dark eyes, rosy cheeks, and a great rope of
chestnut hair wound in a coronet around her head. But
she was not well, and never had been. At her home in
Galesburg she had been able to get along, but her husband had thrown up his good job and put their savings
into sagebrush land, persuaded by speculators to that
madness.

She had come to a shack in the wilderness, tar-paper
covered, like so many other shacks, cold in winter,
broiling in summer. There were no conveniences. But
these were only material hardships. The thing that killed
Sally Howe was seeing the gradual degeneration of her
family. They had come with books, and one of the most
modern of phonographs, and good furniture. She lived to
see them existing in a state lower than the farm animals,
because when a human being no longer aspires, but
simply lives to eat and sleep, he is lower than the beasts
whose habits are the same as his. The father, too, had
the beating habit. A whole family can sink into debase-
ment under the hands of a father who lays violent hands
upon them.

One day, as I sat by the window unable to walk, I
had asked Tom Howe about her condition. "She just lies
in bed," he had said. "She used to be the kindest woman.
But now when I try to wait on her, she says, 'Don't
come near me, Tom Howe, or I'll scratch your eyes out!'"

And Emily Howe, eighteen, the eldest girl in the
family of five, told me, "We surely thought Ma was
dying yesterday. She told Frank to tell us all to come to
her bedside. We did, and Pa was even shaking. He
thought the way we did, that it was her last words. We

stood in a line by her bed, not saying a word, and hardly breathing. She started looking at Pa, and she went down the row, slowly. Then she said, 'You're a fine-looking bunch!' And then she turned her face to the wall."

I could picture it, all of them standing there, slovenly, sunburnt, and she had been so immaculate and dainty. She had no desire to get out of that bed. Of course, she was really ill, too, and nothing was being done to make her better. There was no money to pay doctors. She was a farm woman, and she would have to live or die as nature saw fit.

Mrs. Jean was one of the best managers in our district. She and I were probably the frailest of all the sagebrush women. She had the advantage of me in many ways. Her people had all been farmers as far back as anything was known of them, down in South Carolina. She knew how to do everything and do it well, but she did not do it all herself—she set others to work. I admired her greatly. She saw to it that her children had musical education, taking them to Twin Falls herself, in the car she and Dan managed to get—a good one, at that.

But Dan was a very good husband and father. He was called among us "the workin'st fool ever." That meant he worked whenever possible and did not spend three months of every winter just sitting around settling the Government. When the other men started settling the Government, Dan always allowed he would be "gougin' along."

It was Mrs. Jean who organized the first women's club in our sagebrush community, the Ladies Fancywork Improvement Club, as the women called it; and it was a decided credit to her, for those women often did things for the members of the community much more important than mere fancywork. It was they who had planned this ministration to Mrs. Howe, Miss Butterworth and Mrs. Jean being the acting members of the committee. I was included in the visit because I was a friend of Mrs. Jean, and also because they were borrowing our white-top; very courteously they asked me if I would like to go with them.

We were taking some delicious eatables with us, for
not only was Mrs. Jean proficient in cooking, but Miss
Butterworth had taken prizes at the Fair for her butter
and other things. She was pretty, gray-haired, and had
given her life to her brother's motherless children. She
often wore dainty lavender clothes, and she had a sense
of humor and was "plunk and chuffy," as Tony Work
would have said--Tony, so long gone from our neighborhood.

I was shocked when I saw Mrs. Howe. That glorious
hair was a solid, dingy, repulsive mat on her head. It
could not have been washed or combed for months. We
women dared not cut it off, for we had not the right,
but that is what would have to be done with it. As Miss
Butterworth turned back the covers to bathe her, there
scurried across the grimy undersheet literally scores of big
dark-red bedbugs. They had been feeding on the helpless
sick woman. Miss Butterworth had brought a box of
insect powder, which she instantly puffed over the vile
vermin.

Somewhere we found two clean sheets. We placed Mrs.
Howe in a big chair while the bed linen was changed. I
had been shocked by the condition of her hair; I had
been shocked by those scurrying bedbugs; what next I
saw shocked me more than the other two put together.
Under the hips of the suffering, sick woman a hole had
been rotted entirely through the mattress by the uncon-
trollable flow of excrement from her body, for her
bowels and bladder were paralyzed.

We twisted the mattress around so that the uncomfortable hole would be at the foot of the bed on the other
side. And while Mrs. Jean and I were so engaged, Miss
Butterworth puffed the insect powder over every inch of
the bed-frame and the mattress that she could reach. It
would mean temporary relief for the sick woman, but the
house was alive with the verminous pests.

We used a bread-board for a tray, and I fed my
friend with a spoon while the other two women made
her bed. Fresh raspberries with thick cream; little,
browned, oven-fragrant rolls; Miss Butterworth's prize
butter; white slices of roasted chicken; delicate custard;

and many other things we had brought, with thought of tempting her appetite and in the vain hope that some of the good things might be saved for her. They were a selfish family, the five of them all grown, Harold, fifteen, being the youngest. Perhaps we might have done friendly things for them also. They had been rendered dependent and spineless by a father who had the beating habit. In a family with a beating father the children usually lose all power of independent, elevating action. *Thou shalt not lay violent hands upon the body of another human being!*

My friend had almost totally lost her mind. I could see that easily, for though I was a little girl when I had lived among the insane, I had forgotten nothing. She stared at my face for a while, eating of the fresh, luscious raspberries I gave her, and then I saw that she was making efforts to speak to me. At last I made out what she was saying: "Rhoda...Joe...Rhoda...Joe..." Tears sprang to my eyes.

The Ladies Fancywork Improvement Club wrote to the Red Cross, and soon my friend was in a sanitarium where she could be given proper care. She recovered enough to enjoy sitting there, clean, well-fed, but she yearned not at all for the tar-paper shack, her five children, or her husband. One of them had been kinder to her than the others—Pete, we called him. He went to see her. And there she died. She had enough physical disabilities of which to die. But I believe she might have survived them all had there been hope in her life. She had reached the bottom from which there is no climbing up. She died as a result of the births she had accomplished: she died because of what her children had been compelled to endure and because of what they had become by reason of it. Birthing for her had been a bitter tragedy. . . .

Baseball beside the Willey spillway; rabbit drives everywhere, for the rabbits were everywhere; village and county fairs; and celebrations in conjunction with school doings. Oh, yes, and the movies! The movies came just before we left the farm, kicked off by the Federal Land

Bank, like the rest of the city dream-farmers. But what I write about here occurred while we still believed ourselves likely to pull through, farmers and consumptives never giving up hope, though forced to give up everything else. We farm people were always excited over the Hazelton Fair, and then again over the Jerome County Fair, which followed immediately afterward. All the prize-winning products were taken from the Hazelton Fair to the Jerome County Fair. My vegetables took some prizes, but for some reason, though not through my design, for I am far from being a shrinking violet, my products appeared labeled with Charley's name. Of course, it was a mistake.

For the sagebrush farm people knew that I had raised an extraordinary garden. I sent to Burpee's in Philadelphia for my seeds, and I planted a great many of them in cigar-boxes which I begged from Hank Thorson, the druggist. These had to be crowded in the south bedroom windows day-times and carried to the kitchen night-times, while our bedroom windows were open. Tin cans, with the bottoms nearly cut away, next received the sprouts. I had plants in bloom, some just fruiting, by the time the garden was ready for them. Upstairs harbored the plants until planting outdoors, and the mice and packrats nipped them off until I learned how to deal with them.

After my experience in failing to take the prize for my Golden Bantam corn, I never entered anything again. I should not have minded if I had been beaten. I had raised perfect corn, and I looked the patch over for two ears, the entry required, that would be the exact counter-part of the illustration on the front cover of Burpee's catalogue. I found them, just a few inches long, every kernel as it should be, even to the end—plump, perfect ears. I should have adopted the stratagem of fastening them to the catalogue cover, right over the illustration, but the judges would not have believed their eyes. They were the kind of judges whose only criterion of excel-lence was giantism. They had not learned that vegetables have the equivalent of hyperactivity of the thyroid gland and that oversize is always at the expense of some other important attribute. The Golden Bantam corn that took the prize was at least a foot long, almost snow-white, a thin cob, kernels diminishing and disappearing at the end. It was certainly not the loss of the fifty cents prize-money that left me stunned. It was what this abysmally ignorant award implied of the people who had me at their mercy.

> Oh the years we waste and the tears we waste,
>   And the work of our head and hand,
>   Belong to the people who did not know,
>   And now we know that they never could know,
>   And never could understand!

Moral: Never be a specialist in truck-gardening when the judges of your products are village Babbitts.

But there I do the Hazelton men injustice. There was not a farmer in the Greenwood district who would not have made the award as it was made. At least I think I should have received an award of a tin spoon for being the only person in that part of Idaho who really knew how Golden Bantam corn should look. If I wrong some other Golden Bantam expert at present unknown to me, I will gladly share half of the tin spoon that I did not get with him or her upon receipt of proof, which shall be two perfect ears of Golden Bantam corn tied with green baby ribbon to the illustrated cover of one of the Burpee's catalogues. . . .

We discuss going to the picture-show at the supper-table on Saturday night. I decide against Hazelton's, since my ears are very sensitive, and I can no longer stand the frightful chording of the woman who maltreats the piano there. Even the repertory of two tunes at Eden, with the drum, is better. It is ten miles away, but the faithful flivver will take us there.

Joe, aged nine, has been driving a team all day, helping to haul the red-clover hay, which is being stacked beside the barn. Charles, aged fourteen, for the past three days has been cutting hay for a neighbor, working from seven in the morning until six at night, ten full hours, for two and a half dollars a day, the going wages, as we say in Idaho.

Charles will drive Lizzie. He is five feet eleven inches tall, weighs one hundred and forty-eight pounds, and might well pass for twenty years. And he is an expert, careful driver, although, of course, his driving is permitted only because his mother and father are present. With Rhoda and Joe also, Walter preferring the relaxation of manufacturing his own radio, the car is too full to leave space for Mister, always its guard while we are entertained. Mister does not know we are to leave him behind, and we dread driving off without him, for he is always so disconsolate at being deserted, trotting back from the gate with such a hangdog look.

The family hurry with their supper of some of my famous Boston baked beans, bread and butter, milk and gingerbread, a terribly unbalanced meal, which I did not learn to compose in a home-economics course and know better than to provide; but sometimes over the whole country-side there is the smell of cooking beans, and then we all know that the larder is almost bare, hens moulting, garden stuff gone, hogs sold or not ready to kill. However, on this night the supper is one of convenience as well as necessity, and it is soon dispatched.

Walter, as usual, goes out to feed the stock; Charley goes to irrigate; Charles goes to milk; Joe has gathered eggs and is set to collecting his best clothes; Rhoda is busy about the same task for herself; I am washing dishes. Joe is one of those individuals, such as I was when a child, who has no clothes-consciousness. When he takes off his clothes, they immediately begin hunting places to hide from him. His shirt sneaks one place, his knickers another, one shoe divorces itself as far as possible from its mate, and although Joe is one of the first to get up in the morning, he must hunt for an hour to find enough habiliment to avoid shocking the neighbors. On this night he may go in clean overalls and work shirt, but he must wear the coat to his best suit. So Joe goes prowling upstairs and downstairs, and I even stumble over him making a search among my cooking-utensils in the bottom of the kitchen cabinet.

I call Rhoda to the rescue. It always ends that way. And she has been on the scent only a few moments when she discovers Joe's coat in the unfinished room upstairs. Having washed himself, Joe appropriates some of the dreadful hair-ointment warranted to give the high, patent-leather finish fashionable at this time, and although Joe has pretty, wavy hair, he manages with this evil-smelling stuff to plaster down the top of his head until he looks like a mouse that has been drowned in a mop-pail. But I have not the heart to criticize the little fellow; he enjoys so imitating Charles and Walter, and, like all imitaters, he overdoes it just enough to betray his lack of genius for the thing. I regard what he has done to himself affectionately, remember how willingly he works about the farm from dawn until dark, with never a complaint, never a hankering to stop to play, or, if there be any hankering, hiding it deep in his true, loving heart.

I cannot help thinking, as we speed over the miles in Sagebrush Liz, that there are compensations in being poor--not so poor that your stomach is empty and your feet bare and your back shivering, but so poor that you must ride in an open flivver. For here on one side of the road is the new-cut hay, and there on the other side is a field of white clover. If some manufacturer ever takes a notion to bottle those combined perfumes, his fortune will be made. I make mention often of Cabell's certain place in Heaven for old-fashioned women, which smells of mignonette and where a starling is singing. I hope there is another corner of Heaven dedicated to the smell of white clover and new-mown hay, where laughing women like me can go and be with the little children.

Miles of farming-land we pass: we see the fields of wheat, the fields of barley, the fields of potatoes, the fields of beans--here in a country where there was nothing but sagebrush when the Baron and I came. I know that if I were standing in the middle of that beanfield, looking over it, I should see a constant move-ment of the soil, as the bent backs of the bean-plants push their way out of the darkness. One can actually see them grow, like a purposely accelerated motion-picture. Their growth is so noticeable that there is an uncanny feeling of animal activity, as though they were stretching their bodies up out of the soil where they have been lying.

The next field is wheat, with an odd appearance on account of the many dark-green barley heads raised above the wide expanse of lighter green. Through some inadvertance the barley has been sown with the wheat, and thus each barley stalk, distinctly isolated, lifts its individual banner, as though leading a platoon of wheat in the army of summer. Foolish barley, so brave, so self-deceived! So like visionary mankind, who, like the barley, shall be cast aside when the wheat is threshed. Wheat the great mass of mankind; the barley the dreamers. Dreams are needed to float the banners of inspiration, but the fate of the barley is to be cast aside.

I am not as melancholy as my thoughts appear in print. I see the Jerome Canal in the distance, and "my heart leaps up when I behold" the beautiful, man-made river, standing up out of the valley like those mirages we so often observe on our western horizon, looking outward from our ranch. The Jerome Canal at this point is confined in rock walls, to keep it from flowing into the valley that sweeps below it. Not so far back we crossed our own Jerome Canal bridge, and there the stream is wide and turbulent and deep-blue--so much beauty flowing under that bridge, scarcely noticed each day, but now flowing over my heart forever, never to be ignored.

I think I would rather make a canal or plant a tree than build a house. Especially in making a canal should I feel that I were exercising some of the prerogatives of the Creator. Water has a special sort of mystery which nothing else in nature holds. It is a vibrant, living thing, whose life is so much less understandable than that of plants and animals. It suggests the infinite. No scene is perfect without it, however charming. I feel close kinship to animals and plants, a kinship that is physical and mental, but there is something in my soul that yearns toward the waters of the earth.

We reach the edge of the town of Hazelton, where our mail is distributed, and there, on his lawn, is the rural mail-carrier, feeding a lamb with a baby's nursing-bottle. As hurriedly as may be done respectably, we go on through our town, as it is nearing eight, and always the moving-picture show in Eden has opened doors at eight. A crowd of seven people are strolling up and down Hazelton's Main Street, and five cars are parked against the curbing. Lights are shining in our grocery-dry-goods store, in our grocery-butcher shop, in our grocery-post-office, in our restaurant-drug-store, with two or three people in each one. The hardware store, too, is still open. It is a busy night for the merchants of Hazelton.

On we speed, the scene ahead of us growing more velvety with dusk. The sun is sinking into a lake of rose and gold, so I know there is likely to be a little sprinkling of rain, some wind, and yet generally fair weather. This forecast, which I make to my audience in the car, proves to be correct. I cannot see, in this time of governmental economy, why Uncle Sam does not dispense with all other weather prophets and employ me alone. It is a fact that my study of the sky has never failed to result in a correct prediction.

It is a pretty road on the way to Eden, as a road should be that leads to a place of that name, nor is it guarded by even a cherub with a wooden sword; but at the edge of the little town we see a warning in huge black letters that we must not drive more than fifteen miles an hour, so Sagebrush Liz crawls into Eden on her belly, like a dog that has been scolded for chasing the neighbors' turkeys. I wonder what would happen if we went dashing through at, say, thirty miles an hour. The only official authorized to stop us is probably working on his farm some miles away. Or maybe he leaves the farm for his wife to work, just lounging around Eden "to ketch them pesky smarties that comes hell-bent-fer-breakfast at twenty-thirty miles a-nour" through Eden.

Eden seems much busier than Hazelton. I might be wrong, but it looks as though there are two or more stores than we have in our town. Probably a grocery-barber-shop and a grocery-undertaking parlor. I say probably. I am not sure about it. The unusually crowded Main Street may be accounted for by the fact that the

Ladies Aid of the Union Church has a table on the edge
of the pavement, where home-cooked food is displayed,
the guardians and salesladies being two very large and
amiable-looking women of the kind that seem to bulge at
all corners of public Ladies Aid affairs. As Simon
Heminway had done at the Greenwood-Hazelton ball-
game, these pneumatic ladies are selling ice-cream cones.

Six cars are parked in front of the moving-picture
house, the proprietor of which stands outside in his
shirt-sleeves, and a-few-other-things, loafing and inviting
his soul. No crowd seems to be jamming into its pre-
cincts. Upon inquiry from the shirt-sleeves, and a-few-
other-things, we find that the crowd was late in coming
the previous Saturday, so the time has been changed from
eight to eight-thirty. We have at least twenty minutes to
wait. The bill is Lon Chaney in The Phantom of the
Opera. A little later, as we kill time walking down Main
Street, I overhear a conversation between two highly
illustrated young ladies, the artist's superscription alone
being omitted.

"Goin' to the show t'night?" (Vigorous gum-chewing.
Cleans your teeth--forget which brand, but of course
other brands do not.)

"Y'bet! Wouldn't miss seein' that bird." (Gum here,
too. Cleans her teeth too, I suppose, but they do not look
it.)

"What's the show?"

"It's 'The Panthom of the Opry.'"

"Starved, Stalled, and Stranded"
Meridel LeSeuer

Meridel LeSeuer, born in 1900, is still writing and pub-
lishing works about the land and the people of the
Midwest. In 1945, she published North Star Country, *and*
in a chapter called "Drought" she recreates her bus trip
across the Dakotas in 1930. The chapter ends with the
painful image of a family that has been evicted from their
farm. LeSeuer, however, believes in the ability of rural
people to overcome disasters. At the conclusion of North
Star Country *she writes that:*

> *The people are a story that is a long inces-*
> *sant coming alive from the earth in better*
> *wheat, Percherons, babies, and engines,*
> *persistent and inevitable. The people always*
> *know that some of the grain will be good,*
> *some of the crop will be saved, some will*
> *return and bear the strength of the kernel,*
> *that from the bloodiest year some survive to*
> *outfox the frost.*

Source:
Meridel LeSeuer. North Star Country. *New York: Book*
Find Club, 1945. 261-70.

Drought

*Because the ground is chapt, for there was no rain in the
earth, the plowmen were ashamed and covered their heads.
Yes, the hind calved in the field and forsook it, because
there was no grass. And the wild asses did stand in the
high places, they snuffed up the wind like dragons; their
eyes did fail, because there was no grass.*

> *- Jeremiah, 14:6*

*Instead of fraternity you will get isolation; instead of
inalienable peasant allotment the land will be drawn into
commerce; instead of a blow at the grabbing speculators,
the basis for capitalist development will be expanded. But
. . . it is historically good, for it will frightfully acceler-
ate social development and bring much nearer new and
higher forms.*

> *- Lenin on Karl Marx's answer to Krieg
> as to the opening of free western lands
> in America*

That year, in the early days of the Depression, after
the bank holiday—what has come to be known as the
"crash"—came the drought. I drove through the country
trying not to look at the ribs of the horses and the cows,
but you got so you couldn't see anything but ribs, like
beached hulks on the prairie, the bones rising out of the

skin. You began to see the thin farmer under his rags and his wife lean as his cows.

This was not something sudden. It had been happening a long time and came sooner than Hill had predicted. In the spring, after the terrible winter, added to mortgages and low prices, there was no rain. The village where I lived did not exchange money for two years; they bartered and exchanged what produce they had.

I drove to Dakota in the bus through the hot, stifling country, with dark clouds of dust moving steadily eastward into Illinois and Ohio; Dakota walking east. Everyone talked about horses, cattle, seed, land, death, hunger. The bus went steadily through the bleak country, and they pointed out the window at land now owned by the insurance companies, and we saw it splitting open like rotting fruit after years of decay and erosion, exposing the gashed core; it was the fifth year of the depression.

We stop at a little town and some drivers get on, space-drunk young men, their skin pocked, burnt from the dust and wind, driving from Dakota east, driving trucks back and forth. They like to drive swift and mad over the country, a girl in every city. "We went three hundred miles yesterday," one of them says, slouching down, sleeping on the go—huge, half-man, half-boy; mid-American faces lolling.

There is something about the American earth that is curiously loved. Even like this, with this dark doom of ruin over it, everyone sees it as it originally was: lovely, green, eldorado, with clear streams and broad pastures beside the still rivers.

The country looks so lonely and silent; I realize with a start that the ground has not been plowed or planted. There was no seed. A farmer answers me before I have spoken, "You can't get you no seed. Last year the drought ruined everything and this year they ain't no seed. My farm plumb blew away. The land is sure ruined this year, and mine for a sight longer. It blew right out from under me, clean as a whistle. The fields packed against the barn so you couldn't see the top, the thistles and tumbleweed caught the dust at the fences so you could walk right over them on solid sand. That there land won't grow a Russian thistle."

"What's going to happen?" another says. "People from my home town, pioneers, mind you, gone to Alaska now. Pioneering some more. It beats the Dutch."

"Holy mackerel!" says the grieving man.

And the man talk goes on: "Whole villages ruined! What will they do there?"

This is the bread-basket of the world going up in dust.

Yes, sir, we were starved, stalled and stranded. Dried out three years runnin'. My wife and child jest dried up and blowed off.

Did ye hear this one? A Dakota farmer was waitin' at the hospital for his first baby. The nurse announced an eight-pound baby to the man waiting with him and to the Dakota farmer she announced a three-pound one and to the surprise of the other he seemed very happy. "Man," said the father, "three pounds is a smidgen of a baby. Don't look to me that baby's got a chance. Why are you so happy?" "I'm a farmer from North Dakota." "What's that got to do with it?" "Why, everything. In North Dakota we're darn glad to get our seed back!"

Got to keep movin'. Jest lookin' fer a home. We didn't stop to shut the door.

Dust got so thick the prairie dogs dug their holes right into the air!

Yes, sir, the government bet me a hundred and fifty acres against my belly that I couldn't stick it out. I won.

That land now jest fittin' to hold the world together.

We seen many a time, many a season. We come a far trek and we'll go farther yet. We'll ride through more seasons and buck more journeys yet.

And the folksay echoes back from the years:

My whole place dried up and blowed away.

I didn't sell out, I give out.

Tractors and the wind is our enemy. Should never have plowed up the buffalo grass.

An Indian turned back the freshly plowed prairie sod and said to the new settler who was showing him how to plow, "Wrong side up!"

Another Indian about to be hanged said, "The land you now take by force is the flesh of my fathers."

The conversation continues in a beer joint when the bus stops for lunch. A man in a tattered coat and split shoes joins us in hopes of a free drink, and the young man has been tippling from a bottle in his pocket and makes a speech. The Constitution is a good one, he says; there's a difference between the Constitution and the government, you can bet our bottom dollar on that. According to the Constitution there is no such thing as sedition and the Constitution permits life, happiness, and shall we say the pursuit of freedom—yes, we will say it. "Your mother told you you were going to be President. That's the bunk. Who in hell *wants* to be? All I want is to find some water to go fishing in. Why didn't she tell you you were going to live a good life, that's all—just that stuff, a good life? That's what the Constitution says for a man: life, liberty, and the pursuit of happiness."

The man in the tattered clothes waves his hands surprisingly. "But what about private capital," he says, and you could have knocked us over with a straw. "Yes, sir, what about private capital? Suppose," he says, "I want to put up a skyscraper, or build a railroad, what about it?"

The bus fled through the country and the sun was obscured by the moving dust. The women put wet cloths over the children's noses. And you could see the kind of terror that had grown in everyone. The winter wheat had died; the peas had gone in and fallen down as if mowed by a hot scythe. The corn never came up. The onion seed blew away. And it was too much, at last. A high wind is an awful thing; it wears you down, it nags at you day after day, it sounds like an invisible army, it fills you with terror as something invisible does. It was like the flu terror. No one went outdoors. People shut up their houses as if from some horrible invasion, some massacre on the streets. The radio took to announcing that there was no danger in the dust, which was not true; many children died of it, of dust pneumonia and other diseases that were never named. When you looked out the window you saw the black cloud of dust going over, you saw the fields whiten and die and the crops creep back into the ground.

At first the farmers kept on plowing, first with two horses, then you had to use four to rip the earth open, and when you did a fume of dust went up like smoke and a wind from hell whipped the seed out. Every day the pastures got worse. The grass was dry as straw and the cattle lost their flesh quickly. You had to look for a green spot for them every morning. Children were kept out of school to herd the cattle around near streams and creeks. Some farmers cut down trees so the cattle could have the poor wind-bitten leaves. Some farmers have turned their cows into what was left of their winter wheat, which is thin as a young man's first beard.

Then on Decoration Day all hope went—the wind started again, blowing hot as a blast from hell, and the young corn withered as if under machine-gun fire; in two hours the trees looked as if they had been beaten.

We pass mules hauling a light wagon full of barrels, and with a start I realize that they are hauling water. The wells are dry. The hills are bare and we see no cattle. We pass a freight taking John Deere machinery back to Minneapolis. It is being repossessed. We begin to pass old cars loaded to the gills with household furniture and the back seat full of waving children. They are going west again.

When late afternoon came down not a soul was in sight: the houses closed up tight, the blinds drawn, the windows and doors closed. There seemed to be menace in the air. It was frightening—you could hear the fields crack and dry, and the only movement in the down-driving heat was the dead writhing of the dry blighted tumbleweeds.

There was something terrifying about this visible sign of disaster. It went into your nostrils so that you couldn't breathe: the smell of hunger. It made you count your own ribs with terror. You don't starve in America. Everything looks good. There is something around the corner. Everyone has a chance. Is that all over now?

The dust now becomes so thick, the driver must drive very slowly. It grinds against the windshield. We drive as if going to a funeral; the corpse is the very earth. The houses are closed and stand in the haze hardly visible,

unpainted, like the hollow pupa when life has gone. But
you know that everywhere in those barricaded houses are
eyes drawn back to the burning windows, looking out at
next winter's food slowly burning.

The whole countryside bears not only its present
famine but its coming hunger. No vegetables now and
worst of all, no milk. It is monstrous with this double
doom! Every house is alike in suffering; hundreds of
thousands of such houses from state to state.

An awful thing happened. The sun went down behind
the hot rim of the horizon, and the men and women
began to come out of the houses, the children lean and
fleet as rats, the tired, lean farm women, looking to see
what was left. The men ran into their fields, ran back for
water, and began to water what was left of their gardens
with buckets and cups, running, pouring the puny drops
of water on the baked earth as if every minute might
count now. The children ran behind the cows, urging
them to eat the harsh, dry grass. It looked like an evacuated countryside with the people running out after the
enemy had passed. Not a word seemed to be spoken. In
intense silence they hurried down the rows with buckets
and cups, watering the wilted corn plants, a Gargantuan
and terrible and hopeless labor. One man came out stubbornly with a horse and plow and began stirring up the
deadly dust. Even the children ran with cups of water, all
dogged, mad, without a word. There was a terrible
madness in it, like things that are done after unimaginable
violence.

A farmer gets on and says he's going anywhere. He's
got to get away from the sound of his cows crying for
food. He says that the farmer across from him yesterday
shot his twenty-two head of cattle and then shot himself.

When I shut my eyes, the flesh burns the eyeballs and
all I can see is the sign visible now of starvation and
famine, ribs, the bones showing through the skin, rising
over the horizon.

In the small town, Main Street is crowded and the
farm woman and I look in the window of the grocery
store. "A few nubbins of corn," she says, "is all that come

up. Nobody in our parts could use the tractors, no gasoline, we got out the old mules. We'll be goin' back to the hand plow and the sickle. We lost our mule then and sold the hogs to feed the chickens, and ate the chickens ourselves. Now our place is bare as a hickory nut. I don't think you want to come out. Listen, I haven't got—Oh, it would make me feel bad."

"Never mind," I said, and she looked at me with her bleached eyes, with a touch of strange awkwardness, and bowed quaintly and we got in the old surrey driven by the only son left at home now. The old nag walks through Main Street and the men lounge far back in the shadow of the eaves, the street looks stripped as if buzzards had been at it. We move out into the prairie, through the sulphurous haze; the ruined earth slopes into the sun and, strangely, a young cycle of moon shows white in the scorched sky.

We drop into the smoky pit of prairie and have to cover our faces against the blowing sand which will cut into your skin. The bald prairie, without a blade of grass, is mounded unfamiliarly, some houses almost buried, the marks of fences sticking up. The grasshoppers are ticking like clocks.

We drive in on a road marked out since their departure by shifting sands and one side of the two-room shack is banked with sand. The mother scrapes open the door and I go in with her while the son puts away the horse. It is early but she has to light a lamp to see, and the shivering light falls through the yellow dust onto the chairs, and over a bare table covered with an inch of dust, which she quickly wipes off. There is a picture on the wall of a strong man with black mustaches; perhaps the man, her husband, who plowed this land. The mother moves around the room, her shy eyes on me, her body taking on the grace of a hostess, "I tell Joe not to hang the towel on the line—the grasshopper'll eat it clean out. They are mighty powerful hungry this year, like everything."

We move closer to each other, spreading the scrubbed wooden table. We become tenderly acquainted in the room as she begins to get excited, in the way of lonely people, telling about her husband—birthing her children right in there, she says, right on that bed without hide or hair of a doc. She is like a drunken person, recounting now her lonely pain, bearing children that are gone and will never return. "There was a time," she said, "when I was afraid to look out the window down past the lower forty—afraid they'd be a-comin' to take somethin' away from us. But that's one relief now; we ain't got nothin' now and nobody is a-comin'!"

We ate dinner, the boy shy at first; then he too is hungry for talk and tells about working on the road, about how he wants to work—he's real strong, about the Knutsons, and he gets up to show me their light eerily spread in the dust down the coolie—they are leaving tomorrow for the west, the whole kit and kaboodle of them. They're getting off that farm where they had been all their lives.

"Yes," the mother said, "where all their children was borned and raised. It's shameful. It's a terrible thing."

After supper we can still see the eerie light and imagine the Knutsons moving in their sad tasks. The mother can't keep away from the window and I know she is thinking that they could be put off, too. The boy goes outside and I know he's looking up the hill. He comes in, cracking his knuckles, "They shouldn't do it. They oughtn't get out like that without kicking up a row. What about their money? What about the years of work they got in there? What about it all? You don't hear nothin' about that. The mortgage ain't nothin' to have in that land to what they got there, their whole endurin' lives."

"Be quiet," the mother says. "God'll punish you. We are law-abidin' and that's the law."

We go into the lean-to. I am to sleep with the mother. Joe on the floor where he always sleeps. She tells me shyly she hasn't sheets, but her blanket's clean. She blows out the light modestly and we undress in the dark. I feel good to be near her. We lie side by side in the old bed and I know I am sleeping on the side of her dead husband. Accidently I touch her dry hand and she clutches me, "Do you think they will take it away from us?" I am startled by the fierce vitality of her hand, like a strong bird grasping my fingers. I grasp her hand warmly and she is shaking—not crying, just shaking like a bird captured and straining.

In the morning the sun came up naked as a hot plow in the sky, and there truly seemed as much of the earth in the sky as below it. We start out early for the Knutsons'. Their old Ford is packed and an old rickety trailer sags beneath their household goods. Mrs. Knutson has a baby and is with child, and there must be eight children in the back seat. We stop and we all get out and stand in the dust looking at each other. Nobody knows what to say now. They haven't lived all their lives for this moment. We drive down the hill again. "They have a lot of children," I say inanely, and the mother says bitterly, "That's one crop that never fails—never a crop failure of babies."

The sun is already hot. Before us, standing in the dust, a clot of men are gathered at the gate of a farmhouse; the gate is half buried in dust; the dust sits gray on the clothes of the men, on their slouching hats. The sheriff and three men are standing on the stoop. A man stands in the center of the group of farmers, speaking. As we drive up he calls out, "Join us, brother." Joe stops the horse. "We can't back down," the man is saying. "We can't be afraid. Let him post the notice of an auction; we'll be here. Now is the time to do it. You got rights. We got to begin to go forward. Everything is dry as a contribution box, you can see that. You're willin' to pay but you *can't* pay. We got no wheat, no hogs, no nothin'. We got time to think about it, to figure it out——"

Just then the Knutsons come down the hill and drive by without stopping, the children peering back around the sides, Mrs. Knutson not looking back, not waving; and we watched the old gas buggy go down the road and pass out of sight in the dust.

"They's no use goin' off now," Joe says, "for the West, for Oregon, for Alaska—— They's no use goin' off now——"

A "Textbook Farmer"
Grace Fairchild

Chapter II of Grace Fairchild's memoir opens with a rhyme in which a prairie farmer expresses his disgust with the land:

> *Fifty miles from water,*
> *A hundred miles to wood,*
> *To hell with this damned country,*
> *I'm going home for good.*

Grace, however, had no intention of "going home." She was at home on her South Dakota farm, located near the present town of Philip. As she points out in the introductory paragraph, a good farmer has to learn how to farm. A former school teacher, Grace did not believe in the intuitive approach to farming. Moreover, she had married a man who was more interested in horses than in cattle and crops, so the responsibility of making the farm a success depended on Grace. The chapter presented below, the last chapter of Frontier Woman, *describes the agricultural experiments in which she and her sons Jasper and Byron participated from 1912 through the 1930s.*

Source:
Wyman, Walker D. Frontier Woman: The Life of a Woman Homesteader on the Dakota Frontier. *River Falls: U of Wisconsin-River Falls P, 1972. 103-14.*

"Textbook Farming"

Old Stanley County comprised everything west of the Missouri in South Dakota between the Cheyenne River on the north and west and the White River on the south, a country of 4,146 square miles lodged in between Indian reservations on the south and on the north. It was a great grass empire where thousands of cattle and horses had roamed for years before we homesteaders took it over. After we got through the early years, and the droughts and depressions had frozen out many of the pioneers, we learned that, to survive, a rancher needed to raise both livestock and crops that would grow in a region where there wasn't much rainfall. Most little ranchers looked down their noses at any kind of "textbook farming," but to me it was the only way to adapt to a dry country. The State College at Brookings was to be a great help to all of us who believed in trying new things.

When the County Superintendent of Schools, W.W. Werner, visited our school in 1912, he stayed all night at our house. Jasper was just ten years old, and that is why Mr. Werner wanted to talk to us about 4-H Club work for him. He was in charge of getting it started in Stanley County and wanted us to help set up a club that would try new crops and strains of livestock. He hoped that some of this new "textbook farming" would rub off on the settlers.

Jasper was enrolled as a 4-H Club member and in time his club book came; and though Shy had no interest in "textbook farming," I did, and so I sent for several

bulletins from the Extension Service at Brookings. Mr.
Werner hadn't been able to get other boys to sign up, so
Jasper was the only one. Little did he know how much
depended on him to help us survive in that country! In
time, Jasper received six pounds of Yellow Dent corn
seed, a new variety that had been developed in North
Dakota. Jasper, with the help of his dad, plowed, har-
rowed, and planted a piece of ground, and cared for the
Yellow Dent corn all summer long. That fall, a sample
was sent to the exhibit at Ft. Pierre, along with his work
book. I don't recall that he got any prize, but I do know
that the 4-H Club corn plot opened up doors for all of
us. Our other boys joined the Club as they came along
and so we were always trying new seeds that the experimental stations were developing for the dry plains. It was
a sad and rare day when one of the boys didn't bring
home some prize from the State Fair.

During the first visit with Mr. Werner, he talked
about alfalfa, a new crop in that country. It had been
grown back in Wisconsin, and also in the Black Hills of
South Dakota under irrigation. There were also a few
experimental plots along the Cheyenne River north of our
place. Charlie Haxby was raising it for feed and seed.
Shy had been over to Haxby's and fed some of the
alfalfa to his horses, but said they didn't like it as well
as grass and so he decided that it was not fit feed for
horses. I was anxious to get some started on our place,
but he would not let me plant any. Before Werner left
that day, I asked him if he would send me some seed
anyway and he said he would be glad to send a few
pounds. "Maybe," he said, "you can talk your husband
into planting it for you."

I had to keep that alfalfa seed two years before I
ever got it into the ground. The hired hand had heard
me pleading for a little piece of land to plant the seed
and had heard Shy turn me down, saying that he didn't
want "to get that weed started on the place." There was a
little piece of land ready for oats, so the hired hand said
to me on the sly, "If you want me to plant the alfalfa in
with the oats, I'll do it for you." It was a good feeling
to know that at last we had the seed in the ground even

if it was two years old and had been done behind Shy's back. It wasn't long until we had a swell stand of alfalfa with a few oats scattered in it.

When Shy discovered that he had been tricked, he was as mad as a wet hen. It gnawed at him all summer long. The next spring he hitched up his team to the plow and plowed it all under, and thought he had rid the place of this "weed." But he did not kill it out. The plowing made a better patch. We cut it once for hay and then let it go out for seed, and got a bushel and a peck from that little patch. The horses and cattle ate it and got fat off of it. After that, Shy was sold on alfalfa hay. From that little beginning we seeded over 200 acres and put up hundreds of tons of feed until the drought of the 1930's killed it off. Grasshoppers and beetles made it almost impossible to grow alfalfa until 1948 when a few people got it started again.

4-H Clubs

By 1917 Stanley County was divided into three smaller counties—Jackson, Haakon, and Stanley. Haakon County, in which we now live, hired Freda Morrison as our first Assistant County Agent. She carried on the 4-H Club work and gave home demonstrations. By that time we had several 4-H Clubs in the county and our children were exhibiting their work at the county fair. Joe Morrison was Project Leader one year, and his enthusiasm had the boys excited about trying new things. He gave each boy one bushel of a new kind of soft wheat that had been developed at the State College Experimental Farm. It was a macaroni wheat and it did very well. From these beginnings, we started raising it, and so did the neighbors. We quit growing it when the elevators began to spring up around the country and wheat was shipped out to Minneapolis and other places for milling.

The corn that Jasper grew on his 4-H plot proved adaptable to our land. It was early and the stock liked it, and it was used for many years as a standard seed corn. Later on, a variety of white corn along with varieties of squaw corn were tried out on the boys' plots, and some of these proved to be adaptable to the country. These experiments gave us the edge on many homesteaders since many of them bought out seed from Iowa and Illinois and other states to the east, and found that their crops failed. We learned to make farming pay by planting seeds developed for that dry country west of the Missouri.

One year Byron decided to try a different crop, flax, on his 4-H plot. It was new out there with us and didn't turn out so well. When he mowed it, the mower sickle gummed up. He would wash the sickle and try again, only to have the same thing happen. Then he would clean it with kerosene, try again, bawl awhile, clean it off, and try again. Finally, he came into the house, looked at me grimly, and said, "I'm not going to do anything more with that flax, and no amount of argument from you or anybody else is going to make me." So we turned the stock into the plot and boy, did they ever have lovely coats that fall!

Professor Hansen

For almost ten years after 1929 we were without crops and trying to keep our heads above water on the old homestead. Our alfalfa was gone and most of the feed crops dried up or were eaten by grasshoppers and beetles. It looked as if the whole country west of the Missouri was going to blow away. A lot of the homesteaders who had survived over the years gave up and headed back east. I had read a good deal about crested wheat grass in the farm bulletins and got interested in it. It had been brought from Siberia by Professor Hansen of South Dakota State, and when he visited us his stories about it whetted my appetite for trying it. When the New Deal came along in the 1930's, our chance came to try this new grass. In the new farm program we were asked to lay by some of the land and not use it for wheat. To earn the payments allotted us for this, I seeded sixty acres to crested wheat grass. The first year it looked as if it was a good thing. The second year, I had a good seed crop but like many other new-fangled things in the experimental stage, crested wheat as a feed crop was a flop. It seemed to starve the soil and it rootbound itself so that it didn't get very high. Besides, its nutritious value as a feed was small. We were stung with bumpy fields to mow and got only a good pasture for early spring and late fall. In time, it starved itself out. It never did us much good, though it did help keep the tops of gullies from blowing away and did stop some erosion that was prevalent in the rough country.

Professor Hansen visited our place several times and talked about his experiments. I remembered my childhood days roaming the hills of southern Wisconsin and the nursery stock my father used to bring home to set out. When Professor Hansen wanted me to help with his experiments for getting new plants for the dry country, I was much interested and wanted to help. We worked together on a new berry, a cross between a sand cherry and a choke cherry. I would find the nicest choke cherries, just as I had done as a little girl, and send him cuttings. He would send me many of his plants and I would try them out in our country. These things kept me from just sitting and rotting on our homestead when the going was tough. There were always things to do and to learn, and I find that as true today as it was years ago.

I couldn't see any reason why land which would produce such good grain wouldn't be good for other things such as were grown in the eastern part of South Dakota. Of course, we didn't have water, but that didn't seem to be a problem that couldn't be solved by experimenting with different shrubs and seeds. As the years went by, I found that we could grow most anything adapted to this country, except in the drought years. The settlers who talked down "textbook farming" either got out of the country or turned to other means of making a living.

The country west of the Missouri was covered with a native grass called gama grass by Professor Hansen but bunch grass by the stockmen who used it for a pasture. Actually, there were several gama grasses. We called one of them buffalo grass, another nigger wool, and a tall one we just called wheat grass. Nigger grass was the devil itself to plow up. Its roots were so thick and so deep that they would stay in lumps for years. A harrow with its sharp tines wouldn't break up a clump. The wheat grass was very good feed. We cut it for the livestock in the drought years and sold some of the hay to neighbors. The government offered to buy buffalo grass seed, so we harvested it with special machinery and sold it for reseeding the dust bowl where grasses had disappeared from too much grazing or where wheat farmers had plowed up land that should have been kept as range.

After we had worked with the State College people for a few years, I got interested in knowing what kind of soil we had on our place, and decided to have it tested. I took samples from several areas on the ten acre piece east of the house and sent them to the laboratory at State College. I found that there were seven different kinds of soil, each with different elements in them. Some of it was straight gumbo where nothing would grow. Then there were sandy spots, heavy black loam, and other types. The gumbo would produce good crops if we put a lot of fertilizer on it, but without manure, it just grew a little weed that was sour tasting but which the sheep were crazy to eat. We called this salt weed. The cattle would eat the weed and lick the ground, making big patches on the bare dirt wherever gumbo soil was. I suppose that it furnished the salt for buffaloes in the days before they were killed off.

World War I and After
During World War I we were asked to plow and plant just as much as we could. Food would win the war, they said. We broke up prairie that had never been plowed before and planted wheat and grain, and made money for the first time. We kept this up until the depression began to hit us in 1928 and 1929. Every other homesteader west of the Missouri was doing the same thing. This was a mistake. The dry soil had no protection with the bunch grass gone. Winds picked up the loose dirt and piled it high around buildings and fences and great clouds of dust filled the skies and were carried east. There was a story that went around about an old Indian who saw white men plowing up the prairie and sitting on his haunches, he picked up the dry dirt and sifted it between his

fingers, saying, "Wrong side up." The homesteaders ruined the gama grasses that nature had worked at for centuries to hold that soil down. When the New Deal set up the Soil Conservation program, much of this land was taken out of cultivation. But the damages had been done and it took years to undo it.

Planting an Orchard

It took hard work and time but we did get an orchard started. After a childhood in southern Wisconsin, I just had to have fruit trees and flowers and shrubs around the house. My father who had a nursery at Sac City, Iowa, in 1913, sent out forty-eight apple trees to us, a few plums and cherries, and came out to help plant them. They grew wonderfully well the first year but the next year we had a deep snow that nearly covered the young trees. Hungry jackrabbits fed on the tops and killed most of them. A few came up from the roots but the best trees in the new orchard never made it. The gooseberries and strawberries did well when they did bear. When we picked wild currants, buffalo berries, and June berries, we had plenty for pies and sauce and for canning. But they would skip years so when we did have fruit, we made the best of it.

Prairie Flowers

In the spring the prairie was covered as far as the eye could see with a carpet of beautiful wild flowers. I had names for them but they were not the flower names found in books. Instead, I gave them the names of the tame flowers that they looked like. The first flower in the spring was the anemone which became the South Dakota State Flower. Then we had the little flower that made the ground white in the spring with its tiny petals. The yellow, blue, and white violets sprang up everywhere. There were the yucca, the gumbo lily, and another one that looked like the calla lily; the buffalo pea and the yellow and pink sweet William; snake root which we used for snake bite; wild roses that grew along the creek, buck brush and sun flowers that gave a flash of yellow and brown most everywhere; black-eyed susans, a blue flower that grew like a lady slipper, having many flowers, and there were yellow, pink, and other varieties. Even in dry years, the prairie was abloom in the early spring. Mother nature seemed to make every homesteader a bet: if we could survive the long, hard winter, she would give us wonderful wild flowers in the spring. Even in the summer, the alfalfa looked like an ocean of blue and green over the fields, and this, too, was one of the joys of living west of the Missouri.

Bees

One summer day I looked out over our alfalfa field and wondered if we wouldn't have better seed if we had bees to pollinate it. Besides, bees produce honey for sweetening. Right then I decided to get some bees. I had everything to learn about looking after them but it made sense to me that they would take care of themselves in the summertime when the alfalfa bloomed, so why not get some? We bought two swarms and it was not long until we had several hives. The table was furnished with honey for several years until the drought put us out of the bee business, and about everything else, too.

Our old dog, poor thing, learned to get along with bees early in life. He was in the habit of following me everywhere but one day conditions were not just right and the bees were ornery. They stung him from head to tail, and then took after me. Did they ever! I got stung from head to toe and looked as if I had warts all over. After that, I covered my face and hands and got along pretty well with them. The bees were like everything else. I had my finger in a lot of pies, but the main reason was more that just being curious about something; being a homesteader in a dry country and raising a family without too much help from Shy, I had to make every penny I could or we wouldn't have made it.

Wind Break

In 1912 when Shy came home from the Nebraska Sand Hills he wanted to set out a wind break around the yard. He had seen some native cedars used around some of the homesteads in the Sand Hills and liked them. All hands pitched in and dug big holes for the trees, and the next spring we took the team and went over to the Cheyenne River Breaks after the little cedars. We found all the trees we wanted—two feet high and well-shaped—wrapped the roots of each one in a wet gunny sack, hustled home with them, and put them in the holes. They never seemed to stop growing. Now we have a natural windbreak that slows up the blizzards that sweep across the prairies.

Gardening

It was the garden that kept us alive in the early years, and gave the family something more than beef to eat. I tried out all kinds of wild things and was surprised to find out what grew in South Dakota. One year I planted artichokes. In the fall when we dug them we had sacks and sacks and I didn't know what to do with them. I fed them to the family but they didn't like them, so I put them in the slop pail for the hogs. The boys called this experiment a flop but the hogs seemed to go for the vegetable.

Then I tried wild peanuts and that was also a failure. But some of the little ground nuts produced wonderfully well. They were globules that grew on the end of the roots and were about the size of hazel nuts. We picked them like we would peanuts and found them good eating, but after awhile we got tired of them. When this soil had water, it would produce most anything, and sometimes just overdid itself. I once got started with stubble-berries. These little blue berries darn near took over my whole garden. The berries were delicious when made into pies and jams and I put up gallons of the sauce. It was not until the drought of 1934 that we got rid of them. By that time we'd had enough to do us the rest of our lives.

I always raised more garden than my family could use, so we helped supply the neighbors, too. One of our friends who didn't like to work in a garden brought over a bunch of seeds one spring and asked me to plant it in my garden for her. She wanted to feel free to come over and get things at any time. This seemed to be taking neighborliness too far, so I decided to cut back my garden to what my family needed and quit feeding all of Stanley County. I needed to spend my time on things that would bring in some money, not on things to give away. It was then that I turned to raising chickens.

But I enjoyed the garden even if it was a lot of work. The family all helped with the hoeing, but sometimes I found vegetables cut down and a row of weeds left standing. Shy always hoed down anything he didn't recognize. I always planted flowers in the garden so we could cut them and brighten up the house with them. One day Byron came and said, "Mother, I think I've done a good job. I got all your pansies but one!" When the strawberries were ripe, the children practically lived in the strawberry bed and forgot about hoeing.

After we got the 4-H Club started, the boys had to have plots for their experiments. These plots had to be protected from the livestock and this was quite a problem. One year Byron had his ten-acre plot of corn east of the house. Louie Johnson's hogs kept getting out and coming down to the corn field and helping themselves. The businessmen at Philip had offered a $50 prize for the best corn crop produced by the 4-H boys, and so Byron's heart sank whenever Louie's hogs got in his plot and did a lot of damage yet Byron won the $25 second prize. When any of our hogs got out into Louie's field, he was always pretty mad, but if any of his hogs got into our fields, he would say, "Why, Mrs. Fairchild, my hogs didn't do you any damage. We got them out right away." This was the attitude of most of the homesteaders.

Our township decided to build a pond for watering livestock, but they hoped to make some money on the side with it. Homesteaders don't like cattlemen and sheepmen who let their stock roam loose around the country, jumping over fences and getting into the fields of corn or hay, with their owners never paying any damages. They thought the pond would solve the problem, and got quite a laugh out of taking people's stock and putting them into the corral there, holding them until damages were paid instead of taking them home or telling the owner that his stock was over in some homesteader's field. Since loose stock belonged to homesteaders as well as cattlemen and sheep ranchers, it didn't take long for the township to give up the idea of impounding cattle as a way of raising money.

From Homesteads to Bigger Farms
The country west of the Missouri had been changing ever since the homesteaders began to locate their claims. We were going from open range to fenced farms, from livestock only to mixed farming with both livestock and grain. The people leaving after the drought of 1911 had nothing to go on. They needed ready cash. The homesteaders who had quit the county left behind a lot of good grazing land, and so most of us branched out a little, began to cut the hay on this deserted land or put it into grain or other crops. The county bought various seeds and sold them to settlers, on time, but the seed was infested by the miserable bind weed and anyone getting that seed had his land ruined. We didn't buy any so we didn't ruin any of our land.

Selling Butter and Cream
After a few years, most of the ranchers had a milk cow or two, and some of us started a cooperative creamery. I bought a share although Shy thought it a foolish thing to do. We then got a cream separator, picked out our best cows, and began to milk and sell cream. Up to this time, I had made butter, packed it into jars, and sold it to any homesteader who came to the place after it. But that big old barrel churn that Shy had got for me was a bug-bear. The children hated to do the churning in it and I hated to wash it. It was too heavy to move around, but it did give us a lot of butter for our big family and for selling to neighbors and to the little stores around.
Little stores sprang up wherever there were enough homesteaders around to keep them going. Usually some farmer started one and ran it in a part of the house until he needed more shelves for the groceries he carried. There was usually a post office at the same place. I sold

quite a lot of butter to these little "holes in the wall" until everybody began to milk a few cows. Then we began to sell cream to the cooperative creamery in Philip, taking turns hauling it into town. At one time we milked twenty-five cows. It was such a chore to milk the cows, run the milk through the separator, wash the separator twice a day, and keep the cream cool in crocks in the cellar until we took it to town. In the 1920's we put in a milking machine, and then the price of butterfat fell to twelve cents. Everything we had to sell went down. People drifted out of milking and began to raise beef cattle, and since Shy knew how to buy good stock, we always had good beeves around.

The homesteader who stayed west of the Missouri had to work harder and plan better than he would have had to do back in the Midwest where droughts and grasshoppers weren't such a problem. The droughts drove out many settlers and the rest of us bought their land at tax sales, added more livestock, and turned over more sod for grain and hay. We learned a lot from the 4-H Clubs' plots. If we hadn't learned "textbook farming" from these experiments and from the Ag college, we would have had to go back east, too.

Last Days on the Old Homestead

I suppose if I had known in 1898 what I know in 1950, I might never have left Wisconsin to take my first teaching job at Parker, South Dakota. At that time, the prospect of making $1200 a year instead of $800 or $900 teaching in a little red school house looked pretty good to me. Things look different when you are seventeen than they do when you are sixty-nine. I wouldn't have got married when I was eighteen and I wouldn't have married a widower who was forty-five and had a son as old as I was. But I did. I wouldn't have moved west of the Missouri with a husband who didn't have what it took to be a pioneer on the prairies. Shy was good-looking. People liked to talk to him, especially about horses. But he was as impractical as a man could be, and impractical people have no business pushing into the wilderness where only hard work and sacrifice make life possible.

Over the years, Shy and I drifted farther apart. I finally decided it was up to me to make good on our South Dakota claim.

The Parting of the Ways
    Over the years the rift between Shy and me deepened, and in 1930 we separated. We had a sale that year and divided up the property. He went to live by himself. He had always wanted to move to the Nebraska Sand Hills or to the Black Hills, but some freak of his nature caused him to build a little house within sight of the ranch, and there he batched alone a few years. Then he moved to Philip where he took a room. He came out to see Wayne and Clint, who lived near the home place, any time he wanted to come. In 1939, he got hurt in a poolroom brawl and from that time on he was never well. All his life he had complained about being sick, but I always thought it was in his head and that he was using this to get sympathy from me. I don't think he ever ran a fever and I know that he could always eat his meals.
    When Shy and I separated in 1930, I gave myself five years to straighten out the indebtedness on the land, but never made it in that time. The depression and the drought made me stretch it out to ten years. In a lifetime, I had learned how to live with a mortgage but never really felt comfortable with one. By 1940, I had put together 1440 acres of land and had enough sheep and cattle to keep me out of the poor house, and then some. Though it was tough in the 1930's when prices were so low, I never went on relief. The relief workers told me that I couldn't get any help as long as I had eight cows and other livestock mortgage-free.
    Wayne came to live with me after Shy moved out, and when he got married in 1936, he set up housekeeping on the Louis Johnson land north of the home place. He got a little start with sheep and cattle and settled down close to home, the only one of the eight children who decided to stay with the old homestead west of the Missouri.

After Shy got hurt in the brawl in Philip, the boys brought him back to the home place where he stayed most of his remaining days. When he got worse, Clint and Wayne took him to the hospital in Pierre. Dr. Riggs said he had pneumonia, and gave him sulfa drugs. He didn't respond and this puzzled the doctor. Age may have had something to do with it. The boys sent for me and I went to the hospital to see him. I saw at once that Shy was up to his old tricks and acting contrary as usual. He was taking the sulfa pills out of his mouth when the nurse left the room. I called the nurse and told her what he was doing. She gave him the medicine in another form. But it was too late. The doctor told me that his time had come and that I should let the family know that the end was near. Shy crossed his last divide on May 7, 1940, at the age of eighty-six. I hope that he found a pretty homestead over there, with plenty of hot-blooded horses and country fairs, enough to pleasure him through all the years of eternity. With him I had made my bed, and I had also slept in it. I only wanted a bigger dream than he did—on the South Dakota frontier.

Epilogue
Farming in the 1980s
Lynn Spielman Dummer

Although Lynn Dummer didn't travel across the country by primitive transportation to unknown territory, she is, like many farm women before her, transplanted from the city. Lynn grew up in Hudson, Wisconsin, about sixty miles from where she, her husband and their four children operate a 360-acre farm. They also rent 225 acres from nearby farmers to raise additional crops, and they share-crop with another neighbor who has retired from farming but kept his land. Lynn, a college graduate, combines her role as farm wife with a nursing career, community involvement and family responsibilities. Meeting her, we see that she has the same strong, positive qualities of other farm women who have recorded their lives.

Source: Personal Interview. 13 January, 1989.

To get to the Dummer farm, take Highway 94 east out of Minneapolis for about two hours and turn off on Dunn County Road EE. After a mile, Amy Drive cuts off to the right. Take that road, and the first thing you see is the place that has been in the Dummer family for three generations—a sparkling, square, two-story white house with black shutters, standing against a background of red barns and cement-colored silos. To the left of the house a tall windmill sports a TV antenna in place of the blades that once whirred there—the old functions with the new. A collie and a big gray and white cat lounge on the doorstep. To the right is a mobile home that has a history.

Lynn met Dave Dummer while she was a student at the University of Wisconsin-Eau Claire in 1971. He was playing basketball at the YMCA, and she was watching. They began dating and, Lynn says, "Before I met Dave, I'd never been on a farm. The very first time I came out here, some friends that farm were here around the table having a visit. It was a warm, unique feeling. There's something about rural people, their friendliness."

Dave brought her out to the farm often. While he did the chores, she studied. Before they talked of marriage, he taught her to milk the cows. She says she never hesitated in her decision to become a farm woman, even though she had had a taste of the hard work. They were married in 1972. "That first year, I was a pretty lonely person," she says now. Dave was out in the fields from early morning until after dark, and there were no near neighbors. Like so many other farm women, she adapted to isolation by becoming both creative and productive. She learned to sew, crochet, and work on other craft projects. She sewed a layette during her first pregnancy. She still makes many of her own and her children's clothes.

The farm, which belonged first to Dave's grandfather, then to his father and now to Dave and Lynn, is hilly and rich. They presently milk sixty-five cows. Lynn walks through the main barn that is huge but not big enough for the whole herd to occupy at one time. Curious Holsteins twist their heads and creak the stanchions. The rest of the herd is housed in an adjoining "free-stall" barn where the cows walk around without restraints. This is the way those cows live during the winter: after the cows in the main barn are milked, they are ushered out and the second shift enters. In another connecting barn are sixty-one calves. Unlike most dairy farmers, Dave and Lynn raise all of their calves, usually born in the fall. Each of the many pens holds several calves, except for one occupied by a little black and white calf born only the day before. He pushes his nose through the slats of the pen divider. When Lynn was a young wife with her first two babies, she worked beside Dave in the barn—then they were milking about fifty cows. Dave's grandfather and parents lived in the main house, and Lynn, Dave and the children lived in the mobile home. When Lynn went out to the barn, the grandfather came to the trailer and baby-sat. If something came up with the children that he couldn't handle, he turned the porch light on to signal for Lynn to come and help.

Eventually Lynn's family moved into the main house and a hired man—the only employee on the farm—took over the trailer. Now that the children are old enough to help, Lynn doesn't do the barn work any more. She still helps with special jobs such as driving wagons during haying.

Since Lynn began her work as a nurse at a nearby nursing home, the children have become responsible for much of the routine on the farm and the home. Lynn believes that this responsibility is one of the many advantages of raising children on a farm. Their help is necessary to the welfare of the family—a situation that hasn't changed through the history of farm families. She feels that rural children work hard and must be dependable, and that these qualities will help them in adult life.

On a typical morning when Lynn works, the organization shows. She laughs. "Well, this is the way it's supposed to work." She must be at her job by 6:30 a.m., and she drops five-year-old Daren off at Dave's parents' house in town. The older children, David, 16, and Lisa, 14, take turns with inside and outside duty. Whoever has outside duty gets up at 5:00 A.M. and accompanies Dave to the barn to do the morning milking. The one on duty inside can sleep a little later, but must cook breakfast, pick up around the house, burn the trash and perhaps start something for supper. The eight-year-old, Lori, makes the beds and fills the dishwasher. They all get themselves ready for school and meet the school bus; after school they have other chores, depending on the season. Even Lori works in the barn after school. Rather than resenting their assignments, the children are proud of their farm and attached to both the animals and the machinery. Lynn says that whenever an animal is sold or a machine traded in, somebody says, "Get a picture of that, Mom."

There seems to be no separation of jobs into male and female work. All the children have inside and outside duties. Lisa is in charge of testing milk and keeping those records as well as the breeding records. Lynn is the family bookkeeper. She writes checks and handles the accounting. She and Dave recently took a course in computers, so they can eventually modernize their record-keeping. The Dummer lawn is huge and well-kept in the summer; lawn-mowing and gardening chores are shared by everyone.

Women, especially rural women who may be otherwise isolated, have always banded together to form their own support groups. Lynn belongs to the Elk Mound Homemakers, a group of forty members, active and retired farm women who live in the area. At monthly meetings, members take turns preparing and presenting lessons in some facet of homemaking. Lynn recently presented a lesson on the modern method of canning tomatoes. New varieties, she says, are less acidic and must be canned using a pressure cooker and an addition of lemon juice. The quilting activities of the Elk Mound Homemakers are reminiscent of the quilting bees organized and attended by pioneer women. Every year, each member makes two quilt blocks. The quilts are assembled and two drawings are held—one for older members and one for younger. The winners keep the quilts and withdraw their names from the pool. In this way, every member will eventually win a quilt, Lynn hasn't won one yet, but she has belonged to the club for only four years.

Lynn has other activities besides her job and her farm responsibilities. She serves as a 4-H leader of a Foods and Nutrition project. She is happy that the 4-H rules have changed to allow younger children to belong. She and Dave belong to the Dunn County Farm Bureau, an organization with political clout. She is on the Administrative Board of United Methodist Church in Elk Mound and served on the Building Committee after the church was destroyed in the 1980 windstorm.

The devastation of the 1980 storm is legendary around Elk Mound and the surrounding area. Lynn's family and others had to call on inner and outer resources to pick up and begin again after the destruction. During the storm, the Dummer family took refuge in their basement. After the storm passed, Dave went upstairs and looked outside. He announced that a silo was gone, but the rest of the family didn't believe him until they saw for themselves. The entire north end of the barn roof was also gone. That area had just been filled with hay bales, now vulnerable to the weather. The hay had to be moved. The worst destruction, says Lynn, was that every mature tree on the property was destroyed—broken or uprooted—and trees cannot be replaced quickly. Nevertheless, they recovered from their losses with the help of a positive attitude: Lynn says that the main thing she remembers about the storm is the way that people helped out. Neighbors brought food to those who had no electrical power to keep or cook it and helped one another clean up their properties.

Lynn tells how, after the storm, Mennonite men from Pennsylvania volunteered their time, strength and chain saws to haul away dead trees and otherwise return farms to near normal condition. These men were transported to the disaster area by the Red Cross and housed at the nearby university campus in Menomonie. Besides helping the Dummers clean up, the men moved the hay crop from the north to the south end of the barn, where the roof was still intact. Because the conveyor system had also been destroyed, each bale had to be lifted and carried by hand.

The Dummers and their farm have also survived another disaster, the 1988 drought. Almost the entire corn crop—over 200 acres—was ruined by lack of moisture. They had cattle pastured on rented land, and because the pastures were dried up, they carried hay and water every day to keep their stock alive. Although they didn't lose any animals, they were tempted to sell some young stock because of the feed shortage. When the drought finally broke in late August, the third crop of hay enabled them to keep all of the stock.

As would be expected, the drought occupied everyone's thoughts and conversation. Lynn found support again at her homemakers' group, where the women discussed their feelings and concerns. She also values having been able to talk with a farm woman friend at work. It was impossible, Lynn says, to escape news and speculation about the drought. For the second time in their marriage, the Dummers went on a family vacation to Florida that summer. The vacation was pleasant, but the newspapers and newscasts were full of messages of doom for Midwest farmers. When they called home, Dave's father told them to stay in Florida as long as they wanted because there was nothing they could do on the farm.

How did she get through the crisis? Lynn says, "I guess it's faith. You're going to get through. Hearing of other farmers helping. Several years ago we sent hay to farmers in Georgia, and they did the same for us." She mentions being able to talk to other women about how they and their husbands were feeling; moreover, she read and heard that conditions were even worse in other places.

Lynn says that the disaster payment from the government after the drought was a great help, but that there are inequities for farmers in some laws. For instance, farmers cannot give their farm to their children; it must be sold at fair market value for tax purposes. The Dummer farm has already been purchased three times by family members: Dave's grandfather bought it originally, his father bought it from him, Lynn and Dave then bought it, and if they wish to retire some time and turn the farm over to their children, they will have to sell it to them. She also objects that their own pond—big enough to call a lake—is labeled wetlands and is under the jurisdiction of the DNR. During the drought the Dummers wanted to deepen the pond to provide water for their stock, but the DNR refused permission, claiming that it might ruin the habitat of swans, ducks and Canadian geese that gather there.

Lynn says that she calls herself a farm wife rather than a farmer: the word *farmer* conjures up the image of a man in overalls working the soil. But nearly always in the picture is a woman—working, nurturing and creating. What has enabled farm women to endure and even triumph in adversity? It is the positive, creative spirit that impels women to make islands of beauty in their lives: to sew fragments of outworn and outgrown clothing into quilts that are now recognized as works of art, to embroider color into designs on utilitarian clothing, to plant and nurture flower gardens in the midst of a drought. It is also their devotion to families that exhibits itself in the practical symbols of hand-made clothing, canned and frozen food, service to raising the quality of education. It is certainly some feminine connection to the natural world that compels women to watch and tend the fields.

B.H.

Index

Abuse: child abuse, 327, 328, 331; wife abuse, 327
African Americans: prejudice against, 87
Alberta: 157-70, 301-14
Alcohol: 71, 73, 76, 186, 260, 299
Animals: purchase of, 39, 67, 137, 138; for work, 42, 99, 104, 137, 140, 160-62, 244-45, 253, 271; chickens, 60-61, 91, 200, 250; cattle rustling, 67-68; as pets, 82, 83, 85, 141, 237, 248, 307, 323; herding, 87-89, 109-110, 111-12, 144; as threat, 97-98, 109-13, 139-41, 224, 233-34; wild, 128; effect of drought on, 209, 212, 361, 362; treatment of, 319-23
Army: See Civil War
Birth Control: 290
Celebration and ceremony: 30-31, 70, 76, 77, 109, 158-59, 176-77, 181, 182, 197-98, 228-29, 276, 282
Cheese-making: 115-16
Childbirth: en route to homestead, 37; oblique references to, 71, 73, 107; midwives and doctors, 128, 149; men's role in, see Men as midwives
Children: relationship with adults, 8, 10, 85-86, 90, 104-5, 117, 248, 195; games and play, 24, 84, 101, 104-5, 117, 118, 145, 150, 247; as source of inspiration, 26; work, 40, 81, 105-6, 109-10, 175, 200, 201, 248, 250, 252, 259, 309, 313, 33, 334-35, 353-54, 356, 362, 363, 370-71; behavior of, 50, 54, 81-93, 100, 106-7, 114, 137, 145-46, 168, 176, 177 248, 271, 300
Churches: homes used for services, 41-42, 163; services, 45, 49-50, 100, 166, 174, 175-77, 183; schoolhouses used for services, 45-52; building of, 164-66, 372
Circuit riders: See Ministers